Nicholas Tan Jerome

Low-latency big data visualisation

Low-latency big data visualisation

by
Nicholas Tan Jerome

KIT Scientific Publishing

Karlsruher Institut für Technologie
Institut für Prozessdatenverarbeitung und Elektronik

Low-latency big data visualisation

Zur Erlangung des akademischen Grades eines Doktor-Ingenieurs von der KIT-Fakultät für Elektrotechnik und Informationstechnik des Karlsruher Instituts für Technologie (KIT) genehmigte Dissertation

von M.Sc. Nicholas Tan Jerome

Tag der mündlichen Prüfung: 7. Mai 2019
Hauptreferent: Prof. Dr. rer. nat Marc Weber
Korreferent: Prof. Dr. rer. nat Werner Nahm

Impressum

KIT Scientific Publishing

Karlsruher Institut für Technologie (KIT)
KIT Scientific Publishing
Straße am Forum 2
D-76131 Karlsruhe

KIT Scientific Publishing is a registered trademark of Karlsruhe Institute of Technology.
Reprint using the book cover is not allowed.

www.ksp.kit.edu

Print on Demand 2019 – Gedruckt auf FSC-zertifiziertem Papier

ISBN 978-3-7315-0940-0
DOI 10.5445/KSP/1000095735

Zusammenfassung

Die Exploration großer und komplexer Datensätze ist ein wesentliches Element einer digitalen Bibliothek. Eine effiziente Visualisierung bietet die Möglichkeit über die Suche mit rein textuellen Beschreibungen hinauszugehen. In aktuellen digitalen Bibliotheken haben existierende moderne Visualisierungswerkzeuge allerdings aufgrund der Herausforderungen, die sich durch Datenumfang und Heterogenität der Daten ergeben, noch keinen Eingang gefunden. Und folgerichtig ist eine effektive Suche in sogenannten „Big-Data"-Archiven bislang in der Regel nicht zufriedenstellend.

Diese Arbeit hat sich zum Ziel gesetzt, Methoden aufzuzeigen, „Big-Data"-Archive zu organisieren und zentrale Elemente der enthaltenen Informationen zu visualisieren. Anhand von drei wissenschaftlichen Experimenten werde ich zwei „Big-Data"- Herausforderungen, Datenvolumen (Volume) und Heterogenität (Variety), untersuchen und eine Visualisierung im Browser präsentieren, die trotz reduzierter Datenrate die wesentliche Information in den Datensätzen enthält. Die Herausforderung bei den gewählten Anwendungen besteht darin, große Datensatze von ca. 30 GB und vielfältige Daten mit etwa 100 Parametern pro Abtastzeitpunkt umfassend, sinnerhaltend und interaktiv, d.h. mit Antwortzeiten unter einer Sekunde darzustellen. Es müssen also sowohl große als auch vielfältige Datensätze umgesetzt werden. Um den internationalen Charakter in den großen wissenschaftlichen Experimenten zu berücksichtigen, habe ich mich auf web-basierte Lösungen beschränkt und berücksichtige hier auch Limitationen, die durch Einschränkungen von Bandbreite und Latenz der Client-Hardware entstehen.

In dieser Arbeit präsentiere ich den Entwurf einer web-basierten „Big-Data" Visualisierung unter Verwendung des „data state reference"-Modells. Die vorgestellten Systeme verarbeiten durchgängig multidimensionale Daten.

Für jede der sogenannten „Big-Data“- Herausforderungen schlage ich spezifische Konzepte vor, die sich auch auf andere Anwendungs-gebiete übertragen lassen. Ein wesentliches Element des Designs sind vorprozessierte Bildkarten, die direkt in das „Texture Memory“ der Client-GPUs zu Darstellung geladen werden können. Diese Methode bietet die bestmögliche Interaktivität, da nach dem Laden die vollständige Information auf der Client-Seite vorhanden ist. Diese Interaktivität ist entscheidend, um Datensätze hierarchisch über mehrere Skalen hinweg durchsuchen zu können. Abschließend werde ich den Einsatz des entstandenen Visualisierungssystems an vier komplementären Anwendungsfälle demonstrieren: (1) die Analyse multispektraler Satellitendaten, (2) ein Doppler Lidar zur Messung der Windgeschwindigkeit, (3) Ultraschall Computertomographie für die Brustkrebsdiagnose und (4) die Synchrotron-Röntgentomographie.

Die vorgeschlagenen Entwurfskonzepte tragen zu einem besseren Verständnis der web-basierten „Big-Data“- Visualisierung bei. Entstandene Visualisierungsanwendungen, wie WAVE, BORA oder die optimale Blickwinkelsuche für 3D Objekte befinden sich im Produktiveinsatz und sind schnell zu unverzichtbaren Elementen in der Datenauswertung der Experimente geworden. Wesentlich bei der Realisierung solcher Anwendungen ist es, auch spezifische Anforderungen umsetzen zu können. Das BORA-System verarbeitet beliebige Zeitreihen und kann ohne Programmierkenntnisse angepasst werden. Das WAVE-Framework dient zur Visualisierung von 3D-Daten im Web-Browser und wird ergänzt durch Methoden optimierte Blickwinkel zu ermitteln und so optimierte 2D Ansichten zu generieren. Generell und insbesondere bei weiter steigenden Datenraten, ist es notwendig, schon bei der Aufnahme der Daten, eine hierarchische Datenorganisation anzustreben und so leichter die wesentlichen Informationen extrahieren zu können.

Abstract

Exploring large and complex data sets is a crucial factor in a digital library framework. To find a specific data set within a large repository, visualisation can help to validate the content apart from the textual description. However, even with the existing visual tools, the difficulty of large-scale data concerning their size and heterogeneity impedes building visualisation as part of the digital library framework, thus hindering the effectiveness of large-scale data exploration.

The scope of this research focuses on managing Big Data and eventually visualising the core information of the data itself. Specifically, I study three large-scale experiments that feature two Big Data challenges: large data size (Volume) and heterogeneous data (Variety), and provide the final visualisation through the web browser in which the size of the input data has to be reduced while preserving the vital information. Despite the intimidating size, i.e., approximately 30 GB, and the complexity of the data, i.e., about 100 parameters per timestamp, I demonstrated how to provide a comprehensive overview of each data set at an interactive rate where the system response time is less than 1 s—visualising gigabytes of data, and visualising multifaceted data in a single representation. For better data sharing, I selected a web-based system which serves as a ubiquitous platform for the domain experts. Being a useful collaborative tool, I also address the shortcomings related to limited bandwidth latency and various client hardware.

In this thesis, I present a design of web-based Big Data visualisation systems based on the data state reference model. Also, I develop frameworks that can process and output multidimensional data sets. For any Big Data feature, I propose a standard design guideline that helps domain experts to build their data visualisation. I introduce the use of texture-based images as the primary data object where the images are loaded in the texture memory of the client's GPU for final visualisation. The visualisation ensures high interactivity since the data resides in the client's memory. In particular, the interactivity of the system enables domain experts to narrow their search or analysis by using a top-down methodological approach. Also, I provide four use case studies to examine the feasibility of the proposed design concepts: (1) analysing multi-spectral imagery, (2) Doppler wind lidar, (3) ultrasound computer tomography, and (4) X-ray computer tomography. These case studies show the challenges of dealing with Big Data such as large data size or disperse data sets.

To this end, this dissertation contributes to a better understanding of web-based Big Data visualisation by using the proposed design guideline. I show that domain experts appreciate the WAVE, BORA, and 3D optimal viewpoint finder frameworks as tools to understand and explore their data sets. Mainly, the frameworks help them to build and customise their visualisation system. Although specific customisation is necessary for the different application, the effort is worthwhile, and it helps domain experts to understand their vast amounts of data better. The BORA framework fits perfectly in any time series data repositories where no programming knowledge is required. The WAVE framework serves as a web-based data exploration system. The 3D optimal viewpoint finder framework helps to generate 2D images from 3D data, where the 2D image is based on the 3D scene with optimal view angle. To cope with increasing data rates, a general hierarchical organisation of data is necessary to extract valuable information from data sets.

Contents

To Chui Yee and Abigail, this thesis is affectionately dedicated

You can't manage what you don't measure.

McAfee and Brynjolfsson (2012)

1 Introduction

We are entering an era of data-intensive science where scientific experiments worldwide [1] produces significant amounts of data. Significant refers to the size of the data that surpasses our capabilities to utilise it effectively. Dobre and Xafha [2] claim that we are producing 2.5 quintillion bytes [1] of data every day. Paradoxically, the significant data is not only about the difficulty of managing it; but it also presents the opportunity to prove theories or to discover facts of nature. The Large Hadron Collider (LHC)—particle accelerator—produced 13 petabytes of data in 2010 [3]. The LHC often serves as an extreme case in the data-intensive science, but such large amount of data is also common in many associated applications, e.g., astronomy, atmospheric science, medicine, genomics, biology, biogeochemistry and other interdisciplinary scientific researches [4]. However, the sheer volume of collected data

[1] 1 exabyte equals to 1 quintillion bytes or 1 exabyte equals to 1 billion gigabytes

is overwhelming the world's technological capacity of computation and data storage [5].

Jim Gray, a Turing Award laureate, portrays data-intensive science as the fourth paradigm of science evolution [6]. The first scientific paradigm started humbly with an empirical approach, where natural phenomena were described using primitive methods, such as the comprehensive astronomical and planetary observations made by Tycho Brahe—whom Johannes Keppler assisted—using his astronomical instruments [7]. Then came the second paradigm, a theoretical branch, which sought to craft theories using models and generalisations. Throughout the last few decades, the third paradigm has simulated complex phenomena. Lastly, we have begun to embrace the fourth paradigm, known as data exploration, where theory, experiment, and simulation are unified. We no longer study the weather by staring at the sky, but rather through a monitor screen. We now face the challenge of having an abundance of data as opposed to the situation in the past when there was insufficient data to be evaluated — thus requiring appropriate tools to cope with the size and complexity of the data to efficiently extract relevant information.

These data introduce new challenges to domain experts because of: (a) the large data size, (b) the diversity of data formats, (c) their conceptual dependencies, (d) disperse data locations, and (e) the intensive and systematic nature of scientific queries [8]. These data are also often labelled as Big Data, which is defined by the "four Vs": Volume (scale of data), Variety (diversity of data), Velocity (speed of data), and Veracity (certainty of data) [9, 10]. Without dedicated tools to address these challenges, it would be impossible to process such data [3]. On the one hand, domain experts can enforce their personal or facility hardware to analyse the data thoroughly (high computation capacity); and on the other hand, without powerful hardware (low computation capacity), they have to reduce the data into a manageable size that fits in the hardware memory or scales across cluster resources [4]. Either way, there is no guarantee that domain experts can extract insights from these data on time.

In this thesis, I will focus on selected applications, to develop viable solutions and discuss their impact and limitations. The driving domain of my work was X-ray tomography. In recent years, X-ray tomography imaging is often associated with the *data deluge* [2]. For application fields like biology, several hundreds of small animals such as insects and other arthropods are scanned and stored in a large storage system [12]. Researchers need to perform manual segmentation of each sample ($\sim$ 30 GB); thus each sample would usually take several months to process. A logical approach would be to store all the collected data into a sizeable scalable storage system and analyse the data later. In doing so, we merely shifted the problem from the analysis to the data management domains. With storage hardware being commercially affordable, database engineers seize the opportunity to scale the storage system, i.e., by adding more hard disk capacity or distributed storage systems.

To allow researchers to search and download their desired data, a web-based interface between the server and the user tends to be the complementary product in the storage system. This scenario encourages digital library that serves the scientific data to researchers or even to the public, i.e., CERN Open Data Portal [13], Crystallography Open Database [14], NASA Exoplanet Archive [15], and Sloan Digital Sky Survey [16]. However, these digital libraries rely heavily on textual description, known as metadata, to search for specific data. If the metadata does not describe the data adequately, domain experts will face difficulty in the search for the desired data. Ironically, what seemed impossible before (data too complex to process), is still impossible now (data too complex to search). We are encountering a phenomenon where data deluge is embedded inside the digital library framework.

Since there is no general solution to deal with the large complex scientific data, I have chosen to focus on techniques developed in the field of visualisation which uses visual representations of the data to support understanding and analysis. In particular, I will be discussing how *visual exploration* [17] can provide a valuable *visual cue* from the large and complex data within a

[2]The data deluge refers to the phenomenon where the vast amounts of data are overwhelming the capacity of researchers or institutions to manage and use it [11].

digital library. To determine and prepare a suitable visual output, I study the concept of a data acquisition system that manages a huge amount of heterogeneous data from different sources. It is important to note that we are not going to address all aspects of Big Data, but rather only two distinct subsets of Big Data: Volume and Variety.

In this thesis, I present concepts, guidelines, techniques and study real-world systems that serve as a blueprint approach to address Big Data challenges. Mainly, I answer the challenges raised in Big Data literature survey regarding data visualisation and visualisation approaches [4], that is, how to show the vast amounts of data on the screen visually. The primary challenge is how we choose a proper data representation to visualise the Big Data, e.g., Thompson et al. [18] introduced a compact representation to visualise their large-scale data. To this end, I developed a web-based Big Data visualisation library: WAVE[3], a browser-based data visualisation platform that addresses large data size, multivariate data, and multimodal data [19]. Despite different Big Data challenges, the library generalises various data preprocessing methods thanks to its modular architecture. For any Big Data feature, I propose a standard design guideline that helps domain experts to develop their data visualisation. The guideline is driven by the way they first access their data which serves as a good overview representation. I introduce the use of texture-based images as the primary data object where the images are loaded in the texture memory of the client's GPU for final visualisation. Furthermore, I aim for visualisation with high interactivity. In particular, the interactivity of the system enables domain experts to narrow their search or analysis using a top-down methodological approach. Most available visual exploration tools solve a rather specific use case, but WAVE is applicable to many science domains facing the Big Data dilemma. WAVE contributes to improving current shortcomings of Big Data visualisation tool regarding *poor performances in functionalities, scalability and response time* [4] by its modular web-based

[3] WAVE stands for Web-based Analysis of Volumes

parallel architecture. In the following, I will outline the challenges in detail and raise specific questions necessary to solve these problems.

1.1 Problem Statement and Research Questions

Scientific user facilities—particle accelerators, telescopes, colliders, light sources and more—provide the bedrock for numerous research opportunities where they generate an increasing volume of data with unprecedented quality and rates [20]. Each of the experiments has a scientific focus that drives its programme. What these experiments have in common is that they store their data into a storage system which then introduces Big Data challenges regarding its large data size and diversity of data formats. To cope with large data, it is essential to relate the measured data and the desired information within the data sets. To simplify data processing, it would be desirable to remove unnecessary data as early as possible in the data processing chain. Thus, the central question that arises is:

> How can visualisation of raw/measured data help in searching and understanding Big Data during data acquisition?

In this thesis, I select three distinct experiments that are experiencing a data deluge. These experiments serve as ideal use-cases that introduce Big Data challenges faced within a research facility, with each experiment highlighting a different Big Data aspects on Volume and Variety. I will pose specific research questions to address the core question. I focus on these two Vs because they are the primary Big Data concerns in this data-intensive era; either each data is too large (i.e., gigabytes or petabytes), or there are too many small data to be processed (i.e., 400 million tweets a day) [21]. The lessons learnt from these two Vs will serve as foundations to address further Big Data Vs.

Data too Big

Synchrotron X-ray microtomography offers unique opportunities for the morphological analysis of animals. Internal structures become observable even in opaque organisms in a non-invasive, three-dimensional way with a submicron resolution. At the KIT Imaging Cluster [22] and other synchrotron radiation facilities worldwide, the experiments utilise the X-ray light to scan organisms and store the data in a digital library system. Then, the entomologists will segment the data to study the internal structure of the specimen further. Depending on the scan resolution, the size of each data set ranges from 30 GB to 120 GB. The massive data size is a common Big Data feature where the size is too big to fit into the memory of current computers. The collected data sets are then stored in large scalable storage, and they are made available through a digital library framework. Although I am not dealing with data in the range of petabytes, the size of data lies within the scope of gigabytes which causes high system latency. In this thesis, I aim to visualise these data sets in less than 1 s. Processing, transmitting, and visualising gigabytes of a data set in less than one second is not trivial.

With the digital library filled with hundreds of data sets, entomologists have to rely on the textual metadata description to search for their desired data sets. Often, the metadata descriptions are neither complete nor helpful, which leads to numerous guessing attempts through trial-and-error to find the desired sample. Since the size of each data is in the gigabyte range, downloading and inspecting multiple data sets are cumbersome.

To allow the researchers to work efficiently, we have to introduce additional information to compensate for the incompleteness of the textual metadata. In the context of large data size, the extra information can be in a visual form which contains the main feature of the data. Ideally, we would like to understand the original data immediately without any data latency. Hence the question:

> *Question 1:* How can we visualise Big Data without downloading the whole original data set itself?

Data too Different

In a large-scale experiment, not only is the increasing data size a concern, but also the complexity of the data. The data are usually multivariate—data consisting of different attributes such as temperature and humidity. When multiple sources are present, the multivariate data are described as multimodal data. In climate research, multimodal data can be data from various data acquisition systems that differ in grid resolution and sampling rate. In the medical domain, multimodal data stem from different imaging techniques such as computed tomography (CT), magnetic resonance imaging (MRI), or ultrasound. Despite the data being highly heterogeneous, researchers must, however, combine these data with various attributes and formats to formulate and testify their hypotheses. Often, researchers use *ad-hoc* scripts to process these highly heterogeneous data. Each of the scripts solves one specific task, and the scripts altogether are hard to maintain. With sensors continuously improving, and data formats constantly evolving, researchers find themselves always writing *ad-hoc* processing scripts. Thus:

> *Question 2:* How can we represent and extract scientific insights from heterogeneous data?

While multivariate and multimodal data vary in attribute and format, each different variable requires a dedicated visual format to present its information. As a result, we are left with large amounts of visual representations which will complicate the whole data analysis process. Not only are the many visual representations unable to fit onto a single screen, but using the alternative approach such as *multiple views* [23] might lead to some information being overlooked. Instead, rather than analysing each variable separately, I aim to amplify all relevant information in one visual representation. Hence:

> *Question 3:* How can we merge multimodal and multivariate data into one visual representation?

Data Availability

Research enabled by large research infrastructures is shared among international researchers and collaborations. Thus, it is essential to share data globally. Distributed tools can share insights with other specialists, increase productivity, and encourage more active research. The same technologies can be used to attract a larger audience that may result in promoting the citizen science programme [24]. Hence:

> *Question 4:* How can we exchange data among international research communities?

A primary focus of this thesis is to allow easy data browsing and sharing using the *visual exploration* approach. With data readily available and accessible, the functional blocks used in my design may help connecting scientists and data repository through a common gateway, i.e., web browser. In addition to the traditional textual metadata description, I strive to provide searchable content of the added visual content. Specifically, characterising the visual content can provide a better search experience for users. However, not all data can be sufficiently described in textual metadata, e.g., 3D content, which raises the question:

> *Question 5:* How can we search for non-textual content such as 3D volumes?

1.2 Objectives and Contributions

The problem statements and research questions lay a foundation for the scope and goals of this thesis. In particular, I am going to present the results and contributions of the following objectives:

(i) I will improve the understanding of the visualisation-driven data acquisition system that addresses Big Data challenges. Different visual outputs are identified and described within the scope of flexibility in the design phase.

(ii) I will design an interactive visual exploration system that summarises the core information of the experiments. I will demonstrate my approaches by using experiments in the domain of meteorology, medicine and life science. I will investigate the data acquisition strategy to consolidate all the heterogeneous data in a unified standard manner.

(iii) I will realise all the visualisations using a web-based system which inherently allows one to share data with a wide range of audiences. Since the web-based approach suffers from the bandwidth limitation, I investigate visualisation techniques that reduce the final data size, with the ability to still represent the relevant information. The primary focus will be enabling a broad range of client devices, such as the smartphone, laptop, and powerful workstation, to serve the final visualisation which promotes a multi-resolution visualisation approach. I will also characterise client systems parameters to serve the best visualisation quality to the researchers.

(iv) I will derive searchable attributes from the visual content. As it is unclear how to search a non-textual data content such as a 3D object, I will study and demonstrate how to extract dominant features that best describe a non-textual content.

Given the broad definition of Big Data, it is inevitable that no single scientific experiment encompasses all the Big Data features. Thus, the results and contributions of this thesis are based on many projects conducted in the Institute for Data Processing and Electronics (IPE) in Karlsruhe Institute of Technology (KIT). The institute specialises in the development of custom detector, trigger and data acquisition systems for high data rates and control and monitor systems. It's competences cover the entire signal chain, starting with the physical sensor design, detector assembly through the analogue and digital electronics to the data analysis and archiving. Notably, the institute emphasises in designing and developing data acquisition systems for large-scale experiments. The use case, synchrotron X-ray tomography, is dealt with in the framework of the projects NOVA and ASTOR [12], and meteorology is studied within the KITcube project [25]. Medical aspects are covered by a novel diagnostic device using ultrasound computed tomography (USCT) for early breast cancer diagnosis [26]. As an example for fundamental physics experiments, the Karlsruhe Tritium Neutrino experiment KATRIN [27] is analysed, and finally, the effect of the *Energiewende*[4] are explored in the KIT 1 MW solar storage park [28]. Further information on each experiment will be discussed in Chapter 5. Even with the rich list of experiments, I focus on the two distinct subsets of Big Data (Volume and Variety), which extends our evolving understanding of Big Data in scientific research regarding data management and visualisation.

1.3 Outline

Chapter 2 discusses the current state of digital library framework that embeds visualisation. I present the fundaments of surface and volume renderings that serve as the core visual representations.

[4]Energiewende is a German word for the energy transition. It is a planned transition by Germany to a low carbon, environmentally sound, reliable, and affordable energy supply.

Chapter 3 forms an understanding of designing and developing a visualisation-driven data acquisition system. I study relevant researches and propose a design guideline that applies to various applications based on the user-centric design [29].

Chapter 4 discusses the visualisation techniques for a web-based system. Mainly, the multidimensional raw data is converted into images for further processing within a graphical processing unit (GPU). I present three visualisation modules for the web-based Big Data visualisation system categorised by the multidimensional nature of the raw data.

Chapter 5 presents four use-case studies of Big Data application, where each application consists of a different Big Data challenge. Despite the uniqueness of each experiment, I demonstrate necessary data preprocessing methods based on the proposed design guideline. Each system is built based on the visualisation components discussed in Chapter 4. Also, I evaluate the data interaction between the server and the client to address the system response time. In doing so, the system can provide high-quality visualisation to a wide range of client hardware.

Chapter 6 discusses the contributions and results from the preceding chapters and scrutinises the thesis' objectives. I will give an outlook on possible future work and aspects that are not covered by this thesis.

For some, a library is a dim and dusty place filled with out-of-date texts of limited historical interest...

Traditional library, Kahn and Cerf (1998)

2 Research Background

In this chapter I provide background information that addresses the central question introduced in Chapter 1. Particularly, I describe the digital library domain which is the heart of the Big Data dilemma. Next, I discuss the role of visualisation, particularly how visualisation helps in the process of *knowledge discovery* [1] within the digital library. Following this, I identified a general design guideline to integrate visualisations within the digital library framework. Finally, I explain visualisation techniques in more detail as they provide the foundation of graphical representation used throughout this thesis.

[1] Knowledge discovery describes a complete workflow that starts from recording the data, then cleaning the data, analysing the data, visualising the data, and lastly make sense of the data [4].

2.1 Digital Library Domain

The first use of the term *digital library* dates back to 1988 where Kahn and Cerf [30] presented an open architecture of a digital library system that allows convenient access, either locally or remotely, to geographically distributed users. During that time, this idea was novel because most information was not available in a digital form. They stated their architecture as an extension to the traditional library. The conventional library emphasises storage and preservation of physical items, where users must travel physically to the library to learn from what is available and make use of it [31]. However, the public is losing interest in such community facility in favour of digital technology advancement. For the past two decades, the growth of digital resources such as bibliographic databases and electronic journals are embracing the new library paradigm—digital library [32]. With information resources transforming into digital formats, users no longer need to travel to a library; but instead, they can read and access information through any digitally connected medium, i.e., a web browser. Numerous definitions try to encapsulate what a digital library is [33, 34, 35, 36], where they categorise either by its physical space and collections, by its digital environment, or by its services. In this thesis, I define a *library* by its primary purpose—a community facility which provides public access to its materials. The digital content may be stored locally, or accessed remotely through networks such as cloud services. Hence, a digital library consists of an extensive collection of digital information with public access. Similarly, research facilities have extensive experimental data in which the data are accessible from within the centre or the public. We mainly study the research experiments that store its data into a data repository. In particular, we look at climate research with Doppler wind lidar [25], X-ray imaging for entomology research [12], and medical imaging with ultrasound computer tomography [37].

Each of the experiments tries to capture as much data as possible for better comprehension. Typically, the collected data are stored in storage along with a set of metadata—data attributes which describes the *primary data* [2]. The metadata serve as the tool to enhance the accessibility of *primary data*. The number of stored *primary data* can scale up into the range of millions, and the total size can scale up into the range of petabytes. At such scale, browsing and searching for a particular data set is no longer a trivial task. The current text-based approach is not an ideal solution to present results in this large-scale environment. For example, showing a lengthy list of search results is inefficient, and not intuitive [39]—the items listed at the beginning of the records do not often resemble the best match. Instead, we can incorporate a ranking system that requires users to investigate the top searched results individually [40, 41].

To facilitate the exploration and analysis in a digital library collection [42], existing approaches emphasise metadata analysis, i.e., word-frequency analysis [43], co-occurrence word analysis [44], and probabilistic methods like Latent Dirichlet Allocation (LDA) [45]. While these methods offer a generic solution, they fail to provide information related to a specific domain [46]. Most of the related works focus on a particular data format or application [39, 47, 48]. Instead, my approach is to improve data exploration within a digital library by using visualisation techniques [4, 49, 50, 51].

2.2 The Role of Visualisation

In the scientific research domain, visualisation is often treated as a tool to produce visual outputs that best describe an object. The role of visualisation is to enable domain experts to extract insight from their data [52]. A standard approach to visualisation is to support users' search activities by using information filtering, where the users' interaction defines the attributes of interest that quickly filter out unrelated data [49]. FilmFinder [47] and HomeFinder [48] are classic examples of such visual interfaces that assist users in narrowing

[2]Primary data comprise the original condition of a phenomenon without being processed, transformed, or manipulated into other forms [38].

down the search scope and easily comparing results using the visualisation output. Furthermore, visualisation can be used to understand the relationship between the search query and search results that guide users to formulate a better query in data browsing [53].

In the domain of the digital library, there are numerous visualisation systems available that are reported to improve the overall data browsing experience by using carefully selected techniques [51]. However, these systems are specially designed for their use case. To develop a new visualisation system, I must go through the entire design cycle numerous times. I will discuss the two elements that serve as the bedrock for my design process: general visual interaction guideline and visualisation techniques.

2.2.1 General Visual Interaction Guideline

Visualisation methodologies have long been recognised to improve users' ability to comprehend information quickly [54]. To demonstrate the efficacy of visualisation, numerous applications integrate various visualisation techniques into the digital library domain. Borner and Chen [55] described the three common usages of visual interfaces in the digital library domain: to support identification, to understand the interrelation of retrieved data and to refine a search.

The Envision Digital Library [57] was a prototype digital library for computer science literature. Its user interface allows users to facilitate examining extensive data sets, displaying multiple aspects of the data simultaneously and efficiently, and discovering patterns in the data interactively. Similarly, the LVis (Digital Library Visualizer) project [58] aims to aid users' experience in browsing large document sets. The LVis prototype was based on the data set in the DIDO Image Bank [3]. It uses Latent Semantic Analysis (LSA) to extract relationships between images. This information is vital in the clustering algorithm. To populate the pictures in a 2D or 3D space, LVis modifies

[3]The DIDO Image Bank provides pedagogical images of art historical periods and media. http://dido.dlib.indiana.edu/

Table 2.1.: Summary of visualisation systems implemented for various digital library applications. Each application shows conformance to the path to knowledge discovery based on the *Visual Information Seeking Mantra* [56].

Visualisation System	Data Type	Application	Interaction Design	Visualisation Information Seeking Mantra		
				Overview First	Zoom and Filter	Details-on-demand
Envision [57]	Binary	ACM documents	Dynamic query	Overview of literatures over time.	Cluster relevant documents by its subject.	More information about a literature.
LVis [58]	Image	DIDO Image Bank	Focus-plus-Context, Overview-plus-Detail	Overview about document clusters.	Relate to similar cluster.	More information about an image.
Perseus [59]	Image	Photographs of Greek vases	Focus-plus-Context in wide-angle view.	Overview of vases in eye-level view.	Subset of vases about the vase.	More information
UC [39]	Text document	Research publications	Dynamic query, Zoom	Continuous treemap of a document collection. documents.	Highlight and limit the view to matching	Begins reading with the ReadUp reader.
ActiveGraph [60]	Text document	Research publications	Dynamic query publications.	Overview of with applied filter.	Update scatter plot about the publication.	More information
ResultMap [51]	Repository document	Online repositories	Brushing, Dynamic query	Overview of document's attributes	Brushing an entry in the result lists.	More information about the result.
CodiViz-II [61]	Image	Old manuscripts	Focus-plus-Context, Overview-plus-Detail	Overview of old manuscript's attributes.	Update view base on applied filter.	More information about the page.

the Boltzmann algorithm to compute the spatial coordinates. Shiaw et al. [59] presented a digital library that uses 3D space to display and browse a collection of Greek vases. Unlike a traditional digital library that displays thumbnails and descriptions of vases, the 3D vase museum presents each vase as a 3D object and places it in a virtual room. They combined 3D models and 2D photographs to describe each data set while taking advantage of the 3D capabilities to zoom and navigate around the virtual room. Good et al. [39] presented the UpLib Client (UC) system that uses continuous and quantum treemap layouts to display collections of documents based on the search criteria. They emphasise fluidity in data browsing that allows users to focus on the data, rather than the interface itself. Using the UC system, users can zoom out, zoom in, search in context, limit the view to search results, breakdown to pages and read the document. ActiveGraph [60] is another system that presents multiple perspectives to visualise documents of a digital library. Here, a set of digital library documents are represented as data set in a 2D or 3D scatter plot. The data set can be any digital library objects, e.g., books, journals, papers, images or web resources. The information of the digital library objects is encoded into six visual attributes of the scatterplot: X-axis, Y-axis, Z-axis, colour, size and shape. Clarkson et al. [51] developed a system, known as ResultMap, which emphasises the hierarchy representation of search results within a digital library. They used treemap to organise results in a space-efficient hierarchical display. Their system maps each document in the hierarchical tree structures and highlights the query that corresponds to the outcome. In the digital humanity domain, Chandna et al. [61] presented the CodiViz-II visualisation interface that allows domain experts to find clusters, correlations, outliers, errors in their data by using flexible browsing capabilities. They used parallel coordinates to address the multidimensional nature of the digitised old manuscripts.

Despite the various interaction designs in Table 2.1, the primary goal of these applications is the exploration of the data through visualisations. Few [62] claimed that skilled data seekers tend to converge towards the

Visual Information Seeking Mantra [56]: Overview first, zoom and filter, then details-on-demand [56]. It is a data searching pattern that Few [62] dubbed "the sure path to discovery". Schneidermann, who coined the mantra, provided a useful starting point for designing advanced graphical user interfaces. He summarised this design principle by observing numerous applications which they all have in common:

> There are many visual design guidelines, but the basic principle might be summarised as the *Visual Information Seeking Mantra* [56]:
>
> Overview first, zoom and filter, then details-on-demand
> Overview first, zoom and filter, then details-on-demand
> Overview first, zoom and filter, then details-on-demand
> Overview first, zoom and filter, then details-on-demand
> Overview first, zoom and filter, then details-on-demand
> Overview first, zoom and filter, then details-on-demand
> Overview first, zoom and filter, then details-on-demand
>
> Each line represents one project in which I found myself rediscovering this principle and therefore wrote it down it as a reminder.
>
> — Ben Schneidermann (1996)

From the various interaction designs shown in Table 2.1, I also find myself noticing similarities from the applications as they adhere to the mantra as well. The primary difference between these systems lies in the format of input data, where the format has to conform with the chosen visualisation techniques. Schneidermann [56] and Keim [63] both described taxonomies for information visualisation, which showed a wide variety of visualisation techniques requiring different input data.

To address the various formats for the intended visualisations, Chi [64] proposed a visualisation pipeline, known as the *data state reference model*,

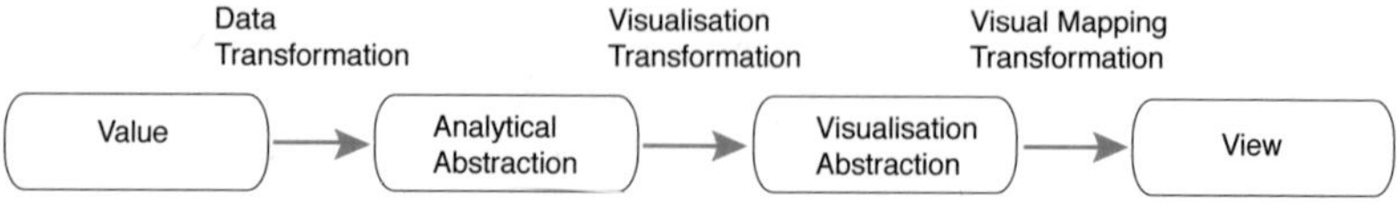

Figure 2.1.: The *data state reference model* by Chi [64]. The black box denotes the state of the data, whereas the arrow shows the action performed from one state to another.

where the pipeline described the transformation of the input data into a visual format. This model uses an operator framework to characterise different visualisation techniques. It breaks the visualisation pipeline into four data stages, three types of transformations (grey arrows in Figure 2.1) and four types of within-stage operators (black boxes in Figure 2.1). The Value stage shows the raw data input which can be an image database or a relational database. In the data transformation, the data structure is altered to suit the application. Data operations such as data reduction and data fusion are commonly applied. In the visualisation transformation, the data structure is transformed into a visual data format. For example, the encoded image format is used as a lookup table within the GPU memory for the final visual mapping transformation [19, 65].

To date, the *information visualisation reference model* [54] and the *data state reference model* [64] are still prominent in describing the conceptual visualization pipeline. While these models are beneficial for understanding visualisation systems, these models need to be refined for each different application domain. Tobiasz et al. [66] adopted the *data state reference model* as the conceptual pipeline for their system. Brunetti et al. [67] developed the *Linked Data Visualisation Model* based on Chi's model to guide developers and designers in the Resource Description Framework (RDF) data visualisations. Cottam et al. [68] included a set of dynamic sources to the *information visualisation reference model*. Treinish [69] proposed a functional-based data model, where he described a taxonomy on the aggregation layer. Elmqvist and Fekete [70] presented a hierarchical aggregation data model with a large demonstration of many visual techniques. Besides the conceptual models, I study the approach demonstrated by the ATLAS experiment at Large Hadron

Collider [71], in which they incorporated data separation as part of their data management pipeline. In their workflow, the raw data set is reconstructed to produce event summary data (ESD) and further processed to create analysis object data (AOD). The data complexity decreases gradually from raw data to ESD to AOD [72].

To this end, I identified commonality from various visualisation systems, where I summarise the process of designing visualisation within the digital library domain into two stages. Firstly, the visualisation must adhere to the *Visual Information Seeking Mantra* [56]. Secondly, the preprocessing of the data follows the *data state reference model* to produce a set of suitable data formats.

2.2.2 Visualisation Techniques

In the early 1970s, the subject *rendering* [4] concentrated on producing a realistic picture. Back then, rendered images did not resemble the real world which motivates research in photorealistic rendering. The primary goal of photorealistic rendering is to reproduce how an object or a scene would look if it were photographed. Photorealistic rendering deals with light interaction on the surface and describes how light reflects, refracts and scatters in a real environment—surface rendering. Later in the early 1980s, medical imaging challenges scientific visualisation to go beyond the surface, and view the internal data structure [73]. In this section, I discuss the two visualisation techniques: surface and volume rendering. Subsequently, I explain the approach to integrate these methods on a web-based platform.

2.2.2.1 Volume Rendering

Instead of rendering a realistic image, we can extract valuable information from the data, i.e., viewing internal organs in medical imaging. Medical practitioners can visualise internal organs and prepare themselves better before

[4] Rendering is a process which creates an image from an object or a scene using a set of mathematical models.

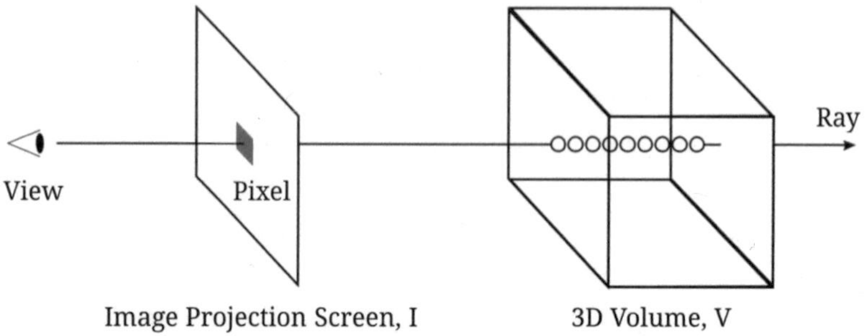

Figure 2.2.: An overview of the direct volume rendering method.

a surgery session, e.g., Grimson et al. [74] described an automatic registration method that enables a visual mix of live video of the patient with the segmented 3D MRI or CT model for planning and guiding neurosurgical procedures. This rendering technique is called volume rendering which refers to the creation of an image from volumetric data—an object with some particular internal structure or distribution of features.

Although the volume rendering approach is mainly applied to medical imaging images, i.e., magnetic resonance tomography (MRT) or computed tomography (CT), the technique is also widely adopted in many fields of engineering and science such as metrology and geology. Volume rendering is commonly used to visualise 3D scalar fields, in which a set of techniques are used to display a 2D projection image of a 3D volumetric data set (Figure 2.2). A 3D scalar field maps a position x in space onto a scalar value.

$$s: \ \Omega \longrightarrow \mathbb{R}, \quad s \longmapsto s(x) \tag{2.1}$$

where $\Omega \subset \mathbb{R}^3$ denotes the 3D Euclidean space [75, 76, 77]. To compute a two-dimensional image of the scalar field, the effects of the optical properties are synthesised by modelling the transport of light along each viewing ray. The scalar field is also known as a participating medium, where light particles interact within the medium in several ways: absorption, emission, and in- and out-scattering. Hence, the particle interactions contribute to the radiance at a single point [78].

Blinn [79] made some assumptions in his model for volume rendering to simplify the light transfer equation and thus reduce the computational complexity. The important assumption is that the volume is in a low albedo environment. The albedo of light particles describes the degree of incoming light reflection. On the one hand, a high albedo environment refers to multiple scatterings of light particles in the medium. On the other hand, a low albedo environment only considers one scattering along the viewing ray. Also, Blinn considered just the absorption and emission components, which simplified the equation to the emission-absorption model [78]. The emission component determines the intensity and colour of a particle inside the volume while the absorption expresses the opacity, respectively.

Volume Rendering Integral To display the 2D display image of the 3D volumetric data set, two approaches are usually performed: the object-order approach and the image-order approach. The main difference between the two methods lies in the iteration direction of the rendering algorithm. The object-order method iterates from the volumetric data set and determines how each voxel contributes to the 2D image projection, i.e., shear-warp [80], marching cubes [81]. Conversely, the image-order iterates from each pixel of the 2D image projection and determines how the 3D volumetric data contribute to the final colour, i.e., ray casting [82, 83, 84, 85]. The lower iterations of the image-order algorithm made the approach more efficient. Given a ray R along the viewing direction v_{dir}:

$$R: \; r(\lambda) = r_{start} + \lambda \cdot v_{dir} \quad \text{with} \quad \forall \lambda \in \mathbb{R} \tag{2.2}$$

where the differential radiance dL of the emission-absorption model at position λ along the ray R is

$$\frac{dL(\lambda)}{d\lambda} = g(\lambda) - \kappa(\lambda) \cdot L(\lambda) \tag{2.3}$$

The source term $g(\lambda)$ describes the amount of light emitted while the extinction coeficient $\kappa(\lambda)$ defines the amount of light attenuated at position λ within the participating medium, respectively. Solving Equation 2.3 for a viewing ray starting from the start position $\lambda_0 = 0$ to the last position ξ yields the volume rendering integral [78]:

$$L(\xi) = L(0) \cdot e^{-\int_0^{\xi} \kappa(\lambda')\, d\lambda'} + \int_0^{\xi} g(\lambda) \cdot e^{-\int_{\lambda}^{\xi} \kappa(\lambda')\, d\lambda'}\, d\lambda \qquad (2.4)$$

with $L(0)$ representing the initial radiance point, the accumulated radiance leaving the participating medium along the view direction is denoted by $L(\xi)$. If the extinction term κ is not constant, the amount of radiant energy reaching the viewer is integrated along the distance from λ_1 to λ_2 which can be represented as

$$T(\lambda_1, \lambda_2) = e^{-\int_{\lambda_1}^{\lambda_2} \kappa(\lambda')\, d\lambda'} \qquad (2.5)$$

Substituting Equation 2.5 into the volume rendering integral (Equation 2.4) results in a simpler form:

$$L(\xi) = L(0) \cdot T(\xi) + \int_0^{\xi} g(\lambda) \cdot T(\lambda, \xi)\, d\lambda \qquad (2.6)$$

Equation 2.6 can be numerically approximated by using Riemann sum where the viewing ray is divided into multiple equidistant segments, n. The length of each segment is $\triangle\lambda = (\xi - \lambda_0)/n)$. Equation 2.5, also known as the optical transparency, can be approximated using Riemann sum between segment i at $\lambda_i = \lambda_0 + i \cdot \triangle\lambda$ and the end point at $\lambda = \xi$,

$$T(\lambda_i, \xi) \approx e^{-\sum\limits_{k=i}^{n-1} \kappa(\lambda_k) \cdot \triangle\lambda} = \prod_{k=i}^{n-1} e^{-\kappa(\lambda_i) \cdot \triangle\lambda} \qquad (2.7)$$

the transparency of the ith segment is defined as

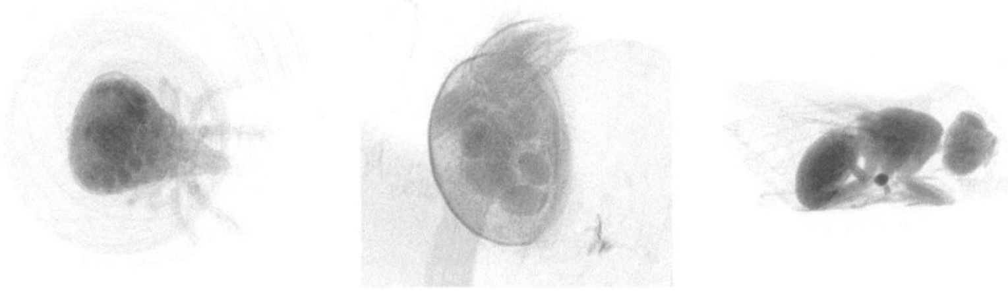

Figure 2.3.: Direct volume rendering (inverted particle model) of the oribatid mite *Archegozetes longisetosus* (left), the box mite *Euphthiracarus reticulatus* (middle) and an unidentified Diptera species—fly (right).

$$t_i = e^{-\kappa(\lambda_i)\cdot\triangle\lambda} \tag{2.8}$$

and the source term g_i for the ith segment as

$$g_i = g(\lambda_i)\cdot\triangle\lambda \tag{2.9}$$

Together with definitions (2.8) and (2.9),the volume rendering integral in (2.6) can be approximated for n segments:

$$L(\xi) \approx L(0)\cdot\prod_{i=0}^{n-1} t_i + \sum_{k=i}^{n-1} g_i \cdot \prod_{j=i+1}^{n-1} t_j \tag{2.10}$$

The resulting discretised integral is adopted in numerous direct volume rendering applications. Whenever a ray casting is performed, the final composition on each pixel of the 2D image projection is evaluated according to Equation 2.10.

The Particle Model Max described a variation from the volume rendering integral, where the intensity $C = C(\lambda)$ is constant along the ray [78]. Thus, resulting in an image similar to an X-ray negative—brightest where the data is most dense, darkest where the data is most sparse. Depending on the background colour, the particle model can be inverted for better contrast.

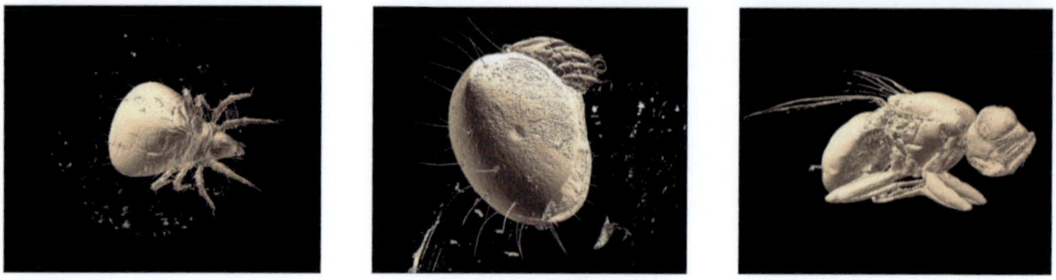

Figure 2.4.: Surface rendering (Phong illumination model) of the oribatid mite *Archegozetes longisetosus* (left), the box mite *Euphthiracarus reticulatus* (middle) and an unidentified Diptera species (right).

Figure 2.3 shows an inverted version of the particle model with a white background. With source term $g(\lambda)$ being composed of $C \cdot \kappa(\lambda)$. The second term of the volume rendering equation (2.6) can be further simplified:

$$\begin{aligned}\int_0^\xi g(\lambda) \cdot e^{-\int_\lambda^\xi \kappa(\lambda')\,d\lambda'}\,d\lambda &= \int_0^\xi C \cdot \kappa(\lambda) \cdot e^{-\int_\lambda^\xi \kappa(\lambda')\,d\lambda'}\,d\lambda \\ &= C \cdot \int_0^\xi \frac{d}{d\lambda} e^{-\int_\lambda^\xi \kappa(\lambda')\,d\lambda'}\,d\lambda \\ &= C \cdot \left(1 - e^{-\int_0^\xi \kappa(\lambda')\,d\lambda'}\right)\end{aligned} \tag{2.11}$$

Substituting the simplified equation (2.11) and the transparency equation (2.5) into Equation 2.6 results in a colour composition equation:

$$L(\xi) = L(0) \cdot T(\xi) + C \cdot (1 - T(\xi)) \tag{2.12}$$

where $L(0)$ denotes the background for the composition of colour C. $T(\xi)$ determines the transparency, and often, the term $(1 - T(\xi))$ represents the opacity—the probability that colour reaches the viewer.

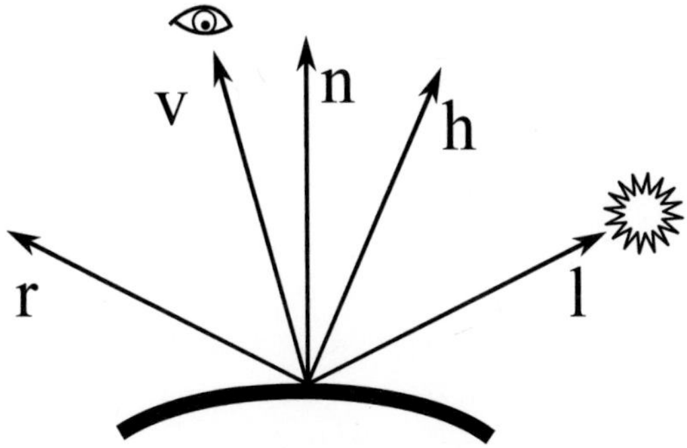

Figure 2.5.: Direction vectors for calculating the Phong illumination model and the Cook-Torrance model: **r**: reflected direction, **v**: view direction, **n**: normal direction, **h**: half-angle direction, and **l**: light source direction.

2.2.2.2 Surface Rendering

Surface rendering deals with how light interacts with the surface of an object by using a lighting model. Figure 2.4 shows the surface rendering of the oribatid mite *Archegozetes longisetosus*, the box mite *Euphthiracarus reticulatus*, and an unidentified Diptera species. A lighting model calculates the behaviour of light, precisely how light sources, materials and geometry interacts. Modelling of light interaction can be categorised into local and global illumination models. The local illumination model is only concerned with how the light behaves at a specific position on the surface, while global illumination deals additionally with shadows and indirect lights. In this thesis, I will focus on the local illumination method. The two most common local illumination models which calculate light per pixel are the Phong model and the Cook-Torrance model. Figure 2.5 shows the direction vectors necessary for the calculation of the Phong illumination model and the Cook-Torrance model. In the following sections, direction vectors will be expressed in bold typeface, i.e., $(\mathbf{l} \bullet \mathbf{n})$ denotes the dot product between the vector **l** and **n**.

Phong Illumination Model Back in 1975, Bui Tuong Phong published a simple model for specular falloff using an integer power of the cosine angle of α—the angle between outgoing view direction and specular direction [86]. His work focused on improving shading methods and also adding realism to renderings of 3D objects. The Phong illumination model consists of three terms: an ambient term, a diffuse term and a specular term. Assuming that there is only one point light source, the illumination intensity at point x can be represented as below:

$$I = I_a + I_d + I_s. \tag{2.13}$$

Figure 2.6 shows the visual illustration of each term that constitutes the Phong model. The Phong illumination model is a local illumination model which considers only direct illumination —it does not consider indirect lightings nor shadows. Hence, the ambient term is included to approximate indirect illumination effects. The contribution of the ambient term is to ensure that voxels with gradients pointing away from light source do not appear pitch black. Let $L_{a,in}$ represents the total intensity of the incoming ambient light. In the Phong model, the surface has an associated ambient reflectivity coefficient k_a that specifies the fraction of the ambient light reflected. The equation for the intensity of the outgoing ambient light is

$$I_a = L_{a,in} \cdot k_a \tag{2.14}$$

The diffuse term simulates the diffuse reflection according to Lambertian law, which states that the reflected light intensity is relative to the angle of incidence. The amount of light that is diffusely reflected is modeled as:

$$I_d = L_{d,in} \cdot k_d \cdot \cos\theta = L_{d,in} \cdot k_d \cdot (\mathbf{l} \bullet \mathbf{n}) \tag{2.15}$$

where $L_{d,in}$ is the intensity of the diffusely reflected light in the viewpoint direction. The term k_d denotes the diffuse reflectivity coefficient which represents the physical property of the surface material.

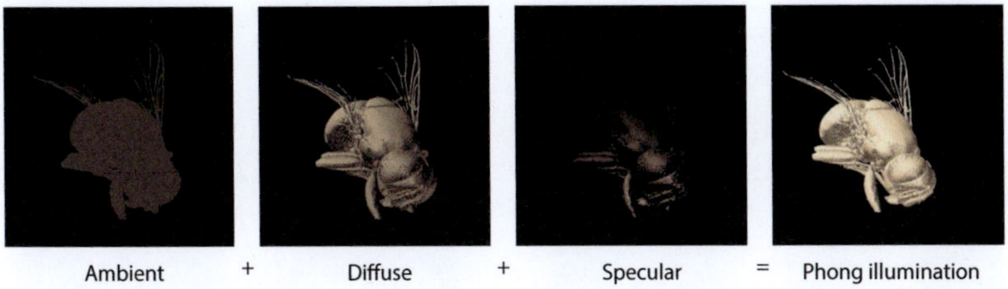

Figure 2.6.: Visual illustration of the Phong equation.

The specular term simulates the shininess of the surface which gives the viewer an idea of light source positions and geometry details. The Phong lighting model uses the factor $(\cos\varphi)^f$ to model the falloff in light intensity in the reflection direction that differs by an angle of φ from the vector direction **r** of perfect reflection.

$$I_s = L_{s,in} \cdot k_s \cdot (\cos\varphi)^f = L_{s,in} \cdot k_s \cdot (\mathbf{v} \bullet \mathbf{r})^f \tag{2.16}$$

where k_s is the specular reflectivity coefficient and $L_{s,in}$ is the intensity of the specular light originating from the light source. In practice, the half vector **h** is used to simplify the calculation of I_s, which is defined to be the unit vector halfway between the light source direction and the view direction [87].

$$\mathbf{h} = \frac{\mathbf{l} + \mathbf{v}}{||\mathbf{l} + \mathbf{v}||} \tag{2.17}$$

The specular term in Equation 2.16 can be defined with the half vector, and the half angle ψ—the angle between **h** and the surface normal **n** as below:

$$I_s = L_{s,in} \cdot k_s \cdot (\cos\psi)^f = L_{s,in} \cdot k_s \cdot (\mathbf{h} \bullet \mathbf{n})^{f'} \tag{2.18}$$

Although Equation 2.16 and 2.18 are not exactly the same, both equations provide qualitatively similar results when f' is set higher than f [88].

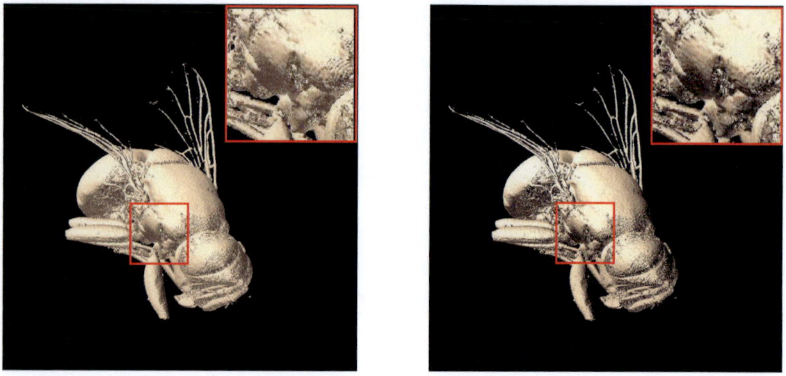

Figure 2.7.: Surface rendering of an unidentified Diptera species using the Phong illumination model (left) and the Cook-Torrance illumination model (right). The contrast between the occluded and non-occluded regions are higher in the Cook-Torrance implementation.

Cook-Torrance Illumination Model The Cook–Torrance lighting model is an alternative to Phong lighting that can better capture reflectance properties of a broader range of surface materials [89]. The visual difference between the Phong illumination model and the Cook-Torrance illumination model is shown in Figure 2.7. Although the Cook-Torrance model shows a better contrast between the exposed and occluded surfaces, the computation cost of the Cook-Torrance model is higher than the Phong model. The Cook–Torrance lighting model is based on a microfacet model for surface reflection, where the incident light either reflects immediately or penetrates the microfacet surface causing further multiple reflections inside the material before exiting the surface in a random direction.

Similar to the Phong model, the Cook-Torrance model is also composed of the three terms: ambient term, diffuse term, and specular term. Thus,

$$\begin{aligned} I &= I_a + I_d + I_s \\ &= L_{a,in} \cdot k_a + L_{d,in} \cdot k_d \cdot (\mathbf{l} \bullet \mathbf{n}) + I_s \end{aligned} \tag{2.19}$$

In contrast to the Phong model, the definition of the specular intensity in Cook-Torrance model is as below:

$$I_s = \frac{(\mathbf{l} \bullet \mathbf{n})}{(\mathbf{v} \bullet \mathbf{n})} \cdot L_{s,in} \cdot s \cdot F \cdot G \cdot D \tag{2.20}$$

where $(\mathbf{l} \bullet \mathbf{n}) \cdot L_{d,in}$ measures the amount of light energy reaching a unit area of the surface, and $(\mathbf{v} \bullet \mathbf{n}) \cdot I_s$ measures the amount of light energy leaving the unit area of the surface. Also, the product $(s \cdot F \cdot G \cdot D)$ denotes the energy ratio of energy reaching to energy leaving the unit area in the direction of $\mathbf{v}$. The constant s is used to scale the brightness of the specular reflection.

The F term is the Fresnel coefficient which shows what percentage of the incidence light is reflected. In practice, the Schlick's approximation [90] is used for better computation efficiency which provides a similar coefficient value. Also, the halfway vector is also adopted in the definition, which gives:

$$F = f_\lambda + (1 - f_\lambda) \cdot (1 - (\mathbf{h} \bullet \mathbf{v}))^5 \tag{2.21}$$

where f_λ is the reflection coefficient for incident light parallel to the normal of the surface.

The geometric term G computes the fraction of the illuminated portion of the surface that is visible to the viewer. The term considers the roughness of the microfacet surface:

$$G = max\left(1, \frac{2 \cdot (\mathbf{h} \bullet \mathbf{n})(\mathbf{v} \bullet \mathbf{n})}{(\mathbf{h} \bullet \mathbf{v})}, \frac{2 \cdot (\mathbf{h} \bullet \mathbf{n})(\mathbf{l} \bullet \mathbf{n})}{(\mathbf{h} \bullet \mathbf{l})}\right) \tag{2.22}$$

The microfacet model D assumes that light incident from the direction of $\mathbf{l}$ is specularly reflected independently by each individual microfacet. Hence, the amount of light reflected in the direction $\mathbf{v}$ is deemed to be proportional to the fraction of microfacets that are correctly oriented to cause mirror-like reflection in that direction. One such model is the Beckmann Distribution function, defined as:

$$D = \frac{1}{\pi \cdot m^2 \cdot \cos^4 \cdot \alpha} \cdot e^{-\left(\frac{\tan\alpha}{m}\right)^2} = \frac{1}{\pi \cdot m^2 \cdot (\mathbf{h} \bullet \mathbf{n})^4} \cdot e^{-\left(\frac{(\mathbf{h}\cdot\mathbf{n})^2-1}{m^2\cdot(\mathbf{h}\cdot\mathbf{n})^2}\right)} \tag{2.23}$$

where m defines the surface roughness—larger m indicates rough and bumpy surface.

Gradient Computation In surface rendering, the surface normal vector, **n**, is essential for calculating the illumination models. Often, surface normal can be derived from the triangle primitives of a 3D object. However, scientific experiment often presents a voxel-based volume. Instead of triangle primitives, the data consists of voxels.

To determine the surface normal from voxels, I compute the gradient of a 3D intensity function vector at all points of interest. The gradient vector is the first order derivative of a discrete volume with respect to all threes directions. Given a function $f(x, y, z)$ the gradient is:

$$\nabla f(x, y, z) = \left(\frac{\partial f}{\partial x}, \frac{\partial f}{\partial y}, \frac{\partial f}{\partial z}\right) \tag{2.24}$$

There are several methods for calculating the gradient vector, i.e., the intermediate difference operator, the central difference operator, the Zucker-Hummel operator [91], and the Sobel 3D operator [92]. The most common method is the central difference method which estimates the derivative by calculating the first terms of a Taylor expansion [93]. By taking the six neighbouring voxels, the gradient can be calculated using the following equation:

$$\begin{aligned} g(x, y, z) = \nabla f(x_i, y_j, z_k) = & \tfrac{1}{2} \cdot \left(f\left(x_{i+1}, y_j, z_k\right) - f\left(x_{i-1}, y_j, z_k\right)\right), \\ & \tfrac{1}{2} \cdot \left(f\left(x_i, y_{j+1}, z_k\right) - f\left(x_i, y_{j-1}, z_k\right)\right), \\ & \tfrac{1}{2} \cdot \left(f\left(x_i, y_j, z_{k+1}\right) - f\left(x_i, y_j, z_{k-1}\right)\right) \end{aligned} \tag{2.25}$$

where x_i, y_j, z_k represents spatial coordinates of the volume. For a better estimation of the gradient vector, the 26 closest neighbours can be evaluated, i.e., the Zucker-Hummel operator and the Sobel 3D operator.

2.3 Web-based Visualisation

A visualisation system is often developed as a desktop application, which permits full utilisation of the machine's capabilities [4, 94]. However, such a visualisation system is restricted to only one machine, and dependent on many software packages [95]. Alternatively, a web-based visualisation system allows multiple users access from various geographical locations. Mwalongo et al. [96] discussed the benefits of web-based visualisation where they emphasise remote visualisation. This approach aligns with the concept of the digital library to provide and share information with the public. In this section, I will discuss caveats and methods to adapt the visualisation techniques in a web-based system.

Since the introduction of the World Wide Web in 1991, data sharing through the web browser was made possible. Limited to a simple scripting task, web browser technology did not utilise the full potential of the client hardware. Fortunately, recent advancement in web technologies has significantly improved the capability of web technology where it can harness the power of GPUs by using WebGL [97] and HTML5 technologies. In particular, major web browsers support resource-intensive GPU-accelerated client-side rendering, i.e., ray marching approach [98] or interactive data visualisation [65].

In essence, the visual information representing the large data should be available to a broad range of users with diverse hardware requirements. On the one hand, users with lower client requirement would appreciate a recognisable visual preview of the data; on the other hand, users with higher client requirements would expect the best quality of visual contents. However, the web-based visualisation is served from a single codebase, and addressing diverse hardware requirements increases the code complexity. Furthermore,

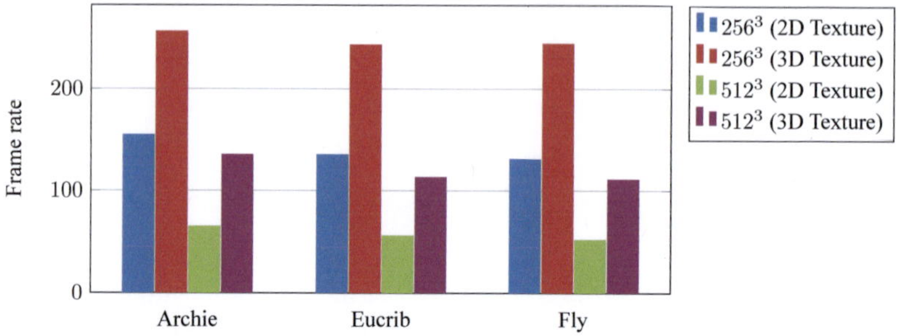

Figure 2.8.: The frame rate of the oribatid mite *Archegozetes longisetosus* (Archie), the box mite *Euphthiracarus reticulatus* (Eucrib) and an unidentified Diptera species (Fly) in two volume sizes (256^3 and 512^3) and textures (2D and 3D). The higher the frame rate, the better.

the different WebGL versions complicate my effort to generalise the codebase. For example, WebGL 1.0 supports 2D texture solely, while WebGL 2.0 supports 2D and 3D textures. Figure 2.8 shows the frame rates of rendering data sets using both 2D and 3D textures. By comparing the same data size, rendering the data using 2D texture leads to lower frame rates due to the slower shader-based interpolation approach in comparison to the hardware interpolation provided by the 3D texture approach. Ideally, we would prefer 3D texture as it offers hardware interpolation that is much faster, but at the same time, we would like to serve the majority of the client systems that support only the 2D texture. Hence, I support both 2D and 3D textures depending on the client requirement.

To render 3D volume using the 2D texture, I emulate the 3D texture function in the fragment shader where a series of cross-section slices can represent the 3D volume, and they are arranged in a mosaic gridded format on one or multiple images. Similar to the term *mipmap*, I dub the resulting grid image as *slicemap*. Figure 2.9 shows how slices are arranged into one or multiple 2D textures. The width, W, and height, H, of each *slicemap* are equal and is set as a power-of-two product, e.g., 256, 512, 1024, 2048, or 4096 texels. Two parameters determine the client hardware requirement: texture size and a tex-

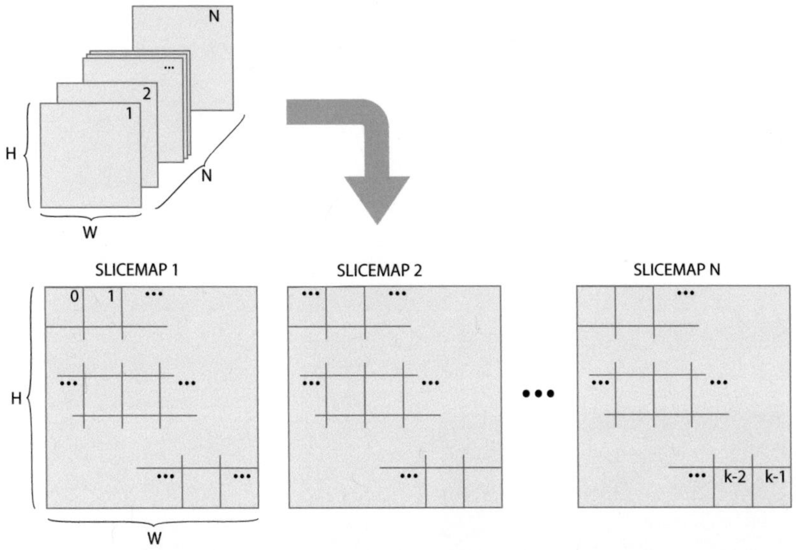

Figure 2.9.: A 3D volume—a set of k 2D slices—is arranged into multiple 2D textures (*slicemaps*). The width W and height H of each slicemap are kept equal and set as power-of-two product such as 2048 or 4096 texels. The index iteration of slices in the slicemap configuration starts from the first slicemap from top to bottom, and from left to right, $[0,\ k-1]$.

ture unit. Since the size of each texture is limited, I enable multiple slicemaps to support a higher number of slices, N. The index iteration of slices in the slicemaps are from top to bottom, and from left to right. The texture size defines the image resolution of the slicemap, whereas the texture unit defines the number of slicemaps that can be rendered. For instance, a *Nexus 5* Android phone (GPU: Adreno 330) can accept up to 16 images with each image not exceeding the image resolution of 4096^2 texels. To exploit the maximum texture capacity of the GPU, I stream multiple slicemaps to load larger volumetric models [19, 99]. In Figure 2.10, a total of six slicemaps are used to render the unidentified Diptera species data set. Each slicemap has an image resolution of 2048^2 texels fitted in an 8×8 mosaic configuration.

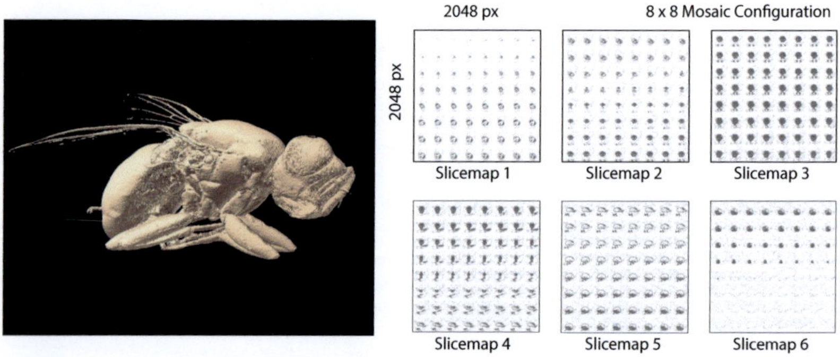

Figure 2.10.: Six slicemaps (right) that are required to render the unidentified Diptera species (left). The slicemap follows a mosaic configuration of 8×8 with each slicemap having an image resolution of 2048^2 texels.

The future cannot be predicted, but futures can be invented.[a]

Gabor (1963)

[a] A quote from Dennis Gabor, a Nobel laureate, for his invention of the holograph.

3 Design Considerations for Big Data Visualisation Systems

With data sets growing beyond terabytes or even petabytes in scientific experiments, there is a trend of keeping data at storage facilities and providing remote cloud-based services for analysis. The tendency arises due to the inconvenience of moving large-scale data which is time-consuming. However, data analysis involves constant data browsing where exploring large-scale data poses high data and network latencies. Moreover, the client hardware varies regarding performance capabilities which further complicates the deployment strategy. To visualise Big Data with low data latency, we can reduce the large size into a manageable size, i.e., the data can be aggregated into multiple smaller data sets that differ in its resolution detail. While providing the appropriate aggregated data to each specific client solves the diversity of client hardware, the primary challenge lies in how well-aggregated data can represent the original data.

In this chapter, I discuss related works that address Big Data management and visualisation: in-situ visualisation, multi-resolution approach, and visualisation software. I begin the overview based on a general data processing pipeline. Then, I organise the considerations of managing and visualising Big Data based on three aspects: the processing model, the data model, and designing a visualisation framework for Big Data applications. Lastly, I discuss the common visualisation techniques that are applicable in most Big Data applications based on the type of data and the degree of interaction.

3.1 Motivation

Most Big Data applications have been designed to solve a specific use-case [4]. Thus, while these applications have its data processing pipeline, their solution is not easily portable to other use cases. Furthermore, the large size and high dimensionality of the data complicate the data visualisation process. Hence, different applications tend to have different solutions that solve a specific Big Data challenge. With the amount of data continually growing, research in designing Big Data system is worthwhile to consider to cope with the massive data scale [5].

However, the requirements of designing a Big Data system varies from experiment to experiment regarding budget and its primary use case [6]. Firstly, the funding of an experiment determines the resource availability and influences the final design of the system—mainly the consideration of whether the system should process the data beforehand or in real-time. Secondly, the visualisation of a Big Data system consists of both an interaction component and a data representation component. Thus, an effective Big Data system needs to address these two aspects during the designing process [100]. Next, I discuss related literature that deals with managing and visualising Big Data. Then, the remainder discusses the type of considerations to design the system, mainly the processing model and the data model. Also, I describe the visualisation outputs that fits into the design workflow.

3.2 Remote Visualisation

Prior works in the processing of extensive data in a data acquisition system focus on the concept of limiting the data movement [1]. The data relates to the experiment or client-side visualisation of simulation data. Mainly, I emphasise visualisation-driven data acquisition system. Since the limited network bandwidth is the bottleneck, reducing or restricting data movements will improve the latency of the system. These prior works mainly revolve around the concept of *in-situ visualisation* which allows users to connect directly to a running simulation, examine the data, do numerical queries and create graphical output while the simulation executes. Alternatively, *multi-resolution technique* is a conventional approach that prepares a hierarchy of similar data that varies in resolution details. Rather than serving the experiment large data set, the server sends smaller aggregated data that can represent the original data adequately. Although the multi-resolution technique has earlier been presented in 1983 by Williams [101], such an approach is still valid, as the system bottleneck continues to remain at the network bandwidth because advancement in data acquisition far exceeds the advancement in data transmission [102]. Finally, I study similar visualisation software that addresses Big Data challenges.

3.2.1 In-situ Visualisation

Rivi et al. [103] described three different approaches in the field of in-situ visualisation: they are tightly-coupled, loosely-coupled and hybrid approaches (Figure 3.1). The tightly-coupled setup describes a system where the visualisation and analysis compute nodes have direct access to the memory of the sim-

[1] The data movement refers to the cost of transferring data from one compute node or resource to another.

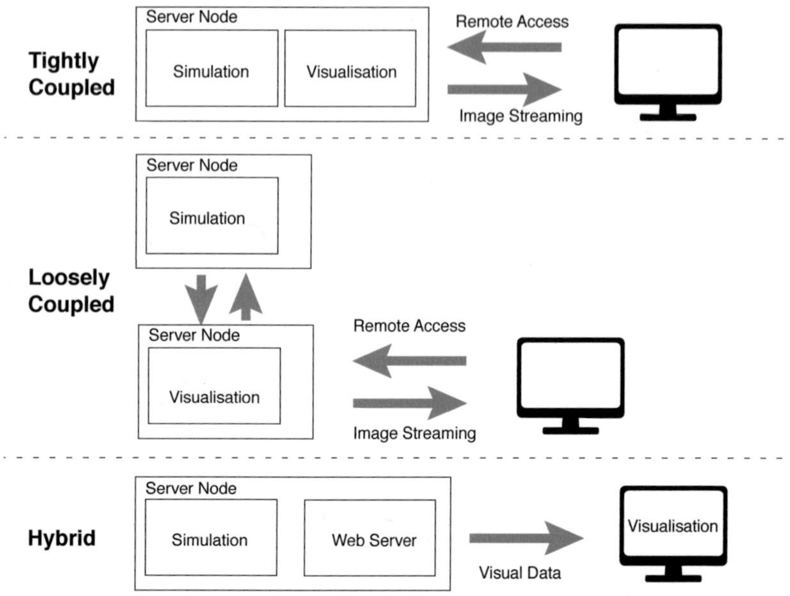

Figure 3.1.: Three in-situ visualisation setups: tightly-coupled, loosely-coupled, and hybrid approaches.

ulation code. The tightly-coupled approach does not require any data movement since the visualisation and computation running on the same node or machine. There are numerous applications based on the tightly-coupled setup as can be seen in SCIRun [104], Hercules [105], YT package [106], ADIOS and CoDS (Co-located DataSpaces) [107] and Damaris/Viz [108]. The tightly-coupled setup benefits from images rendered directly from the original data which provide the optimal quality. Due to the small size of the rendered image, users can query the information of the large data continuously—image streaming. However, this approach requires large investments in visualisation equipment and sound knowledge in the experiment's simulation. Also, the maintenance effort is high due to tightly-coupled software between the visualisation and simulation.

By separating the resources into simulation and visualisation components, I present the loosely-coupled approach where visualisation and analysis nodes run on concurrent resources. The approach introduces a minimal data movement over the network between the simulation node and the visualisation node (server-side). This approach offers flexibility but at the expense of being restricted by the network bandwidth—latency for memory copies between simulation and post-processing hosts. Applications using the loosely-coupled approach are EPSN [109], PreData and ADIOS [110, 111], an adaptive framework for critical climate applications [112], Catalyst [113] and Strawman [114]. In contrast to the previous tightly-coupled setup, these applications have a clear separation between simulation and the visualisation nodes that eases the maintenance effort.

A third variant is a hybrid approach where it inherits the advantages and the disadvantages of both tightly-coupled and loosely-coupled methods. The hybrid approach reduces the data size at the server before distributing the reduced data to a concurrent resource. Typically, the hybrid approach employs the web browser for better data sharing across various platforms, e.g., ParaView Web [115], Cinema [116] and, WAVE [19].

These approaches are still widely used in most HPC facilities. There is no single universal technique for in-situ visualisation where each method has its particular use case. The choice depends on the domain expert and experiment needs. For instance, the tightly-coupled approach is not limited by the network bandwidth in a local setup, but the process is synchronous. If an error occurs within the software, both the simulation and the visualisation components will suffer a downtime. On the other hand, the loosely-coupled approach involves data movement over the network, but the operation is asynchronous. In this setup, an error in the simulation code will not affect the visualisation code and vice versa. Recently, the hybrid approach focuses on collaborative visualisation that helps domain experts in sharing their knowledge among one another. Also, the flexibility of the hybrid setup allows itself to operate even in a resource-constrained environment [65].

To address the Big Data visualisation, I propose a strategy to provide the optimal visual output with aggregated data sets. My approach follows the hybrid setup where I focus on supplying aggregated data that match the client hardware requirement. Also, I include the tightly-coupled approach where I stream images that are rendered directly from the server.

3.2.2 Multi-resolution Approach

Isenberg et al. [44] presented an analysis regarding recent visualisation techniques and categorised multi-resolution techniques, view-dependent visualisation, and level-of-detail (LOD) under the main category *abstraction, simplification, approximation*. These subsets of methods complement each other to achieve an efficient rendering at interactive rates. Burigat and Chittaro [117] studied the feasibility of overview-and-detail visualisation [118] on mobile devices. In their study, they firstly loaded a map with the coarsest level of detail, and subsequently a map with a higher level of detail only on a higher zoom level. Lu et al. [119] introduced a flexible LOD control scheme to efficiently explore the flow structures and characteristics on programmable graphics hardware. In their control scheme, the output textures were created according to a sparse noise model, taking the depth distance of a point and the corresponding brick contribution into consideration. Kimball et al. [120] introduced a level of detail algorithm which enables interactive visualisation of massive, unstructured, particle data sets. They created a multi-resolution pyramid of volume slabs that stacks slabs into a volume. Each slab varies in level of detail, and they selected the slab with the best resolution based on the closest view distance. Zinsmaier et al. [121] proposed a technique that allows straight-line graph drawings to be rendered interactively with an adjustable level of detail. They used the density-based node aggregation and the edge aggregation to select visual patterns at different levels of detail. They were able to interactively show graphs up to $\sim$ 107 nodes and up to $\sim$ 106 edges. The commonalities among these applications are that they first prepare a series of LOD data governed by its different visual detail, e.g. resolution; and then secondly the system selects the best LOD data according to the target requirement.

3.2.3 Visualisation Software

In this section, I present visualisation software that is commonly used to address the various Big Data challenges.

VTK/ParaView The Visualization Toolkit (VTK) [122, 123] is a visualisation library which consists of a C++ class library and interface layers such as Tcl/Tk, Java, and Python. The library supports a wide variety of algorithms, e.g., scalar, vector, tensor, texture, and volumetric methods. The toolkit supports parallel processing and integrates with various databases on GUI toolkits such as Qt and Tk. VTK is a seemingly personal visualisation library among research insititutions [124, 125, 126] due to its ability to include various custom algorithms.

VisIt VisIt [127] is a visualisation application that aims to solve large simulation data sets. In particular, the application is often used to perform in-situ visualisation, e.g., [128], [129], [130]. Its system architecture is highly modular which adopts the plugin-based approach. Users can write a custom plugin that serves their needs, a feature that most researchers will appreciate.

COVISE The Collaborative Visualization and Simulation Environment (COVISE) [131] is a distributed software environment that integrates simulations and visualisations together. The primary motivation of COVISE is to foster collaborations between engineers and scientists. The supported environments are planar and curved power walls or CAVEs in which immersive data evaluations are made possible.

SCIRun SCIRun [132] is a visual programming environment that emphasises problem-solving in scientific domains. The high-level workflow allows domain experts to customise their workflow to achieve their desired outcome. The high flexibility of SCIRun made the software famous where domain experts can easily duplicate networks and create new modules.

Cinema Cinema [116] is an image-based approach for extreme scale in-situ visualisation and analysis. Rather than rendering the raw data directly, Cinema produces a set of intermediate images that serve to build the final 3D visualisation at the client-side. The concept is to minimise the size of the data for better data transmission over the limited network bandwidth. To produce the intermediate images, Cinema takes a snapshot of the object in various angles that covers the whole surface area. Then, in the client visualisation, Cinema retrieves the images to emulate interactive navigation around the object. The result seems as if users are interactively rendering images from a 3D model. Recently, Cinema is gaining popularity as can be seen by the number of applications adopting the framework, e.g., [133], [134], [135].

X3DOM X3DOM [136] is a plugin-free declarative 3D framework for web technology, i.e., HTML5, CSS, and Javascript. Users can create any 3D visualisation by adhering to the document object model (DOM) of an HTML document. The framework is used in the medical domain to provide light-weight volume rendering on web browsers. X3D introduces the concept of 3D graphics through Nodes, Components, and Profiles, i.e., lighting such as point light can be defined at the Nodes and grouped as one component. Then, these multiple components into one profile. The X3DOM is mostly used in medical domain, e.g., [137], [138].

3.3 Data Processing Pipeline

Challenges in Big Data management include data inconsistency and incompleteness, scalability, and timeliness [140, 141]. We can describe the Big Data system using the data processing pipeline (Figure 3.2), which is mainly used in

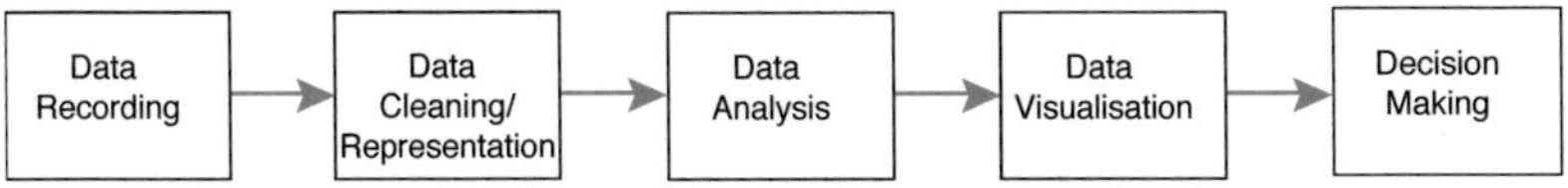

Figure 3.2.: The workflow of the knowledge discovery process [139] that serves as the outline for this chapter.

the field of data mining [4, 139]. Before data analysis, data must be prepared in a structured manner. However, given the large amounts of heterogeneous data, the main consideration to improve data analysis is to perform a series of data processing steps within a specified timeframe that is specified by the experiment requirement. Although the general data processing pipeline offers a good guideline to study the process, I adopt the *data state reference model* by Chi [64] to accurately emphasise the user's analysis process as well as the intermediate results. The model categorises the data processing pipeline into the Within-stage Operator, the Transformation, and the Domain Space (Figure 3.3). The model describes not only the processes involved but also the state or structure of the data at each stage, which provides a comprehensive overview of the experiment. The Within-stage Operator shows the structures or formats of the data at each stage, e.g., image, text vectors. Often, the experimental data can be transformed into multiple formats for various visual outputs. The transformation describes the actions to manipulate the data from one state to another. The Domain Space shows the resource environments, i.e., the Data Space and the View Space. The different space defines the available resources and possible user interactions that will affect the data processing pipeline, which plays a major role in my considerations of designing a Big Data system.

3.3.1 Data Space

The Data Space describes a set of procedures that process the experiment data into visual data formats. The visual data format is the required input data

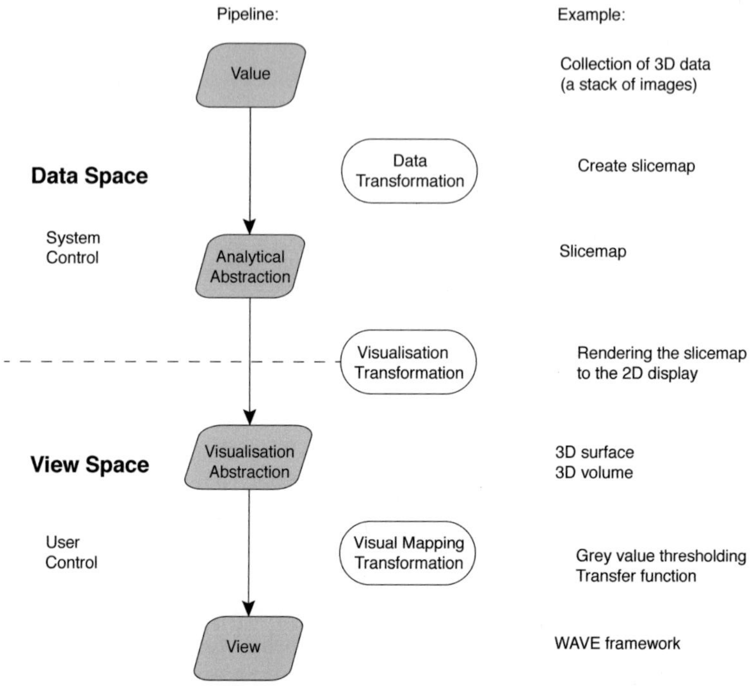

Figure 3.3.: The *data state reference model* by Chi [64]. The dark boxes represents the within-stage operators; whereas the white boxes represent the transformations.

structure to perform the final visualisation. In the context of a web-based Big Data system, I emphasise reducing the size of the data for better network transmission—transferring data from the server to the client suffers from limited network bandwidth. Within the Data Transformation, several data processing steps are essential and must be considered within a standard workflow:

I Data Filtering

II Data Reduction

III Data Mapping

IV Data Mining

Data Filtering Data filtering has the task to reduce the content of noise or errors from the experiment. Often, data recorded are inherently coupled with noise that masks the essential features from the data and limits their usefulness. The goal of data filtering is to provide noise-free data that helps domain experts in their research.

Data Reduction Data reduction is necessary for dealing with Big Data. Mainly, I enable data transfer through the network where data with smaller size ensures the responsiveness of the overall system. A conventional technique is the usage of the multi-resolution method that creates multiple down-sampled data sets and then serves the data with appropriate size according to the network requirement. Typically, the data with the smallest resolution is sent first, followed by the high-resolution data loading in the background. Also, reducing the size of the data beforehand guarantees the data availability where the system does not require complex real-time data processing.

Data Mapping Data mapping is the process of transforming raw data into a visual data object. The visual data object is the required input data for the Visualisation Transformation process. For example, the 3D data is transformed into a slicemap [2] and later can be loaded in the client's GPU texture memory. Here, the slicemap is the visual data object that helps in rendering the final 3D visualisation.

Data Mining Data mining is the process to analyse and generate new information from the raw data. The new information is useful for the later Visual Mapping Transformation process. For example, data mining can find the optimal threshold value that allows the grey value region filtering of 3D data.

[2] Slicemap is discussed in Chapter 2.3.

The new information is an add-on feature that helps explain the visualised data.

3.3.2 View Space

The View Space consists of two Transformation processes and two Within-stage Operators where they mainly describe the visualisation space. The Visualisation Transformation renders the visual data object into the defined visual outputs. The Visual Mapping Transformation is responsible for handling the user interaction which can be categorised by its degree of interaction. The Visualisation Abstraction Operator describes the final visualisation such as 3D surface rendering or volume rendering. The View Operator manages the interaction capabilities of the client visualisation system.

In this thesis, the purpose of integrating visualisation into the digital library (Chapter 2.1) is to provide a better data browsing system that allows domain experts to narrow down and find the relevant data quickly. Since domain experts drive the process primarily, different experiment emphasises on different features where there are many visualisation possibilities [29]. Keim [142] classified the visualisation techniques based on three criteria: the types of data, the visualisation assets, and the interaction method. To achieve the final visualisation, 1D, 2D, or 3D data (types of data) must be processed using available resources (visualisation assets). Also, the final product has to be equipped with interaction methods for seamless user experience (interaction method). It is thus attractive to study the possible visualisation techniques that are essential in large-scale scientific experiments. Here, I design the pipeline by first identifying the required visualisation outputs. In this section, I derive the possible visualisation techniques based on the types of data and interaction methods. Mainly, I focus on one-dimensional (such as temporal data), two-dimensional (such as a geographical map), and multidimensional (such as relational tables) where they are common in research facilities. Also, the visualisation techniques differ regarding the level of interaction. As user interaction plays a vital role in Big Data exploration, I follow the *Visual In-*

formation Seeking Mantra [56] which serves as the initial design guideline (Chapter 2.1). The mantra categorises the visualisation techniques into three primary components where each component differs from one another regarding the degree of interaction, i.e., Overview First (low degree of interaction), Zoom and Filter (medium degree of interaction), and Details on Demand (high degree of interaction).

Overview First : The Overview First describes the big picture of the data structure, a summary display that entails most prominent features. The display is static, and there is low to no degree of interaction. The display serves as the first clue for further investigations.

Zoom and Filter : The Zoom and Filter provides a display with more granular details than the Overview First display, where users can select any arbitrary region of interest and request for data with higher resolution. Mainly, users can narrow down the search and focus on the region of interest.

Details on Demand : The Details on Demand provides the full interaction capacity where users can analyse and interact with the data in real-time. For instance, users can perform multi-parameter filtering and study the relationship between the parameters.

Given the diverse applications and the many visualisation techniques [142], it is difficult to choose a suitable visualisation technique that fits a given application. Table 3.1 shows the possible visualisation techniques based on the type of data and its degree of interaction. In the followings, I describe the visualisation techniques presented in detail.

Icon-based Display The icon-based display has been proven to be effective for the visualising multivariate data [143]. It maps data variables onto geometric and non-geometric visual attributes, e.g., shape, size, orientation, colour and texture. The approach is used to convey the meaning of measurement

Table 3.1.: Possible visualisation techniques based on the type of data and the interaction method.

Interaction Method	Data Type		
	One-dimensional	Two-dimensional	Multidimensional
Overview First	1D Display, Icon-based Display	2D Display	2D Display, Small Multiples
Zoom and Filter	Small Multiples	Dense Pixel Display	3D Display, Dense Pixel Display
Details on Demand	2D Display	3D Display	3D Display, Dense Pixel Display

data through visual attributes. For example, Nocke et al. [144] showed the maize conditions in a scattered, regular, and quadtree-based multi-resolution layouts (Figure 3.4).

Small Multiples Small multiples are thumbnail-sized representations of multiple images displayed at once. They can be a shrunk time series graph or small representative images. The main idea is to provide users with a broad overview of a broad range of data that helps in narrowing down the search. Initially, Tufte [145] described the small multiples as illustrations of postage-stamp-size like the frames in the movie. There are no restrictions on the type of visualisation for the small multiples; hence information visualisation is commonly used to add additional information to the original visualisation. Figure 3.5 shows the data exploration method using small multiples where users can select between a large overview display and small multiples for comparison using a filmstrip metaphor [146].

Dense Pixel Display The dense pixel display describes the manipulation of each pixel on the target display, resulting in a scatter plot. Typically, a scat-

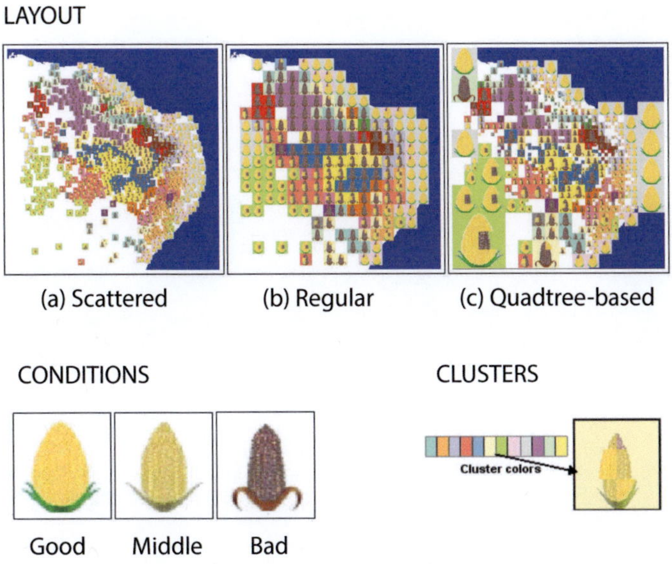

Figure 3.4.: An icon-based display that shows the maize conditions over an area. The conditions are categorised in good, middle, and bad where each category is represented by a visual attribute. The clustering of the type of maize is performed by different colours. Copyright ©2005 IEEE [144].

Figure 3.5.: A data exploration method using small multiples to represent the original data for comparison and guidance [146].

ter plot maps input data into the final visual output—a static display. In this thesis, I use the dense pixel display profoundly because the approach allows high interaction between the data and display, e.g., multi-parameter filtering.

Mainly, I use GPU's shader-based approach where I define the resulting colour on each pixel by using a series of decision logic [65]. Figure 3.6 shows a dense pixel display that describes the vertical wind velocity of a Doppler wind lidar [65].

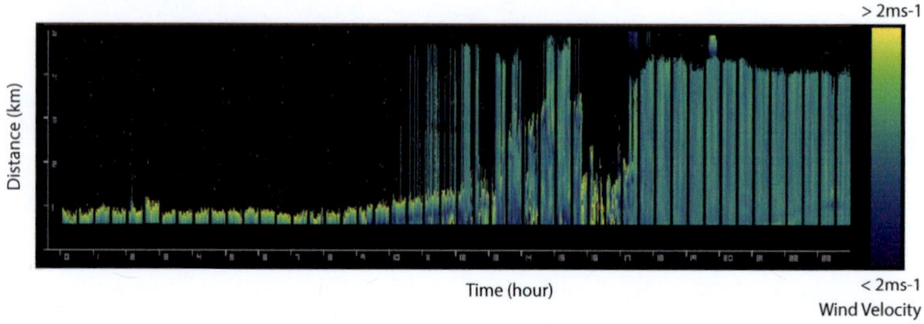

Figure 3.6.: A scatter plot that shows the vertical wind velocity profile of a Doppler Wind Lidar. Each pixel is evaluated by the shader logic prior to the final rendering [65].

1D Display The 1D display represents scalar values of a given time. Since the display only shows one value without dependency parameters, such display is only used to indicate the operational status of an active experiment, mainly providing an overview of the system. Often, extra hints are present to evaluate the scalar value, e.g., last refresh time (Figure 3.7).

2D Display The 2D display remains as an indispensable plot among research institutions where it describes the conventional x-y plot, mainly temporal data that produces a time series plot. The degree of interaction for the 2D display depends on the visualisation system, where there can be no interaction, or there is a rich interaction between the server and the client. For example, the Advanced Data Extraction Infrastructure (ADEI) system allows users to browse large-scale time series data interactively [147]. ADEI uses bin aggregation technique to create aggregated data sets as temporary caches.

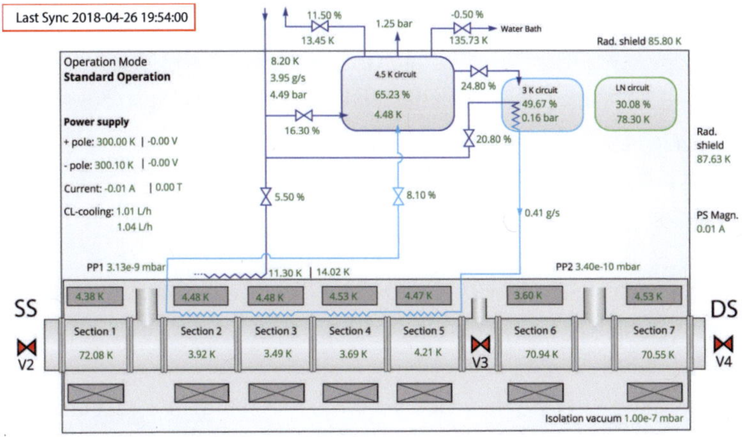

Figure 3.7.: A 1D display showing the latest value of a series of sensors within an experiment. The last refresh time is shown on the top left of the display. Chapter 4.2.1 describes the 1D display framework in detail.

3D Display The 3D display provides a visualisation where users can interact with the data by rotating and moving in the 3D space. Typically, the 3D display has one extra dimension in comparison to the 2D display that is the depth. The extra dimension allows users to analyse and inspect the data in 3D space. The WAVE framework [148], which I will elaborate more in Chapter 4.2.3, can provide a 3D display where users can switch mode between surface and volume renderings. Also, users can slice the 3D data to emphasise on the region of interest.

3.3.3 Designing Big Data Visualisations

Even though the *data state reference model* (Section 3.3) provides a good guideline to design a Big Data visualisation system, the model, however, emphasise little on the real-world considerations such as the resource issue and the latency issue. Often, the adopted methods are based on the available resources allocated for the experiment, which might differ vastly from a small to large-scale experiments. Also, the limited network bandwidth is a concern regarding remote data visualisation. In this regard, I will discuss the Data Space and the View Space from the model and refer them as the *server-side* and the *client-side*. As discussed in Section 3.2, I focus web-based remote visualisation solution which is a hybrid in-situ visualisation for better system response.

Latency Issue The latency issue refers to the delay between the data transfer between the server and the client. If the client requests a set of data, the server has to respond in a short time, typically in less than 1 s to ensure a responsive system [149], in which the system responds within an interactive rate.

There are two approaches to achieve an interactive and responsive system. Firstly, the data has to be readily available where the network latency is the only consideration. However, the data has to be processed beforehand, and this setup does not allow arbitrary data generation. Liu et al. [150] described the benefits of precomputing data tiles for an interactive visualisation system and stressed its importance in providing seamless user experience. Secondly, the data can be created in real-time which allows arbitrary data generation, but the setup includes an extra consideration on top of the network latency where the total time for data processing has to be small, preferably in the range of milliseconds. To ensure real-time data processing, the second approach requires a high-performance infrastructure, e.g., cluster computing, GPU parallel computing. Also, the system can adopt approximation methods used in BlinkDB [151] and online aggregation [152] to provide a coarser resolution that can later be enhanced with more details.

Concerning network latency, the data has to be small enough to be transferred through the network within the desired time frame, i.e., less than 1 s. Shorter network distance between the server and the client can handle more extensive data, whereas a longer network distance can only handle smaller data. In response, multi-resolution approach and progressive loading are commonly seen to provide a better user experience, e.g., Google Maps, Hotmap [153], WAVE [19], imMens [150]. The WAVE framework has been developed in this thesis and will be discussed later in Chapter 4. The multi-resolution approach prepares a series of aggregated data varying in its resolution from fine to coarse and sends the data that fits the network and client requirements. The progressive loading serves the lowest resolution for instant data preview while loading a high resolution in the background.

Resource Issue The Data Space and the View Space dictate the possible resources for our experiment. On the one hand, the Data Space refers to the server environment and we can safely assume that our server infrastructure can scale to handle more processing loads. On the other hand, the View Space refers to the client hardware where the requirements vary from the mobile phone up to a powerful workstation. Despite the varying client requirements, I describe the client environment as a platform with limited resources to have a solution applicable to most client devices.

Like any real-world projects, funding is needed to create a set of generic tools that cover the whole data processing pipeline—from data recording, data validation, data analysis, finally data archiving. The number of resources available defines the requirement for each stage. For instance, less coding efforts are required if we can launch our processing tasks across a large number of computing clusters. Jim Gray [6] observed that the U.S.-Canadian ocean observatory—Project Neptune [154]—allocated approximately 30 per cent of its budget for cyberinfrastructure. Also, he categorises experiments by its scale in a pyramidal format where small-scale experiment typically has only the budget to buy MATLAB and Excel. To design a Big Data system, it is thus crucial to understand the available resources and how can we generalise the design considerations.

Turning tiny insects into Big Data.[a]

Microsoft Research (2017)

[a]A Microsoft research project called Project Premonition where it aims to monitor virus spread by using mosquitoes as field agents to collect blood samples from animals.

4

Visualisation Techniques for a Web-based System

The data processing pipeline, as discussed in Chapter 3, laid an excellent foundation to design a Big Data visualisation system. However, there are many visualisation techniques available that the subject of choosing a suitable visualisation method is an art by itself. To improve the process of designing a new system, I use the *data state reference model* [64] as my reference guide. In this chapter, I study the process of selecting appropriate visualisation techniques. Mainly, I emphasise the View Space that consists of two visualisation aspects: Visualisation Abstraction Operator and View Operator. Firstly, the Visualisation Abstraction Operator describes the types of final visualisation. Secondly, the View Operator presents visualisation systems that manage user interactions. Mainly, I developed three frameworks that help in visual-

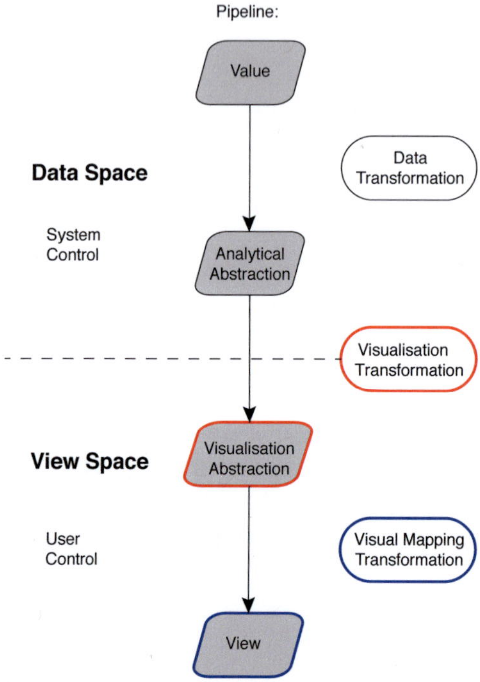

Figure 4.1.: The *data state reference model* by Chi [64]. The red boxes describes the type of visualisation techniques; whereas the blue boxes represent the final visualisation system with its interaction methods.

ising multidimensional data: the BORA framework, the 3D viewpoint finder framework, and the WAVE framework.

4.1 Visualisation Abstraction Operator

The Visualisation Abstraction Operator produces the final visualisation based on the visual data object [1]. For better network transmission, the data size has

[1] Visual data object is discussed in the Data Mining section of Chapter 3.3.1.

to be small. Firstly, the input data can be processed into small images on the server and placed on the web browser display. Secondly, the input data can be transformed into an intermediate visual data object which later serves as a lookup input data for the client. On the one hand, the first approach requires no client performance where the central processing tasks are performed on the server. However, the information of produced images cannot be altered afterwards. On the other hand, the performance of the second approach depends on the client requirements where the client is required to render the visual data object. The advantage is the high interaction between the client and the data. The visual data object can be composed of multivariate data and users can visualise different parameters interactively, without suffering from any network latency, e.g., multi-parameter filtering [65].

4.1.1 Image Data Transformation

Transforming the multidimensional data into an image format offers the flexibility of scaling the size and dimension of the data to match the target display. Regardless of the different data types as shown in Table 3.1, they can be transformed into images. In the case of 1D input data, the scalar value is categorised and assigned a visual representation that can best describe the data—icon-based display (Chapter 3.3.2). In the case of 2D input data, the data are plotted into an image and later being scaled down before sending to the client [147]. Often, the image is a line graph that consists of the X-Y axes. Even when the image is scaled down, users are still able to interpret the trends and patterns of the figures. To transform 3D data into a 2D image, I adopt the perspective projection that creates a 2D image based on the 3D data.

4.1.2 Shader-based Display

The shader-based display is a dense pixel display where it manipulates each pixel of the final target display. The method offers high interaction between users and the data, in which the data is loaded in the memory and later served as a lookup table. Thus, the size of the data must be small enough to fit the client memory. The format of the input data is in the image format that will be loaded into the texture memory of the client's GPU. In the case of a 2D display, the horizontal axis of the image is used as the time dimension, while the vertical axis is used to store the distance parameter. Each pixel consists of 4 channels, i.e., RGBA, and this data structure allows multivariate representation. Figure 4.2 shows the input data that are being passed through the shader code block, producing a series of 2D displays. To allow 3D rendering, I use the slicemap format which resembles a 3D structure (Chapter 2.3).

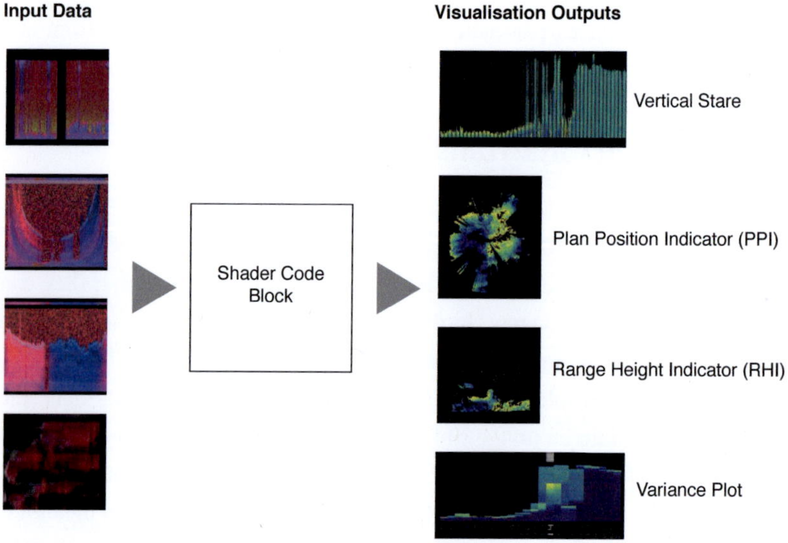

Figure 4.2.: The shader-based approach that transforms a series of visual data objects into 2D displays.

The shader code block contains the programming logic that transforms the horizontal-vertical image structure into the desired visualisation output. Also, a colour map can be applied interactively to adopt different use case. For example, the vertical stare plot requires a one-to-one coordinate transformation; whereas the Plan Position Indicator (PPI) plot transforms the input data into a spherical coordinate system, and the Range Height Indicator (RHI) converts the input data into a hemisphere coordinate system. The variance plot is similar to the one-to-one data transformation of vertical stare plot, but the plot further includes variance calculation before displaying the final value. As a result, the shader-based display offers high interaction and flexibility of presenting the final visualisation. Depending on the dimensions of the input data, the shader code block can render a 2D image or a 3D object.

4.2 View Operator

The View Operator describes the interaction between the visualisation system and users. For instance, the way we interact with a 1D display is different than a 3D display. The additional dimension allows users to have more options such as navigation in a 3D space. In this section, I develop three frameworks that manage the final visualisations of multidimensional data (as discussed in Section 4.1).

1D Display For 1D display, I present the BORA [2] framework that helps domain experts to generate a web-based monitoring display. The final visualisation shows a series of scalar values which depict the latest value of each sensor. Mainly, BORA is used in real-time monitoring of the experiment's operation status, whereby a subset of up to a few hundreds of data is displayed out of a set of thousands of status variables.

2D Display To provide a 2D display, I provide a 3D viewpoint system that creates a 2D image from a 3D data according to a set of view parameters. The system is part of the server-side processing component that allows high-quality image streaming. Both the BORA framework and the 3D viewpoint system transform the experiment data into images that are later served to the client.

[2] BORA stands for Build-Once-Run-Always

2D/3D Display The third system is the WAVE framework where I render a 2D or 3D displays by using the shader-based approach (Section 4.1.2). The WAVE framework allows high degree interaction due to the parallel computing capability of the GPU. Despite the different visualisation outputs, these systems are modular and can be merged easily.

4.2.1 Framework I: A Personalised Collaborative Display

In this section, I present the BORA framework that mainly generates an icon-based display to monitor the status of an experiment. Although there are numerous libraries and templates available, each experiment has its unique requests which require an in-depth knowledge of any library. The difficulty in building the desired web-based data display is the reason why there are numerous web developer tasks offered at research institutions. Rather than creating many custom-made web-based data displays, I enable the domain experts themselves to take full control of their data displays, with no necessity in learning any toolkit internals. Hence, BORA is a framework that allows domain experts to design and manage their own proxy data displays. Mostly, BORA helps domain experts to create multiple status displays. Multiple status displays are used even within a single experiment for different components and phases.

Data monitoring in scientific experiments is crucial to ensure smooth operation and to foster collaboration among scientists [155, 156]. Due to the complexity of a scientific experiment, multiple data monitoring displays are necessary to describe various parts of the operation. Hence, to develop these custom data displays, domain experts need to collaborate closely with computer engineers which are time consuming [157]. Moreover, a large-scale scientific experiment is continually evolving thus requiring continuous maintenance on the displays. The conventional visualisation technique used in monitoring displays is by using an icon-based display, where the latest value of each sensor is represented visually.

To effectively communicate the data among geographically distributed domain experts, I display the data through the web browser. One of the great successes of the web as a platform is data availability across most client devices. These devices can visualise data in a web browser by combining three different technologies: HTML for page content, CSS for visual styling, and JavaScript for interaction. They share the same page content representation called the *document object model* (DOM), which defines the logical structure of the HTML documents and how we access and manipulate the HTML document. This shared representation allows visualisation tools to be deployed across devices from a single code base [95]. There are many visualisation toolkits available such as D3 [158] and Javascript InfoVis Toolkit [159] for web browsers that enable standard data visualisation methods, e.g., line graphs, bar charts. However, implementing custom displays that deviates from conventional visualisation methods requires in-depth knowledge of toolkit internals.

The primary challenge in this thesis revolves around the difficulties of bringing Big Data onto the client's browser. Hence, the purpose of this section is to demonstrate how I enable data sharing for arbitrary experiments that allow domain experts to manage and share their data. I describe how I design my system to address the challenges regarding *efficiency* and *scalability*. The *efficiency* refers to reducing domain experts' efforts to create data displays; the *scalability* refers to the ability of the system in coping with the increasing number of collaborators accessing the experiment data. Based on these two aspects, I structure BORA in data and visual spaces. In the data space, I poll the data regularly and update the data in a cache file. Then, in visual space, I transform the cache file into HTML document for final display. By identifying commonalities in most experiment monitoring displays, BORA allows domain experts to build the data display with minimal effort using user-friendly features, e.g., drag-and-drop, dropdown list, text input.

In this section, I demonstrate how I design BORA to address data availability regarding efficiency and scalability. The efficiency refers to reducing domain experts' efforts to create data displays; the scalability refers to the ability of the system in coping with the increasing number of collaborators accessing the experiment data— a large number of data queries. Based on these two main challenges, I structure BORA in data and visual stages. In the data stage, I poll the data regularly and update the specification file. In the visual stage, I transform the specification file into an HTML document for final display.

My contributions are two-fold: First, I provide a generic system that allows domain experts to build arbitrary data displays with minimal effort; Second, I address the high user connections by introducing an intermediate data interface to preserve the performance of the experiment database. Given the simplicity of the framework, BORA is readily applicable to any experiment setups.

4.2.1.1 Web-based Data Monitoring

Data monitoring displays are common in experiments which involve control systems. Process engineers rely on these monitoring displays to receive feedback allowing them to take appropriate actions. Oceanographers at the University of Washington created a visualisation display based on a scientific workflow management system called Trident [160]. Beran et al. [161] developed SciScope that manages geoscientific data, in which they show the information on a simple map-based interface in the browser. Beglarian et al. [162] use a web interface to monitor the temperature variation of a highly vacuumed spectrometer in the KATRIN experiment [27]. Their visualisation display is built on top of a LabVIEW [163] control system. Also in the KATRIN experiment, various software packages are used for data acquisition and control purposes. The system has web interfaces which provide visual feedback of the operation [164]. However, all the monitoring displays as mentioned above are tailored to a specific application or technology. Extending these existing interfaces to accommodate various data sets or technologies is cumbersome, in which creating a new interface from scratch is often the better approach.

There are numerous web-based graphics libraries that allows user to create visualisation from their data [158, 159, 165, 166]. A most used library is the D3 [158] as can often be seen in the Visual Analytics Science and Technology (VAST) Challenges [167]. D3 allows designers to selectively bind input data to arbitrary document elements, applying dynamic transforms to produce 2D visualisation displays. D3 introduces an abstract representation to simplify web technologies, which helps the new user in the world of web development. Taking a different approach, using Processing [166] requires no understanding of web technologies. Instead, users are required to learn their language called the Processing language. Using the Processing language, they aim to bridge the gap between software developers, artists, and data visualisers to produce the final visualisation product. Instead of 2D visualisation methods, Three.js [168] enables users to express their data in a 3D environment. Three.js abstracts the complexity of native WebGL implementation by exposing intuitive and straightforward API. Although these graphics libraries offer convenient abstractions to generate visualisations, users are required to learn each particular library. If the library is not able to produce the desired visualisation, users are then forced to study the internals of the library.

Often, non-programmer domain expert in a large-scale experiment requires only a custom display that shows the most prominent values and trends. Instead of introducing another library, my system is built on top of the previously mentioned web-based graphics libraries exposing only the needed visualisations through easy-to-use features, i.e., drag-and-drop approach. Rather than providing a comprehensive visualisation toolkit, I address a smaller yet essential problem: efficient communication of experiment data. Thus, I extract data directly from the archived database and display them through the web browser.

4.2.1.2 The BORA Architecture

BORA is designed to help domain experts building proxy data displays for their experiments. The proxy data displays act as multiple smaller displays

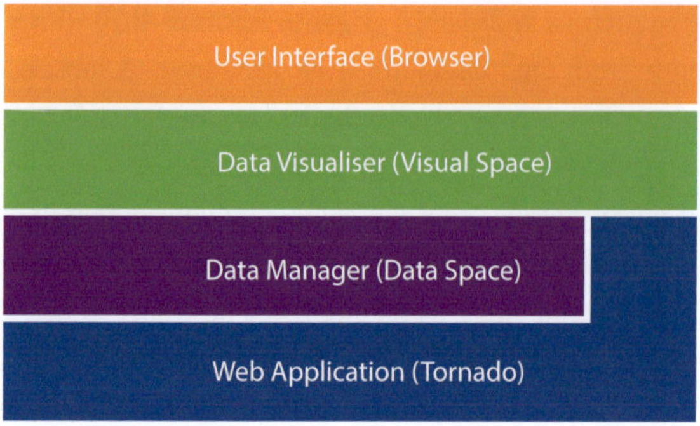

Figure 4.3.: The architecture of the BORA framework.

that as a whole describe the status of the experiment comprehensively. BORA, which stands for *Built Once Run Always*, aims to minimise the maintaining effort on the page and offers a flexible way to add and remove data items. The philosophy behind BORA is to set up the data display once and let the domain experts manage their data. Besides, BORA addresses the redundant data queries by building a retrofit interface that is capable of handling concurrent connections.

Figure 4.3 shows the fundamental structure of the BORA framework. In a nutshell, the working principle of BORA can be categorised into two main components: data manager and data visualiser. The data manager, on the one hand, is responsible for organising the data attributes where the latest value for each data is stored in a temporary file. On the other hand, the data visualiser accounts for the aesthetic appearance of the data display.

A significant drawback of the data display is the difficulty in showing the age of the data. Since the colour code is used for experiment-specific warnings or errors, the standard approach is to use the tooltip for additional information such as the age of the data when users hover over a data item in the display with the mouse cursor. In the following example applications, I show the tooltip in different forms, e.g., trend graphs or static display. Figure 4.4 shows

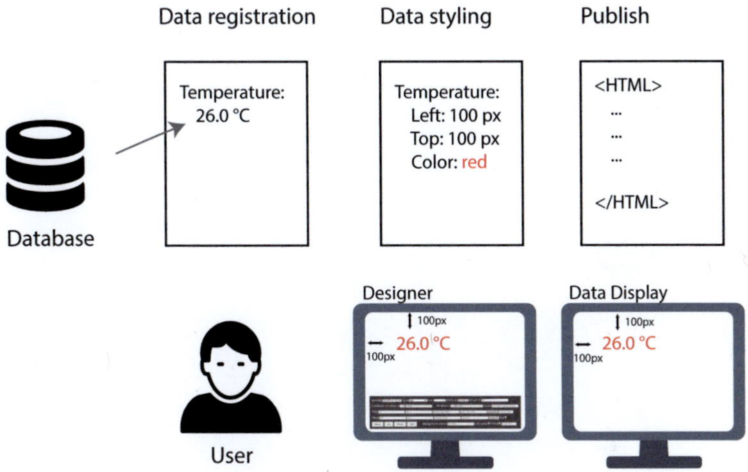

Figure 4.4.: The workflow of BORA. The user first register the data, then assigns the visual attributes to the data. Finally, the user published the results which the final output reflects the visual output designed in the designer user interface.

the workflow of implementing BORA. Given the simplicity of the workflow, BORA can be adopted into any experiment with ease.

Data Manager The BORA framework serves as a web-server that handles the request of users in managing their data displays. Mainly, users can add their desired data items by passing the necessary parameters together with the URI. Internally, the BORA framework queries the data from the experiment data server, e.g., MySQL, ADEI [147].

Here, the data manager polls the database server regularly based on a specification file which contains a list of data. Users generate the specification file through data registration where users specify the required data during the initial setup. To address the redundant calls, I set up a standard interface for each experiment that polls the data from the server regularly. The data is temporarily stored in a cache file, and proxy data displays query their data from

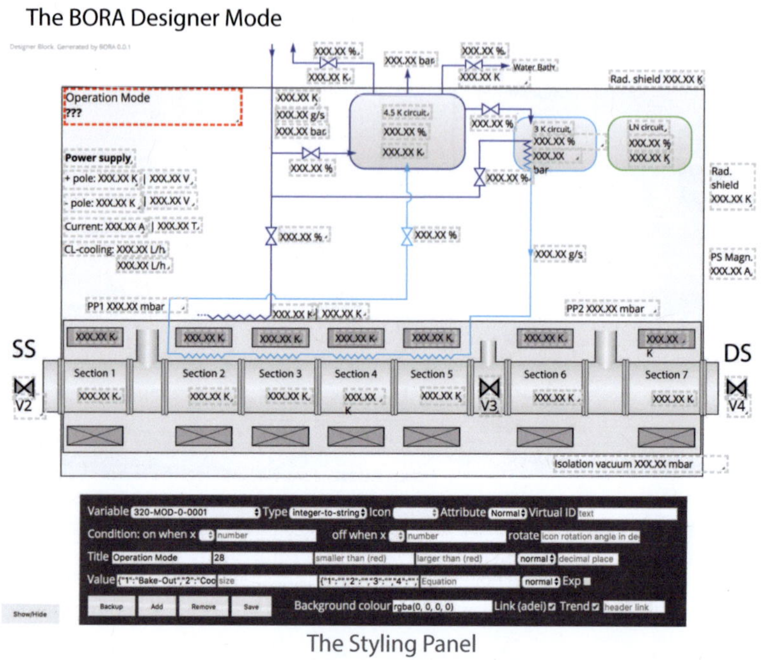

Figure 4.5.: The designer mode of the CPS proxy data display. The styling panel at the bottom of the page allows users to assign various style attributes to the data.

this intermediate cache file. Regardless of the number of proxy data displays, the total data queries depend on the number of unique data items.

Data Visualiser Users can update the visual attributes of each data which the approach follows the WYSIWYG [3] philosophy. Then, the browser continuously requests for data from the data manager together with its respectively visual attributes from the data visualiser and update them on the final data display.

[3]WYSIWYG stands for what-you-see-is-what-you-get which implies a user interface that allows the user to view the final output similar to the design input [169].

I provide a designer mode where users can style their data items on the browser. Figure 4.5 shows a proxy data display in the designer mode where the styling panel is shown at the bottom of the page. The styling panel allows users to insert the registered data, assign a piece of information under a category, insert a header text, perform a mathematical calculation of a data item or between multiple data, and represent the boolean data value with an icon.

4.2.1.3 Example Applications

To implement BORA, users have to register their desired data into a specification file. Then, for each data, users can assign visual attributes that describe the visual appearance of the information on the screen, i.e., position, colour. Finally, the data are summarised into web technology files such as HTML and CSS files. In the following sections, I demonstrate the implementation of BORA in the Karlsruhe Tritium Neutrino experiment (KATRIN) [27] and the KIT 1 MW photovoltaics facility.

KATRIN As a brief introduction, KATRIN measures the neutrino mass in a model-independent way through a very high precision measurement of the kinematics of electrons from beta-decay. To detect the subtle effects of a massive neutrino on the kinematics of the beta electrons, the provision of a reliable gaseous windowless Tritium source is essential to the experiment. The Tritium source is equipped with well-known properties and precision control, and a high-resolution spectrometer (MAC-E filter) with a large diameter (10 m) to analyse the electron energies from the source precisely [27].

KATRIN is a large-scale experiment where the international KATRIN Collaboration consists of world-wide collaborators that specialise in tritium-β-decay. The research field is paramount in astroparticle physics. There are altogether more than 150 scientists, engineers, technicians and students from 12 institutions who are located at geographically distant locations, i.e., Germany, the United Kingdom, the Russian Federation, the Czech Republic and the United States.

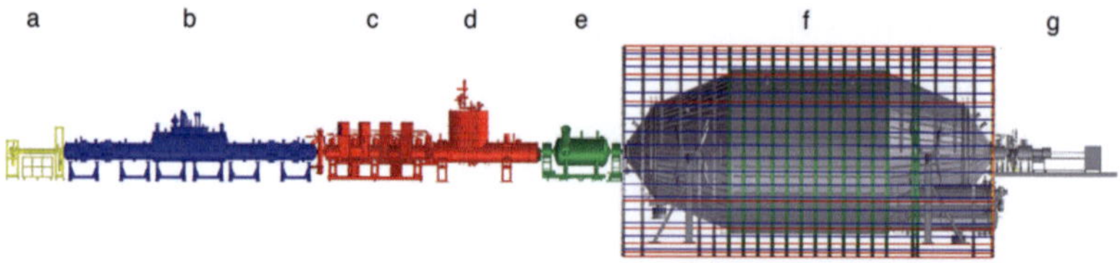

Figure 4.6.: Schematic overview of the 70 m KATRIN experimental beamline: (a) rear section, (b) windowless gaseous tritium source (WGTS), (c) differential-pumping section (DPS), (d) cryogenic-pumping section (CPS), (e) pre-spectrometer, (f) main spectrometer in air-coil framework, and (g) focal-plane detector system. Reprinted from Amsbaugh et al. [164] Copyright (2015), with permission from Elsevier.

The setup of the experiment consists of multiple segments as shown in Figure 4.6 where each section has a dedicated working group that ensures the operability of the particular part. Each segment contains hundreds of sensor measurements where a subset of data is selected to be displayed on a display. To date, there are 10 BORA displays that cover the operation of the experiment. Figure 4.7 and 4.8 show four of the many data displays from the KATRIN experimental beamline. The windowless gaseous Tritium source (WGTS) segment has two data displays, which shows how one segment can have multiple variants of data displays that emphasise different aspects. The domain experts provide a different background image, and it is placed in the background of the HTML page in which the image provides spatial information for better data interpretation.

By hovering over the displayed data item, I provide a thumbnail trend graphs for the past 24 hours. The concept follows the details-on-demand [170] whereby it allows users to inspect the data item more thoroughly. The thumbnail trend is an image generated by a graphics software that updates the trend graphs regularly.

KIT 1 MW photovoltaics facility In addition to the 2D data displays, the BORA framework can be extended into a 3D context. The KIT 1 MW photo-

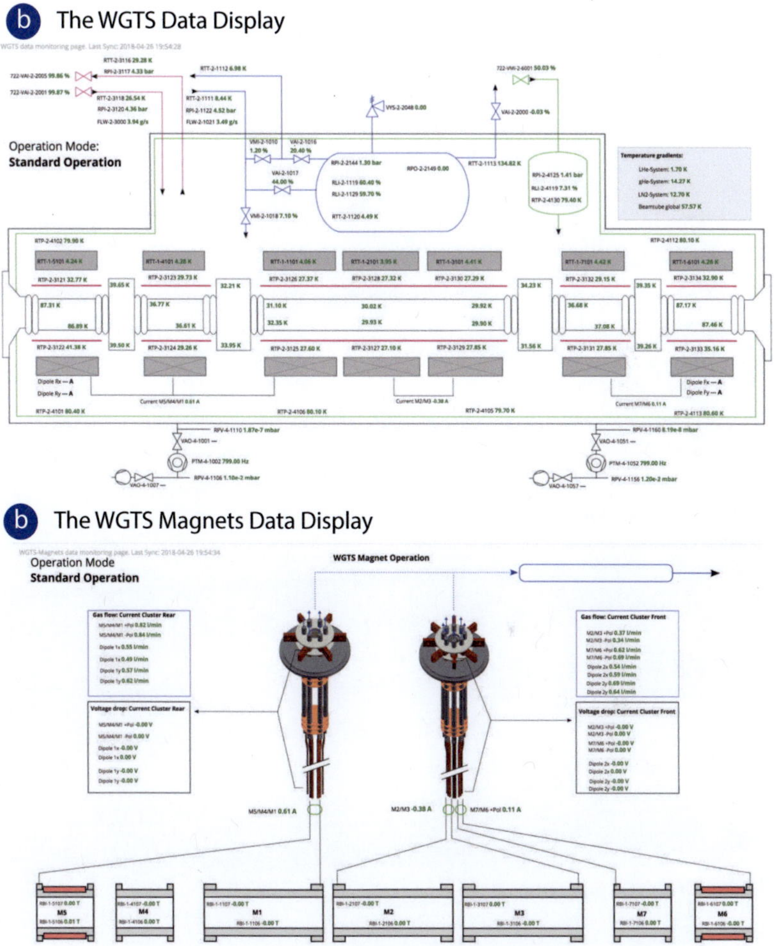

Figure 4.7.: The WGTS and WGTS Magnets proxy data displays. Even from the same segment, there can be multiple data displays that emphasise in different aspects. WGTS stands for windowless gaseous Tritium source.

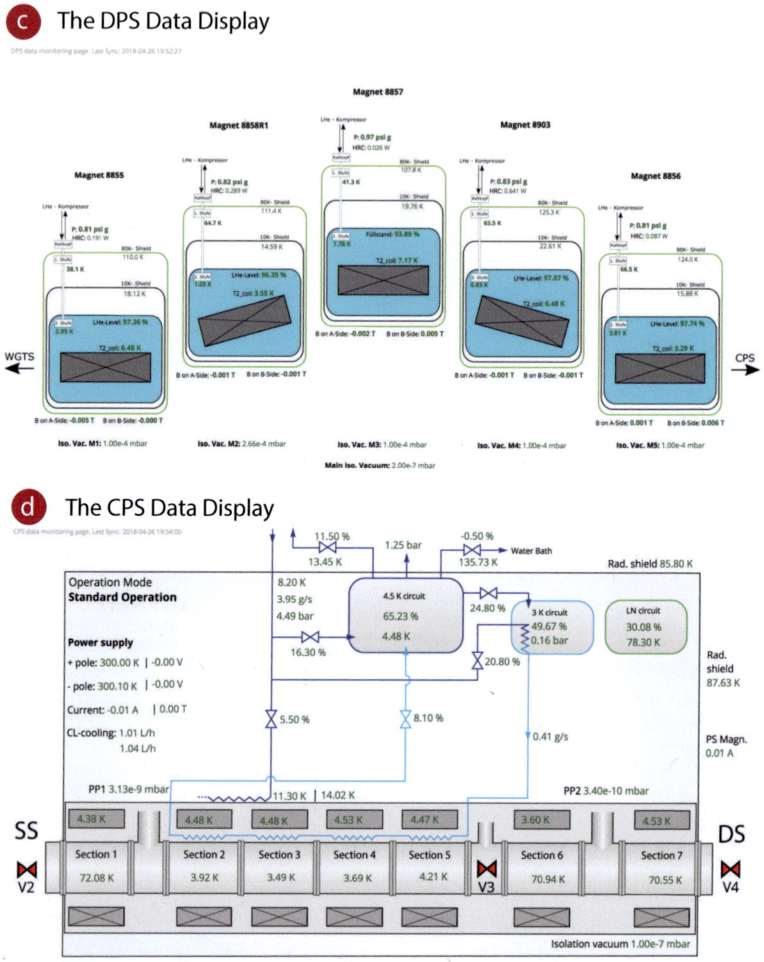

Figure 4.8.: The cryogenic-pumping section (CPS) and differential-pumping section (DPS) proxy data displays.

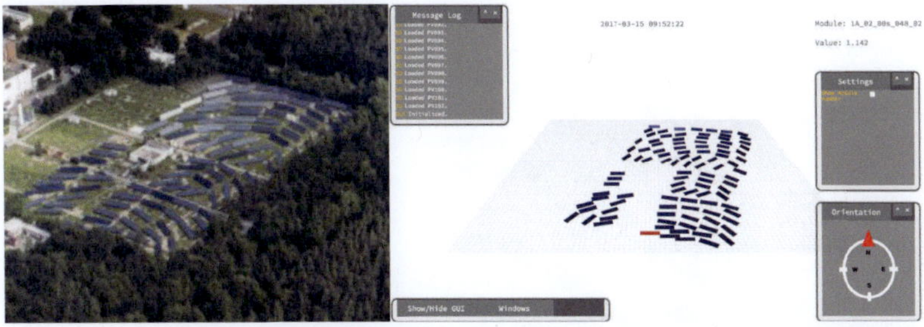

Figure 4.9.: Left image shows an aerial view of the KIT 1 MW Solar Plant at the Karlsruhe Institute of Technology, Eggenstein-Leopoldshafen. The right picture shows the data display built with the BORA framework. Blue colour represents the solar panel that is generating power; whereas the red colour represents no power generated.

voltaics facility installed at the Karlsruhe Institute of Technology (KIT) serves as an ideal use case (Figure 4.9). KIT has established the largest photovoltaics (PV) facility for its consumption in Germany and produces energy from renewable sources for its supply. The facility not only is used to cover its power consumption but also to conduct research [28, 171]. Hence, continuous monitoring of the solar park is essential.

Table 4.1.: Solar array numbers sorted by orientation (rows), inclination (columns) and inverter type, where types A, B, C, D are green, magenta, blue and red, respectively [28].

	2°	15°	30°	45°	60°
60° E		1, 2	3, 4	5, 6	7, 8
45° E		9, 10, 11	12, 13	14, 15	16, 17
30° E		18, 19, 20, 21, 22, 23	24, 25	26, 27, 28	29, 30, 31
15° E		32, 33, 34	35, 36, 37	38, 39, 40	41, 42, 43
0° S	46, 47, 48	44, 45	49, 50, 51, 52, 53, 54	55, 56	57, 58
15° W		59, 60, 61	62, 63, 64	65, 66, 67	68, 69, 70
30° W		71, 72, 73, 74, 75, 76	77, 78, 79	80, 81, 82	83, 84, 85
45° W		86, 87, 88	89, 90	91, 92	93, 94
60° W		95, 96	97, 98	99, 100	101, 102

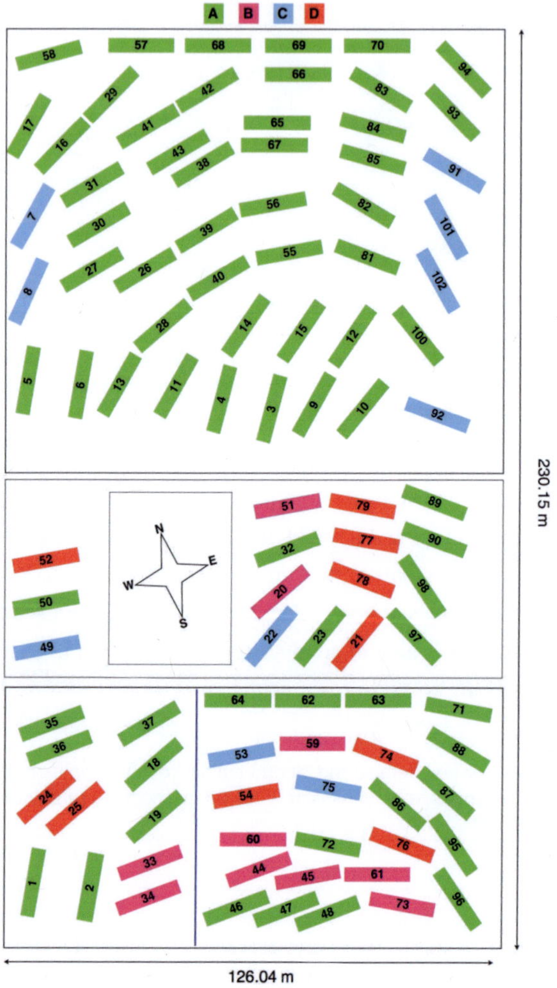

Figure 4.10.: Schematic diagram of the photovoltaic field layout, with array numbers and colours corresponding to those in Table 4.1 [28].

Figure 4.10 shows the solar park configuration according to its orientation and inclination as shown in Table 4.1. There are altogether 102 solar arrays, with each solar array consists of 16 solar modules. At every time interval, the operational data of each solar array are recorded. Based on the various positions with different inclination angles, I build a 3D data display on top of a 3D web-based library (Three.js) to emphasise the various module setups. The domain experts are interested in knowing whether: (1) the operation status of solar modules, and (2) the power harvest by each module. Hence, I translate the requirements into two modes: the status mode and the gradient mode. In the status mode, domain experts can have a glance whether there is any outfall of any modules. The ability to identify the operability of solar modules is essential especially when domain experts are performing data analysis on the whole solar modules in the field—a defective module can lead to misleading results. There are three states implemented (Figure 4.11: Status Mode):

Healthy (green) : There is regular incoming data from the database server.

Faulty (red) : There is no incoming data from the database server.

Late (yellow) : There is a lag of more than 15 minutes between the data updates.

In the gradient mode, I use the normalised power value and apply a colour map to visualise the power variation over the field. Since trees are surrounding the photovoltaic area, the low power observed at the right side of the image (Figure 4.11: Gradient Mode) implies that the shadow of the trees is covering the solar arrays. By hovering over the solar module, I display the information on the static placeholder on the display [170] which provides the information about the age of the data.

4.2.1.4 Evaluation

The BORA framework was initially meant to solve the massive server queries, but later gained popularity and it is implemented for 13 experiment groups, i.e., ten sub-groups from the KATRIN experiment and three sub-groups from the 1 MW photovoltaics facility. The high number of requests are mainly due

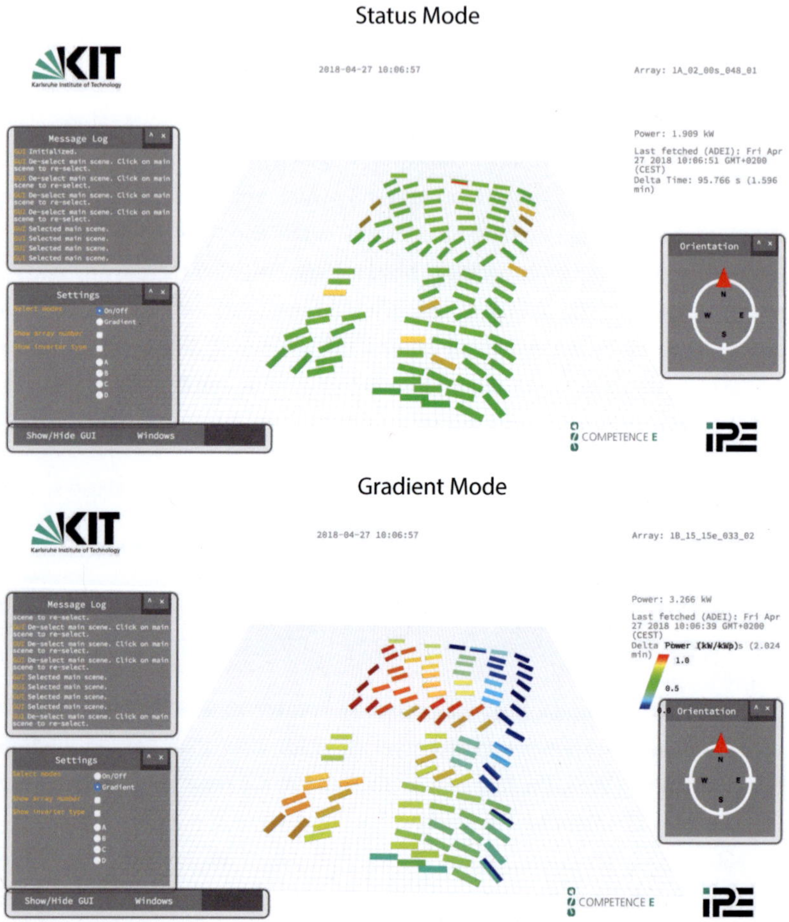

Figure 4.11.: The status and gradient modes in the 3D data display.

to the high redundancy of calling the same parameter; hence the BORA framework removes redundant parameters. In Figure 4.12, we see a drastic drop in the number of requests. Several spikes in the graph show the debugging or software development phase, where I test the reliability of the server by in-

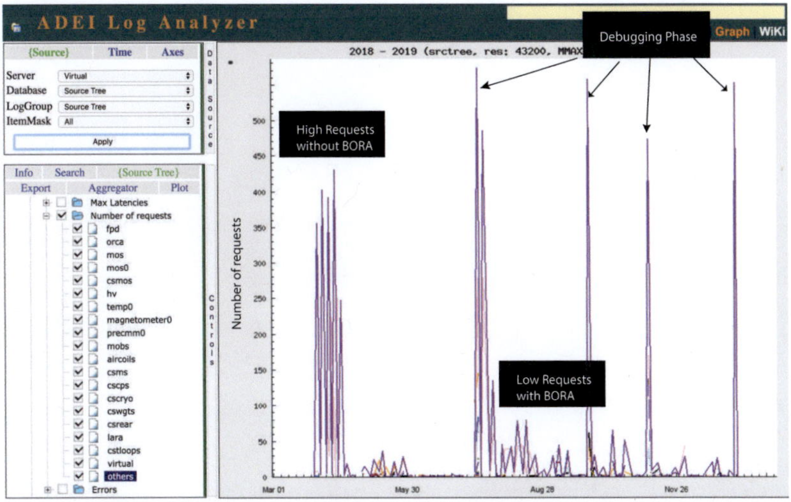

Figure 4.12.: The number of requests made by BORA displays to the server (purple line).

creasing the number of server requests. After the introduction of the BORA framework, there are more displays included, and yet the number of server requests remains low (lower than 50 requests per minute). In Figure 4.13, I perform a load test by testing on multiple concurrent user connections to the server. Even when there are 100 concurrent user connections, the BORA page yields a good load time at 240 ms.

4.2.1.5 Software-as-a-Service (SaaS)

I have discussed the architecture of BORA and its applications. However, each different application consists of different attributes. Hence, I deploy multiple BORA systems across heterogeneous applications by using Software-as-a-Service (SaaS). The SaaS allows users to design and manage their own proxy data displays where there is a single code repository used for various research groups, each research group with its unique settings and styles. The code repository simplifies software maintenance issues. The SaaS is based on

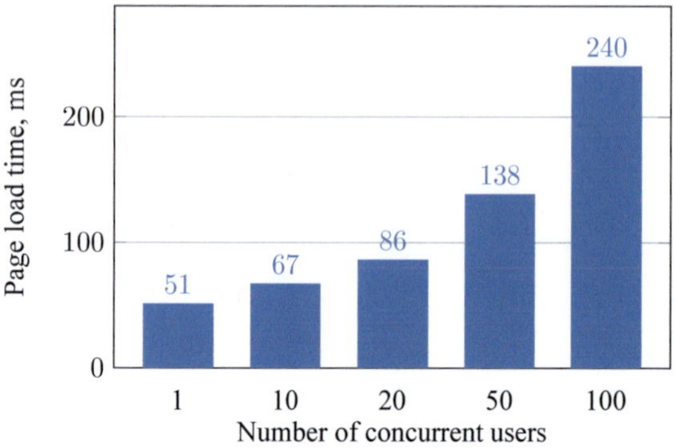

Figure 4.13.: Page load time on multiple concurrent user connections.

the service-oriented architecture where I prepare the data monitoring service by application components, i.e., OpenShift platform [172] and Pull-based approach [173]. To use BORA as a SaaS, users have to develop their displays locally and later push the changes on the server.

To develop the display, I enable the pull-based development model [174] where the changes performed by users can be merged into the BORA's codebase. By using **git**, users can work locally in different branch or fork of the primary code base. During the development phase, users update the content in Data registration and Data styling of BORA. Whenever users are ready, they can push their changes or updates to the central repository. The update will trigger a request on the OpenShift platform to perform a content update. The workflow does not require any intervention from other parties such as computer engineers where users can manage their own data displays independently. This workflow is used in the research environment that requires continuous updates on the data items.

4.2.2 Framework II: An Optimal 3D View Point Finder

In this section, I describe a system that finds the optimal viewpoint of a 3D data, in which the final 3D view space is projected onto a 2D image. Optimal refers to the viewpoint that contains the most information in a 2D image. The advantage of the method is the high-quality of the rendered image, where I render the 2D image directly from the raw data.

However, the principal challenge lies in finding the best view angle that conveys the most information, that is, the view angle that allows domain experts to recognise the type of specimen. Furthermore, the number of data sets can scale indefinitely. Hence, the process of determining the best view angle has to be automated, so that no human operator is required. For this reason, I set the Shannon entropy criterion[175] as my search metric. In this section, I will not be discussing the search paradigm but rather the metric that can be used to describe a 3D context. The Shannon entropy, H, describes the statistical measure of randomness to characterise the texture of the rendered image:

$$H = -\sum_{i=0}^{m-1} p_i \log_2 (p_i) , \tag{4.1}$$

where p_i contains the normalised histogram counts of the image. The higher entropy value means that more information is present in the rendered image, and hence, the better domain experts can recognise the data. Figure 4.14 shows an additive blending visualisation of the tachinid fly *Gymnosoma nudifrons* (Herting, 1966) data set in various rotation angles. The additive blending approach is chosen due to its simplicity that leads to faster rendering time. Although the visual quality of the additive blending approach is less appealing than the surface rendering method, the difference regarding visual quality is not noticeable due to the small viewport size. Hence, better rendering schemes such as surface rendering will not benefit much regarding visual quality.

Arguably, the sample can be rotated along X and Y axes, in which a more comprehensive study of image entropies can be studied. In doing so, we indirectly introduce a higher computation time. Since the samples are placed inside a container with an inverted conical base, the samples do not lie flat on the container base; therefore, a rotation along Z-axis alone can give us a sufficient amount of information. In this example, the tachinid fly data is fixed

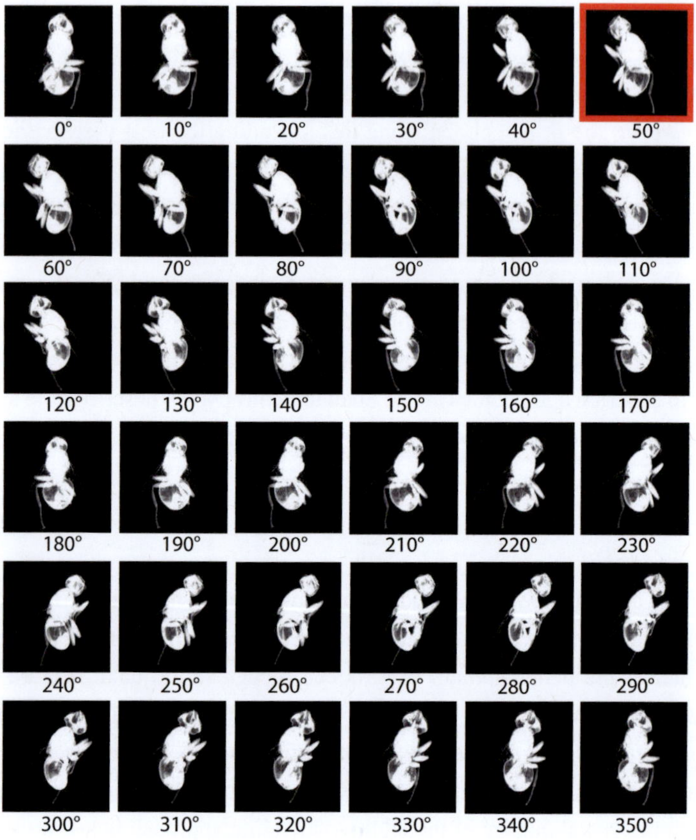

Figure 4.14.: The 3D rendered images of the tachinid fly *Gymnosoma nudifrons* (Herting, 1966) data set in various rotation angles along the Z-axis. The red label shows the image with the highest entropy value.

at its Z-axis and makes a full rotation. At every rotation interval of 10°, I continuously make a *snapshot* hence producing a series of 2D images. Then, I calculate the entropy value for each image and select the image with the highest entropy value (Figure 4.15). As a result, the image with the highest entropy has the best posture where the features are not overlapping. The image with

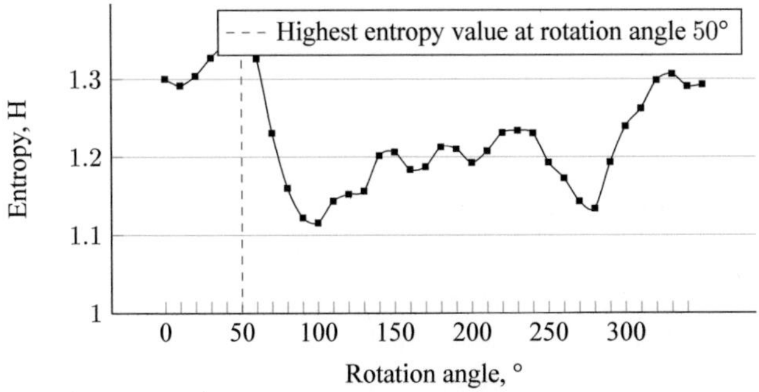

Figure 4.15.: The entropy values for the 3D rendered images for a full rotation with a 10° interval between images. The red dotted line shows the highest entropy value.

50° (highest entropy value) exposed four of the specimen's legs; whereas the image with 100° (lowest entropy value) exposed two of the specimen's legs. Visually, the images that have similar entropy values are not easily differentiable, but the entropy value provides us with a decision criterion to find the optimal representation.

To evaluate the effectiveness of the system, I selected five 3D data sets and performed the Z-axis rotation to find the highest entropy value. The information of the data sets are described in Table 4.2. The total time taken for each process is recorded in Figure 4.16. It is shown that the system takes in average 3.21 s to find the most informative 3D image along the Z-axis rotation.

In the presence of an HPC infrastructure, the optimal 3D viewpoint finder can be extended as an image streaming component for distributed clients. The images are rendered directly from the primary data which guarantees high-quality visual outputs. The image renderer is written in OpenGL and C++ and delivers a 3D image base on the given viewing position. There are two approaches to operate the image renderer: non-persistent and persistent instances.

The non-persistent instance first loads the large primary data renders the content by producing a projected 3D image, and finally closes the instance.

Table 4.2.: The information of data sets used in the evaluation.

Label	Type	Size
A	Oribatid mite	$512 \times 512 \times 384$
B	Box mite	$512 \times 512 \times 384$
C	Gammasid mite	$512 \times 512 \times 512$
D	Pseudoscorpion	$512 \times 512 \times 423$
E	Tachinid fly	$512 \times 512 \times 485$

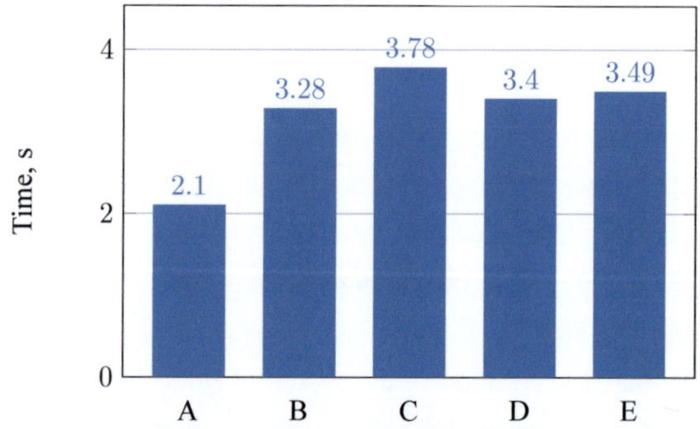

Figure 4.16.: The performances of finding the optimal 3D view point along Z-axis rotation using data sets described in Table 4.2.

The advantage of this approach is that the image renderer frees up the GPU memory after finishing its rendering. However, the method suffers from the data latency of reading data from a hard disk. If the user is rotating the 3D object, the image renderer will produce a series of the projected 3D image with each image generation suffering from the data read-out latency.

The persistent instance, on the other hand, does not close itself after finishes the rendering and it continues to wait until the users load a different data set. The benefit of this approach is that the user only expects for the data read-out latency once and further image generation of the same data set will not incur additional lag time. However, the data read-out latency will still occur when the user is requesting a different data set.

Since the bottleneck remains at the data read-out from the hard disk, deploying the persistence instance approach while having ample memory in the GPU seems like an ideal solution. The ideal solution will need to incorporate more technologies such as CPU and GPU clustering to address scalability.

4.2.3 Framework III: An Interactive 3D Web Visualisation

I develop the WAVE framework to provide 3D visualisation of Big Data in a web-based platform [176, 177, 178]. Although the framework is built around 3D visualisation, the framework can be adapted to 2D visualisation in the GPU shaders [179]. Hence, the WAVE framework serves as a component that provides a 2D/3D display. The 2D WAVE framework processes the input data in X and Y dimensions only, whereas the 3D WAVE framework processes an additional Z dimension that shows the depth of the volumetric data. The advantage of the 2D variation is due to its ability to perform GPU parallel processing at the client side.

To specify the framework requirement for visualising large data sets, I study the existing systems where Jomier et al. [180] presented a web-based remote visualisation system that addresses large data sets by using MIDAS and ParaViewWeb [115]. In their use case application, they present the drawbacks which serve as references in designing a web-based framework for dealing with large data sets. The challenges, which align with my application, are as follows:

C1 : Remote rendering assumes that you always have connectivity and, therefore offline rendering is not possible.

C2 : High-quality rendering is sometimes necessary and particularly difficult to achieve via distant rendering.

C3 : The infrastructure needed to support remote rendering is much more expensive compared to client rendering only.

The challenges serve as the cornerstone of a better web-based visualisation system where I present techniques to address perceptual and interactive scalability which then constitute a hybrid system combining remote and client rendering. Mainly, the framework reduces the data into manageable size while including the image streaming service if the HPC infrastructure is available. I address **C1** and **C2** where low-resolution LOD has to be loaded only once. Then, users can analyse the data without maintaining active connectivity. Furthermore, I address **C3** where the visualisation performance depends solely on the client hardware in which expensive server architecture is not a necessity.

To this end, a useful large data previewing framework must address two main challenges across various client hardware: substantial data processing and interactive scalability. The large data can be either processed in parallel or reduced in size. I use the latter approach, where the framework mainly handles the data in offline processing, online processing, and client-side visualisation. In Figure 4.17, the offline processing is data-driven where it monitors new incoming data from the experiment using a cron service (Step 1) and caches the LOD data (Step 2). In online processing, the framework selects the best cache data that provides excellent visual quality and a reasonable bandwidth transmission based on the client requirement (Step 3). Also, the processes in the online processing are triggered by the client requests. Lastly, the client

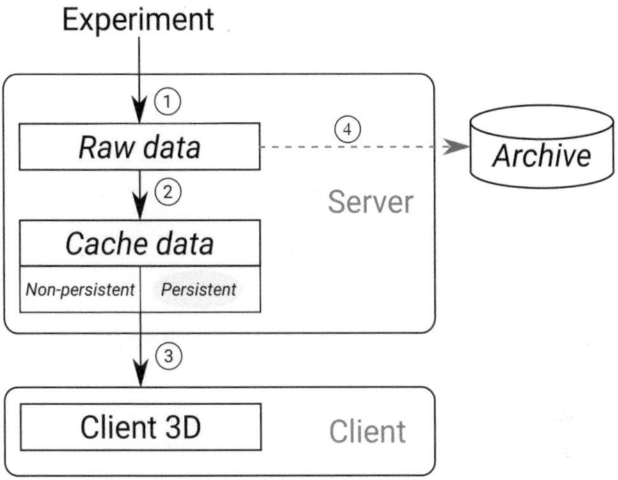

Figure 4.17.: The data flow of the WAVE framework.

visualisation renders the selected data producing the final display. To deal with the growing data size in the server storage, data that are no longer in active use, are pushed to a dedicated remote archive (Step 4). At the same time, non-persistent caches are flushed while preserving persistent caches. The persistent cache data is the smallest LOD data that does not take much storage space and yet able to represent the large data.

In the presence of HPC infrastructure, I further augment my approach by utilising the HPC server. The image rendering is performed from the primary data directly and generates rendered images (in situ visualisation). These resulting images, which are small in size, are served to the client. Mainly, I address **C2** to provide a high-quality rendering despite being at a distant location. The overall system does not emphasise substantial investments in rendering infrastructure where the presented approach can operate with any consumer machines, e.g., laptop or personal desktop with rendering quality reflecting the performance of the client hardware requirement (**C3**). Optionally, when

HPC infrastructure is available, my approach seizes the opportunity to stream high quality rendered images.

4.2.3.1 Server Architecture

Figure 4.18 shows the WAVE server architecture, where each data undergoes the data reduction, the data caching, and the data summarisation stages. A cron service monitors new incoming data and triggers a series of batch jobs. The batch jobs reduce the size of the primary data by generating multiple LOD data. The data summarisation stage collects general information of the data structure that can be used as a reference value for later use, i.e., providing an optimal threshold of grey values for the final 3D visualisation that filters the unwanted details. Next, the cache selection allows progressive loading to improve the user experience where the low-resolution data is loaded first, followed by high-resolution data. Furthermore, the server-side support online generation of arbitrary LOD. To address the scaling size of data, only the low-resolution LOD is stored as a persistent cache, whereas the other caches are non-persistent.

4.2.3.2 Client Architecture

The client is implemented in Javascript, which is written based on the ThreeJS library [168] that utilises WebGL [97]. The Javascript language offers platform independence, and it can be interpreted at every major client browser. Figure 4.19 shows the client architecture, which is consist of a core layer, an event handler layer, and an application programming interface (API) layer. The core layer is responsible for rendering the visual data objects into the final visualisation. For instance, the renderer and the shader components can perform the direct volume rendering based on the work from Kruger and Westermann [181] and the local surface illumination model using the Blinn-Phong model [86]. The event handler manages the communication between the client requests and the core functionality. Furthermore, I provide a layer of application programming interface (API) where users can control the visualisation

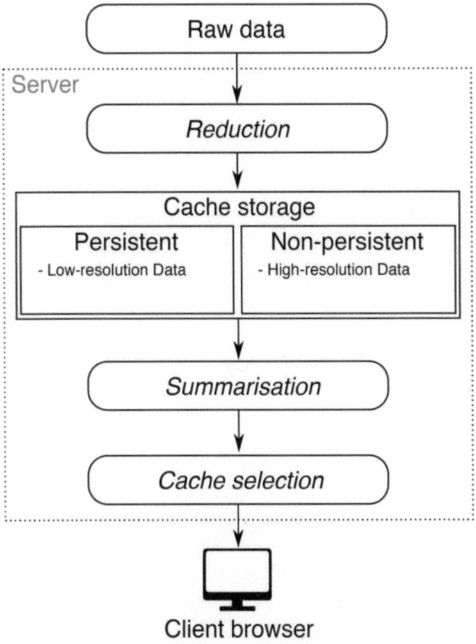

Figure 4.18.: Detailed server architecture.

output by using Javascript that allows users to integrate the library into arbitrary user interface designs.

The WAVE frontend module exposes a set of APIs that allows users to access to its primary functions. Mainly, users can use the browser's developer console tab to interact with the WAVE frontend (Figure 4.20). For example, users can switch between surface rendering and direct volume rendering modes interactively. Also, users can set the minimum and maximum grey values, the bounding box boundaries in all three dimensions as well as the mapping of colours to grey values of the data.

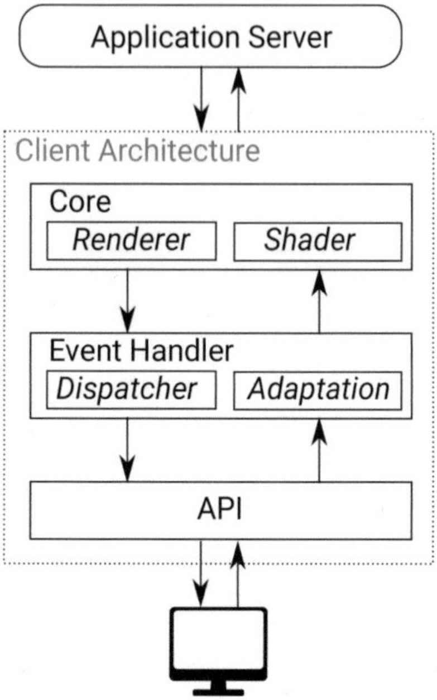

Figure 4.19.: Detailed client architecture.

4.2.3.3 Multi-resolution Support

To support a wide range of web-based clients with varying hardware requirements, I propose the use of multi-resolution slicemaps that vary in resolution details. The interactive 3D visualisation is a 3D display that offers the highest interaction possibilities to analyse the 3D content.

In my approach, I prepare a hierarchy of multi-resolution slicemaps that vary in resolution. For the most favourable client performance, I send the optimal size of slicemap according to the client hardware. "Optimal" is quantified as the data size that provides the best visual quality with the best data latency. Thus, I study the relationship between the varying sizes of slicemaps and the frames-per-second of multiple client devices (Table 4.3). In this study, I chose a wide range of client devices, starting with a less powerful mobile

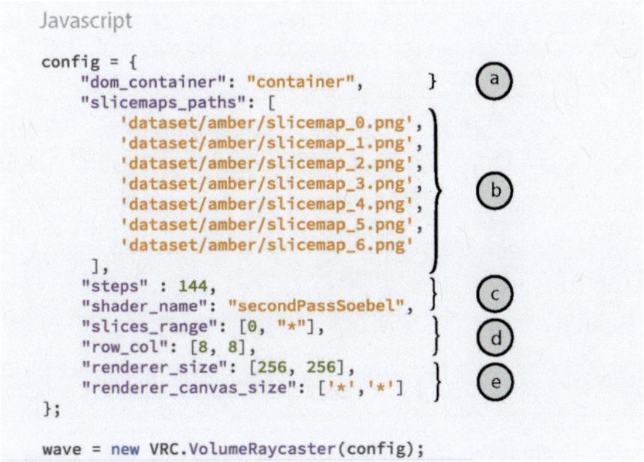

Figure 4.20.: Example of the required WAVE settings: **a**—DOM container used for the visualization. **b**—Paths to the input data. **c**—Shader parameters. **d**—Input data format. **e**—Size of the target canvas and viewport.

phone and reaching up to a more powerful desktop computer. The data size is inversely proportional to the scale of data transmission. In other words, a smaller data size results in faster data transmission, whereas a more extensive data size results in slower data transmission. To interpret the performance metric—frames-per-second, I follow the study conducted by Claypool et al. [182] where the quality of the user performance and perception starts to drop significantly when the frames-per-second goes below 15 fps.

The data set with 128^3 voxels provides the best frames-per-second across the selected client devices; whereas data sets with 256^3 voxels and 512^3 voxels are imposing problems on the smaller client device. Despite the unacceptable frames-per-second (<15 fps) of 256^3 data set on the mobile device, there is room for improving the client rendering with an optimised code, i.e., using a limited number of ray iterations, or using the nearest neighbour interpolation scheme. In recent web-based 3D visualisation reports [95, 184, 185], Noguera and Jiménez [99] introduced the use of non-uniform voxel size. In doing so, I extend the variety of input data by varying the z-dimension of the data for more granularity regarding visual improvement.

Table 4.3.: Relationship between the varying size of the slicemap and the frame rate of the client devices.

Device (GPU)	Texture Unit	Texture Size	GFXbench[a] (frames)	Voxels (fps) 128^3	256^3	512^3
Desktop (Titan)	32	16384^2	107898	1301	649	245
Laptop (GT750M)	16	16384^2	8821	200	112	45
Desktop (HD4000)	16	8192^2	3362	102	32	11[b]
Phone (Adreno330)	16	4096^2	1601	30	12[b]	1[b]

[a] The frame metrics are taken from GFXBench benchmarking suite tested with *T-Rex off-screen 1080p* [183]. This metric shows the performance of each GPU (higher the better).
[b] < 15 fps. Unacceptable user perception quality [182].

4.2.3.4 Performance

In this section, I would like to evaluate performance as a function of achievable display quality. Mainly, how does each downscaled data set affects the visual quality and overall system performance? To illustrate the visual quality of the slicemaps[4], I use the box mite *Euphthiracarus reticulatus* data set as my use case. The visual results illustrate a minimal gradual visual improvement (Figure 4.21) using the multi-resolution scheme. However, the introduction of the additional data granularities, in all its infancy, contributes very little to visual improvement. The varying-z-dimension variants require careful data scaling which is cumbersome. The data preparation of such anisotropic data strives to maintain the aspect ratio of the original data despite the non-isotropic format. Although there is a gradual improvement through varying the z-dimension, the question is, whether the effort to prepare the data is worth the minimal benefit achieved in the results.

To determine the performance of the prepared multi-resolution data sets, I look into aspects regarding system interactivity and latency. Particularly, how

[4]The slicemap format is discussed in Chapter 2.3.

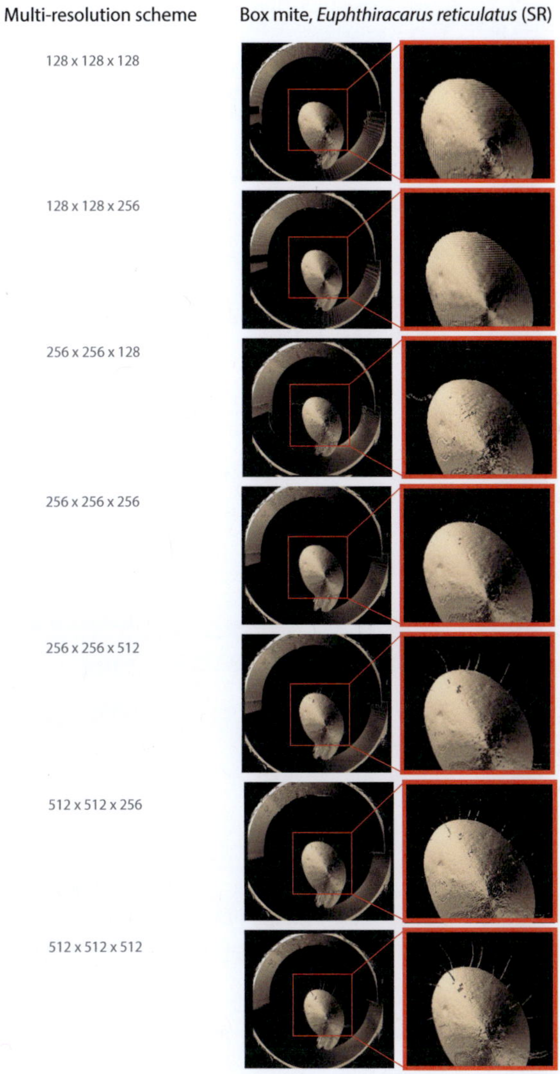

Figure 4.21.: The visual outputs of Eucrib in various multi-resolution schemes.

Table 4.4.: A series of slicemaps generated from the box mite *Euphthiracarus reticulatus* data set.

Scheme	Voxels	Size (MB)	Reduction Ratio[a]	Slicemap		
				Grid	Quantity	Dimension
$128 \times 128 \times 128$	2097152	0.85	3200	8×8	2	1024^2
$128 \times 128 \times 256$	4194304	2.10	1295	8×8	4	1024^2
$256 \times 256 \times 128$	8388608	3.40	800	8×8	2	2048^2
$256 \times 256 \times 256$	16777216	7.80	349	8×8	4	2048^2
$256 \times 256 \times 512$	33554432	17.40	156	8×8	8	2048^2
$512 \times 512 \times 256$	67108864	30.10	88	8×8	4	4096^2
$512 \times 512 \times 512$	134217728	67.30	40	8×8	8	4096^2

[a] The reduction ratio quantifies the amount of reduction in bytes. The original data set consists of $1536 \times 1536 \times 1152$ voxels (2.72 GB).

Table 4.5.: The network profiles created for bandwidth trottling.

Network Preset	Download	Round Trip Time
Ethernet	100 Mb/s, 200 Mb/s, 400 Mb/s	6 ms
Wifi	30 Mb/s	2 ms
DSL	2 Mb/s	5 ms
2G	750 kb/s	100 ms

data size affects the local client data and the network latencies. The slicemaps information is shown in Table 4.4. The reduction ratio is defined as:

$$ReductionRatio = \frac{orignalSize}{reducedSize} \tag{4.2}$$

where $originalSize$ and $reducedSize$ are represented in bytes. For optimal storage of the texture memory, I ensure that the x-and y-dimensions have the same length and are a power of two, i.e., 128, 256, 512. In conjunction, I vary

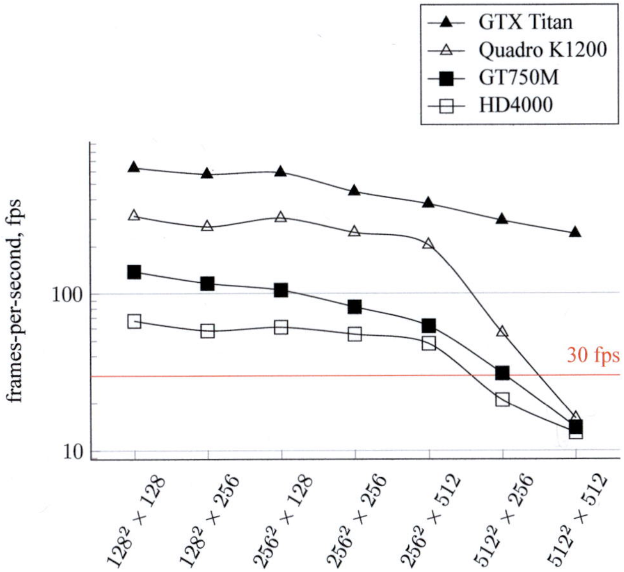

Figure 4.22.: The frames-per-second for multi-resolution slicemaps of the box-mite *Euphthiracarus reticulatus* data set, tested on various client resources (sampling step=512).

the z-dimension to study the performance of each multi-resolution scheme. The rendering performance is related to the size of the slicemap and client hardware. Figure 4.22 shows the frame rate of multi-resolution slicemaps rendered on various client hardware. The GTX Titan performed superior across all the data sets, which is one of the high-end graphics cards available on the market. For the other graphics cards, the data sets with xy-dimensions of 128^2 and 256^2 resulted in optimal performances (frame rates larger than 60 fps). However, the xy-dimension of 512^2 suffers significantly with frame rates below 30 fps. The first tests measure the responsiveness of the client-side rendering; this represents the average frame rates across various client devices. The slicemap with higher detail requires better client hardware for greater performance.

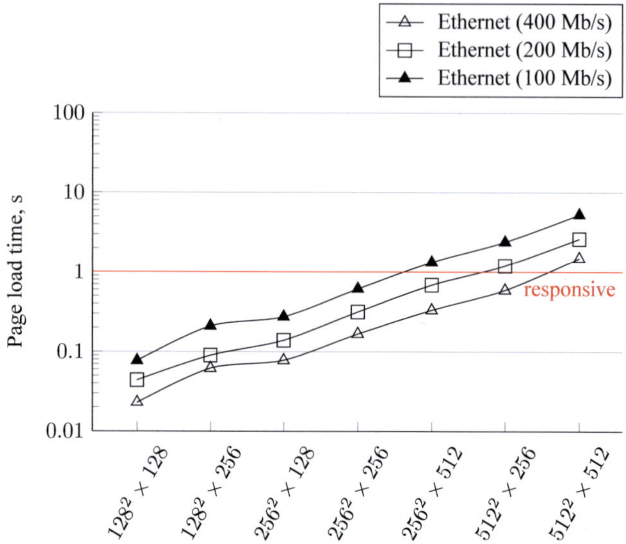

Figure 4.23.: Latency for *multi-resolution slicemaps* based on Ethernet download speed of 100 Mbps, 200 Mbps, and 400 Mbps.

However, the frame rate alone does not give us an adequate representation of the overall performance. The latency between server-client interaction also affects the perceived system interactivity. Hence, I performed tests to measure the content load time for various data sizes. In this context, content refers to the slicemaps that I prepared. Other Javascript files are loaded, although I solely study the varying size of slicemaps on different network presets. In this test, I conducted a bandwidth throttling using the profiles created in Table 4.5. Figure 4.23 shows the content download time of the different slicemaps with Ethernet infrastructure that is common in most research institutions. The results showed that data size smaller than $256 \times 256 \times 256$ guarantees a responsive system where the content is ready in less than one second [149]. Figure 4.24 shows the performance of slicemaps over slower network presets. It is evident that the slower network renders the system unusable since the response time is longer than one second. For slower network connections, it is thus desir-

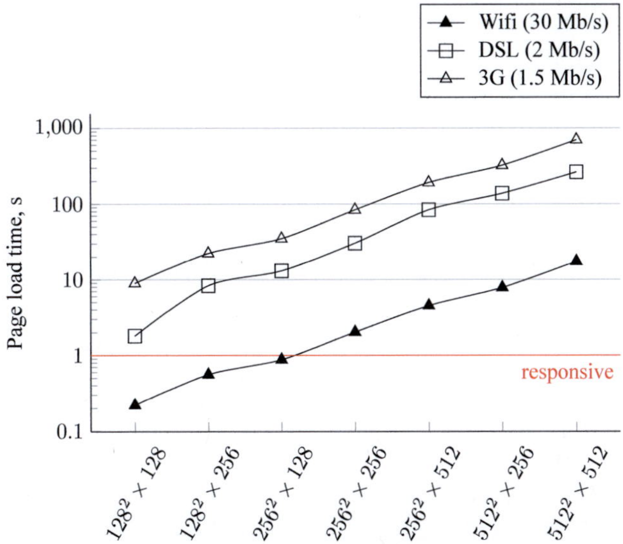

Figure 4.24.: Latency for *multi-resolution slicemaps* on slower network presets, i.e., Wifi, DSL, and 3G.

able to operate entirely offline in which users can send the slicemaps to the collaborators by using mail or file sharing platform, and later view the data on their local machines.

The overall results are as expected where smaller slicemaps load faster than larger slicemaps. Interestingly, if I combine the results of visual quality, frame rates and content download times, I notice that the z-dimension variations do not account for better visual quality nor better performance, but instead suffers during the network transfer. Hence, I propose to use only isotropic slicemaps that provide gradual improvements regarding visual quality, rendering performance, and download time. The multi-resolution scheme for slicemaps is shown in Table 4.6. The data sets $128 \times 128 \times 128$, and $256 \times 256 \times 256$ can be utilised by a broad range of clients, whereas the data set $512 \times 512 \times 512$ can only be used by the client who has the powerful supporting hardware. In this regard, the progressive loading approach is suitable where the $128 \times 128 \times 128$

data set can be first loaded while the $256 \times 256 \times 256$ data set is loading in the background. If the client has a high-end GPU and a fast network connection, the $512 \times 512 \times 512$ data set can be served as well.

Table 4.6.: Multi-resolution hierarchy scheme definition.

Level (N)	Scheme	Voxels	Format
0	$128^3 \times 8^0$	2097152	$128 \times 128 \times 128$
1	$128^3 \times 8^1$	16777216	$256 \times 256 \times 256$
2	$128^3 \times 8^2$	134217728	$512 \times 512 \times 512$

Table 4.7.: The resulting level of detail (LOD) based on the cache selection criterion (Equation 4.3).

Device	GPU	GFXbench (frame rate)	Texture Unit (TU)	Texture Size (TS)	LOD
Google Nexus 5	Adreno 330	1601	16	4096	0
Desktop	HD4000	3362	16	8192	1
MacbookPro	GT750M	8821	16	16384	2
Desktop	GTX Titan	107898	32	16384	3

Given the three slicemap's level of details defined in Table 4.6, the Cache Selector aims to serve the appropriate size of slicemap that allows interactive and responsive system. To select the proper cache data for a particular client, I evaluate the client processing power by its Texture Mapping Units (TMUs): texture unit (TU) and texture size (TS). The reason is that I load the input data for the final visualisation in the texture memory, which the texture memory is a subset of the TMUs block. The TMUs process and filter the loaded textures in conjunction with pixel and vertex shader units. The TMU is thus responsible for applying texture operations to pixels that will be projected onto the display. The number of texture units and maximum supported texture size in a graphics processor are used when comparing two different cards for texturing performance. Hence, I assume that the card with more TMUs will be faster at processing texture information.

Using the texture unit and texture size, I determine the appropriate level of detail, LOD, by:

$$LOD = \left\lfloor \log_2 \frac{TU \times TS}{BP} \right\rceil + 5 \tag{4.3}$$

where BP is the multiplication product of the smallest slicemap size, i.e., $128 \times 128 \times 128 = 2097152$. Table 4.7 shows the resulting level of detail (LOD) based on the different client's TMU specifications. The cache selection can yield LOD higher than 2, and in this case, I will still provide the highest defined LOD, i.e., $LOD = 2$, to the clients.

A central goal is to synthesize different types of information from different sources into a unified data representation.

Thomas and Cook (2006)

5
Scientific Data Visualisation

In Chapter 4, I presented three view operators that can handle multidimensional input data and produce 1D, 2D or 3D visualisation output. The view operators are modular systems that can fit together in the same data-processing ecosystem. In this chapter, I demonstrate designing Big Data systems using the proposed guideline and the view operators. Mainly, I address the Big Data challenges faced in large-scale scientific experiments by building a visual system as part of a digital library framework. The system should show the vital information of each data set, which helps users in discovering their desired data set. I follow the general design guidelines elaborated in Chapter 3 and apply them in four use cases: satellite imaging with analysis of multi-spectral imagery [167], climate research with Doppler wind lidar [25], medical imaging with ultrasound computer tomography [37], and life science research with X-ray microtomography (SRμCT) imaging technique [12].

In each application, I show essential details in the visualisation in which the chosen features are selected based on continuing discussions with the domain experts—mainly driven by "how they look at their data"—known as the user-centred design [29]. Table 5.1 shows the features of four applications in the context of Big Data. The challenges set forth the discussion in later sections. Mainly, I show the consideration process of designing the visualisation, and the data processing adapting to the final visual design. Despite the different applications, they share the same goal which is to summarise and merge core information of data on a single display.

5.1 Use Case I: Analysing Multi-spectral Imagery

In this use-case study, I demonstrate the feasibility of my design guideline based on the data sets from Visual Analytics Science and Technology (VAST) Challenge [167]. One of the challenges is to find a novel approach to analyse the multi-spectral image. The goal is to provide a system that helps to analyse the urbanisation and environmental change of the nature preserve and possibly relates to the decreasing population of the Rose-Crested Blue Pipit. I use the WAVE framework (2D display) as the view operator and process the images into 2D visualisations.

Since the satellite image consists of six bands of information, the main question is how can we encode all six information in our limited hardware display (3 colour channels). If we omit any of the information, we risk of not detecting useful features. Furthermore, this study demonstrates the usage of the WAVE framework as a 2D visualisation system.

5.1.1 Design Strategy

Using the WAVE framework as the view operator, the multi-spectral image has to be converted into an RGB 2D image. Each multi-spectral image con-

Table 5.1.: Overview of the selected use cases in the context of Big Data.

Use Case	Multispectral Imaging Analysis [167]	Doppler Wind Lidar [25]	Ultrasound Computer Tomography [37]	X-ray Computer Tomography [12]
Domain	Satellite imaging	Climate research	Medical imaging	Entomology science
Display	2D	2D	3D	3D
View Operator	WAVE	WAVE, BORA	WAVE	WAVE, Optimal 3D View Point
Application	Detecting urbanisation	Study of wind characteristics	Early breast cancer detection	Morphological analysis of animals
Big Data	Variety (Multimodal)	Variety (Multivariate)	Variety (Multimodal)	Volume
Data Type	Excel file	Database	Images (3D stack)	Images (3D stack)
Scale	Hundreds of items	Billions of items	Gigabytes of data	Gigabytes of data
Multifacet	6 imaging modalities	Multiple parameters	3 imaging modalities	Multiple segmented data
Challenge	Merging multimodal data	Representation of heterogeneous data	Merging multimodal data	Compact representation

sists of six information (bands) of (Table 5.2) that can be mapped onto the image's channels. However, only three bands can be assigned to an RGB image at a single time. Assigning an arbitrary band to the RGB colour channels will result in a different visual result, thus highlighting a specific set of features. For example, assigning B4 to the red channel, B3 to the green channel, and B2 to blue channel, emphasises the urban areas depicted in cyan colour (Figure 5.1). Moreover, the cyan colour also shows the road network on the map. The combination is applied across the data of three years from 2014 to 2016 where each year is represented by each year is represented by four quarterly multi-spectral images (Figure 5.2). A histogram analysis is present to show the contribution of each colour channel in the image.

I propose to provide an overview that shows the trend of the multispectral images throughout three years (Figure 5.2). The summary shows the final visualisation of each multispectral image based on the three selected band information and their histogram characteristics. On the other hand, users can choose one multispectral image for further analysis where the band information can be updated interactively (Figure 5.3).

5.1.2 Data Space

In the data space, the multi-spectral bands are encoded into two images where each image contains three bands of information respectively, i.e., the first image contains B1, B2, and B3; whereas the second image contains B4, B5, and B6.

5.1.3 View Space

For this use case study, I used the WAVE framework that offers high interactivity with its shader-based approach. Assigning B6 to the red channel, B4 to the green channel, and B2 to the blue channel, the water reservoir is highlighted in deep blue (Figure 5.3). Many possible combinations extract different features as can be seen in recent works [186, 187, 188, 189, 190]. Furthermore, users

Table 5.2.: Multi-spectral bands and their utility.

Band	Colour	Wavelength (nm)	Useful for Mapping
B1	Blue	450-520	Penetrates water, shows thin clouds and general visible brightness
B2	Green	520-600	Shows different types of plants and general visible brightness
B3	Red	630-690	Vegetation color and certain mineral deposits
B4	Near Infrared (NIR)	770-900	Partially absorbed by water, sensitive to vegetation structure and chlorophyll
B5	Short-wave Infrared	1550-1750	Completely absorbed by liquid water. Sensitive to moisture content of soil and vegetation; penetrates thin clouds
B6	Short-wave Infrared	2090-2350	Insensitive to vegetation color or vigor, shows differences in soil mineral content

can perform multiple index calculation, i.e., Normalized Difference Vegetation Index (NDVI). The index calculation results in a one dimension values normalised between 0 and 1. Figure 5.4 shows the vegetation intensity on the map. I assign the NDVI index onto the green channel which the vegetation intensity corresponds to the degree of greenery in the map. The index is used to study the feature variation over time, i.e., the trend of vegetation growth around the area. Figure 5.5 shows the vegetation growth over the three years. Rather than predefining the combination beforehand, I promote interactive data update where users can perform any combination in the provided shader editor.

The execution model handles the shader updates since users can interactively change the colour channel assignments to narrow down the search. Also,

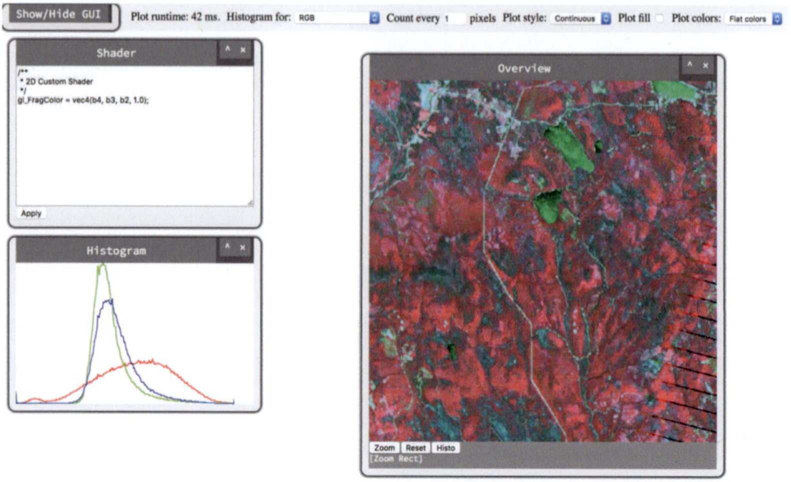

Figure 5.1.: The WAVE analysis display of the multi-spectral image. The overview shows the image composition based on the combination $(B4, B3, B2) \mapsto (R, G, B)$. The cyan colour depicts the urban area and road networks.

I generate a histogram analysis of the image colour's distribution. Moreover, users can zoom on a particular area and study the region of interest for three years. For this application, I provided only the 2D mapping module that maps the extracts the slicemap information onto the viewport.

5.1.4 Discussion

As it stands, I provide an Overview-Detail navigation pane that helps users to detect anomalies in the satellite images. Users can interactively update the mapping of satellite bands which allows high flexibility in analysing the images. However, the application requires further methods to be reliable, i.e., contrast stretching, cloud removal. The occasional occurrence of clouds and different imaging contrast obstruct the clarity of the imaging. Also, the study demonstrated the usage of the WAVE framework in a 2D visualisation system. The guideline serves as an excellent reference to structure the entire system.

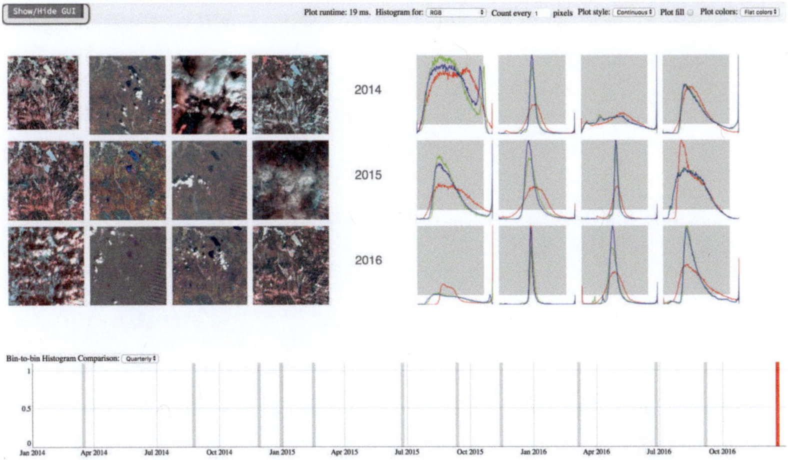

Figure 5.2.: The trend of the multi-spectral images over the course of three years. The histogram analysis shows the contribution of each colour channels in the resulting image.

Also, this study demonstrated the flexibility of the WAVE framework for various 2D visualisation applications.

5.2 Use Case II: Doppler Wind Lidar

By using Doppler wind lidar, researchers can gain insights into daily phenomena such as rain, updraft, downdraft, fast moving low clouds and nocturnal low-clouds [191, 192]. In climate research, a major visualisation purpose is to explore hidden patterns and structures [193]. From the available parameters measured by the Dopper wind lidar, we can identify important events based on lidar's three primary attributes: wind velocity, backscattering coefficient, and signal-noise-ratio. During each measurement campaign, experiment operators orchestrate the lidar's illumination direction in azimuth and elevation angles to cover more area for better analysis. The measurement modes are as follows:

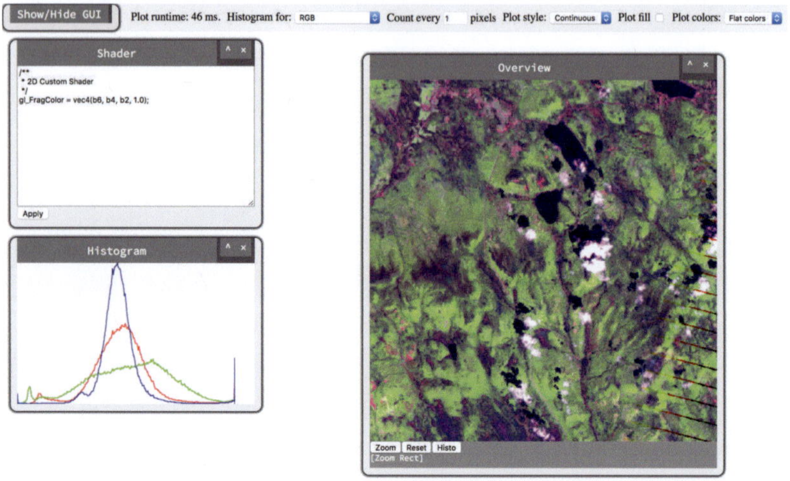

Figure 5.3.: The WAVE analysis display of the multi-spectral image. The overview shows the image composition based on the combination $(B6, B4, B2) \mapsto (R, G, B)$. The blue colour depicts the water reservoir.

Vertical Stare : A fixed arbitrary azimuth angle and a fixed elevation angle at 90°.

Plan Position Indicator (PPI) : Varying azimuth and fixed arbitrary elevation angles.

Range Height Indicator (RHI) : Fixed arbitrary azimuth and varying elevation angles.

Despite various setups, the measured data (multivariate) are stored in one repository which complicates the overall data processing and visualisation. The data with different configurations must be preprocessed and presented in a variety of standard visualisations [194]. Moreover, the large-scale of the collected data poses further challenges in perceptual and interactive scalability [150]. For example, a Doppler wind lidar system with 10 Hz sampling rate produces approximately 10 million data items per day. Based on the survey

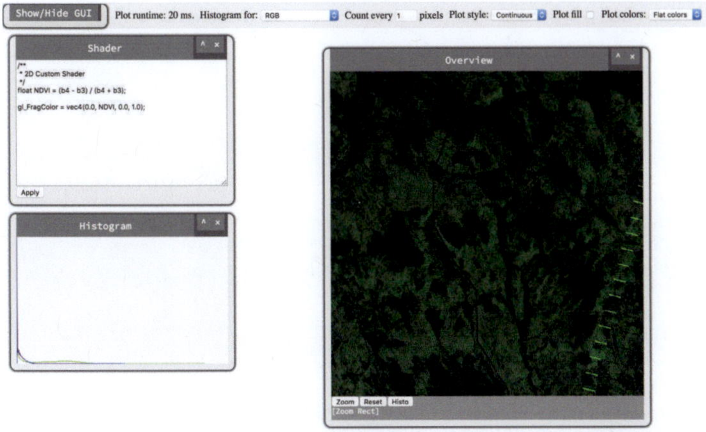

Figure 5.4.: The WAVE analysis display of the multi-spectral image. The overview shows the image composition based on the NDVI index. The green colour depicts the intensity of vegetation growth.

by Tominski et al. [195], domain experts often use script-based tools such as Matlab and Ferret to process and produce static images for visual inspection. However, these traditional tools were not suitable for the scale and heterogeneity of such lidar data [196, 197, 198].

As the Doppler wind lidar system often comes with a dedicated user interface for online monitoring, there is no demand to have a separate offline visualisation system [199]. Furthermore, standard displays for the Doppler wind lidar are readily producible in offline mode using any conventional graphics display packages. Hofmeister et al. [200] evaluated their Doppler wind lidar using a custom LabVIEW display tool. Prasad et al. [201] also assessed their lidar system using a custom display tool called Windimager. However, they often use a script-based approach such as Matlab [202] and Ferret [203] for offline data processing and analysis [195]; thus, suffering in performance due to the data size and complexity [196, 197, 198].

Although most lidar visualisation systems are attached to the hardware, there are also standalone systems available. Wang et al. [204] presented a dis-

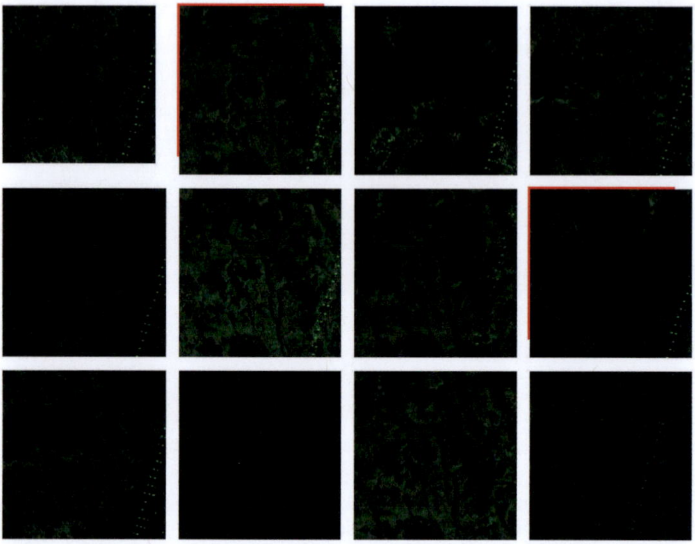

Figure 5.5.: The trend of vegetation growth in the map. The trend shows low vegetation growth during the first and last quarter of the year which is largely due to the winter season.

play system that integrates Google Maps with a microscale meteorological model to improve its overall system's functionality. They extended their system to visualise Doppler wind lidar data as well. Cherukuru and Calhoun [205] developed a smartphone application to perform lidar visualisation in augmented reality. Their work opens up visualisation opportunities in lidar visualisation and spun idea for virtual reality implementation [206]. These applications emphasised overlaying lidar data on terrain or a 3D environment to increase spatial awareness. Coupling with the lidar hardware, their systems rely on external resources, i.e., the system by Wang et al. [204] requires an interface to Google services and the lidar smartphone application by Cherukuru and Calhoun [205] where a virtual reality goggle is needed.

So far, the lidar visualisation system emphasises the displaying of lidar data in real-time, meaning, data acquired from the lidar has to be displayed immediately. My work aims to provide a visualisation platform for better performance that supports online and offline measurement phases. Thus, my approach does not rely on external dependencies, where I store cache data at the server for high-speed data browsing. Since the lidar data have to be represented in its distinct formats such as PPI and RHI scans, there are high data preprocessing steps involved in displaying them onto the screen. In response, I avoid the preprocessing costs by preparing a set of cache data beforehand.

5.2.1 Design Strategy

To design a visual display for each data set in a digital library, I apply the client-server paradigm that extracts information and encodes primary lidar attributes into the images' colour channels within the server. On the client-side, I load these encoded images (cache data) and display lidar data in multiple forms. In contrast to having many static images, my approach allows researchers to begin analysing the extensive data using a more top-down methodological approach by introducing a daily view and an hourly view. Regarding interactions, I implement features such as zooming, multivariate filtering, and hourly variance heat map.

In conjunction with the Dynamics-aerosol-chemistry-cloud interactions in West Africa Campaign (DACCIWA) [207], I use the Doppler wind lidar data collected throughout two months from the KITcube mobile observation platform [25]. The KITcube experiment is a portable measurement platform that is deployed in various places in different seasons. In each measurement campaign, domain experts aim to understand the wind characteristics in a particular geographic location within a preselected period. In other words, domain experts want to analyse everything that they can measure. Any anomaly or conformance of data under the prior hypotheses is valuable to their research. Hence, I summarise their data into a single compact visualisation that provides an overview of the data structure (Figure 5.6). Mainly, I show the vertical stare profile (Figure 5.6: B) which can provide initial information such as cloud coverage or a raining event. The detailed view (Figure 5.6: C) allows

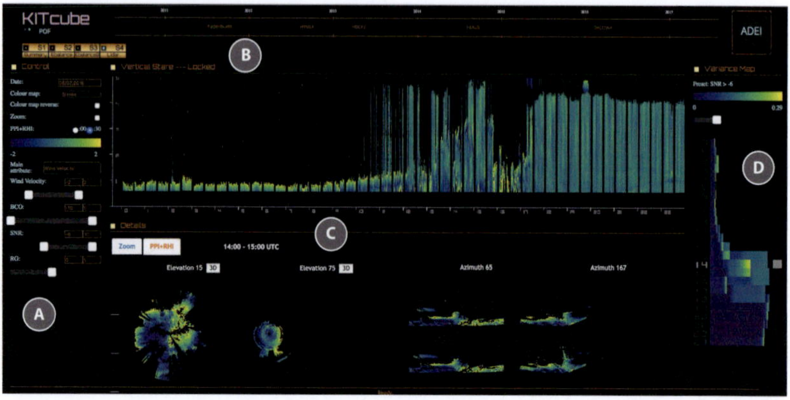

Figure 5.6.: In the Visual Display, there are (A) parameter selection to perform multivariate filtering method, (B) daily overview of the vertical stare plot, (C) hourly vertical stare, PPI, and RHI schemes, and (D) hourly variance heat map.

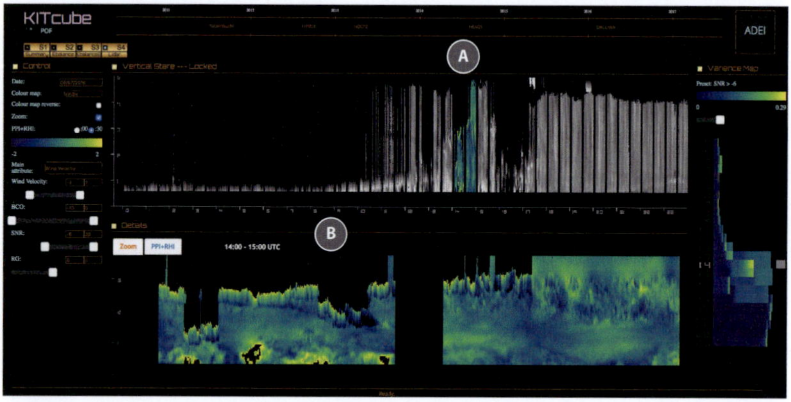

Figure 5.7.: A zooming interface with two views: A daily view (overview) and an hourly view (zoom). The daily view consists of 24 equally divided hourly segments, (A) with the selected segment highlighted. (B) The details view shows the selected hourly segment with more details (time resolution in minutes).

domain experts to analyse any hourly segment further through the vertical

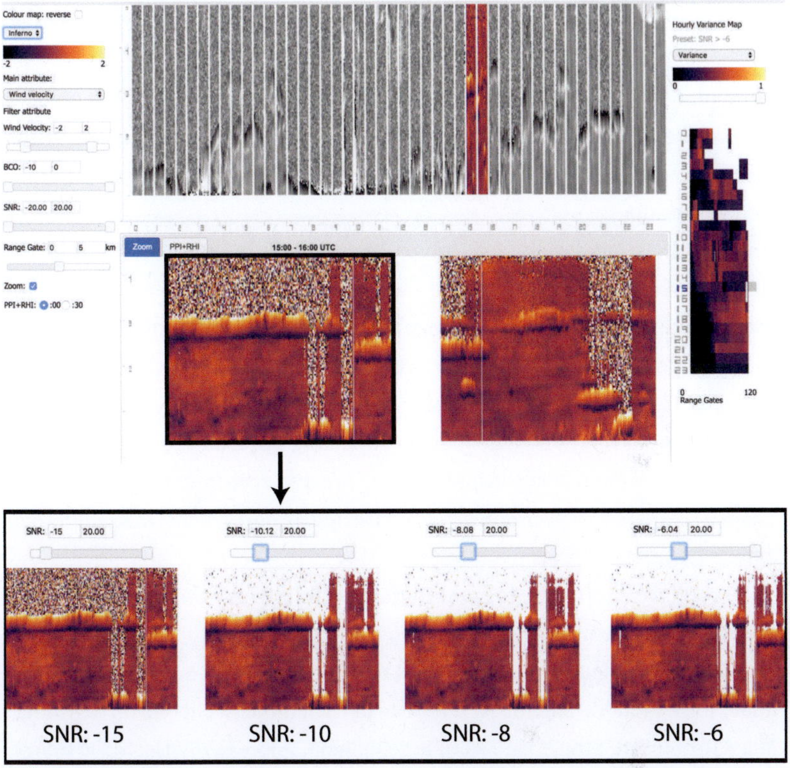

Figure 5.8.: Image shows the filtered wind velocity display that satisfies signal-noise-ratio (SNR) range. The visualisation demonstrates the use of a different colour map which is updated interactively. The lower image shows the progressive change of the wind velocity representation.

stare profile, the PPI scan, and the RHI scan. For the PPI scans, I provide a 3D visualisation of the PPI mode which complements the existing 2D PPI scans.

Due to the limited screen viewport, it is inevitable that visualising large amounts of temporal data results in a loss of details. In response, numerous works emphasise multi-focus interaction [208, 209]. Amongst these techniques, I adopt the zooming interface approach (Figure 5.7) that uses a temporal separation between views [118]. The daily view (Figure 5.7: A) consists of 24 equally divided hourly segments, $(a_0 \cdots a_{23})$. By hovering over each segment, I provide a more detailed hourly view (Figure 5.7: B). The combination of the daily view and the hourly view allows domain experts to detect atmospheric events, such as low-level nocturnal clouds, rain events, updrafts, and downdrafts.

A demanded feature in data browsing is the ability to inspect multiple attributes interactively [210], where I show and filter data based on the wind velocity, the backscattering coefficient, and the signal-noise-ratio parameters. To investigate the vertical wind velocity profile, domain experts often start with range criteria between $-2\,\mathrm{m\,s^{-1}}$ and $2\,\mathrm{m\,s^{-1}}$. Then they can update the wind velocity displays by adjusting and updating other attributes interactively (Figure 5.8). Colour maps can also be updated in real-time to emphasise the features of interest. These adjusted criteria update and synchronise all the data content across viewports interactively.

To produce the various visual outputs, I follow the *data state reference model* for a systematic data processing overview (Figure 5.9). First, I categorise the heterogeneous data into its respective mode, i.e., the vertical stare mode, the PPI mode and the RHI mode. In each mode, I encode three primary data attributes into the image's colour channels. Also, I downscale the images for better network transmission. The encoded images serve as the input for the final visualisation, mapping the data onto its respective plot.

The lidar scanning strategy applied during the DACCIWA campaign is described in Figure 5.10. Within every 30 minutes interval, the Doppler wind lidar performed two PPI scans, four RHI scans, and is followed by a vertical stare sweep. After each lidar scan, measured data are sent to a central server for data archival and processing. To generate the encoded images for the final visualisation, I convert the incoming data through a series of data preprocessing steps. Figure 5.11 shows the UML activity diagram of the whole process. I follow the suggestion proposed by Liu et al. [150], in which pre-

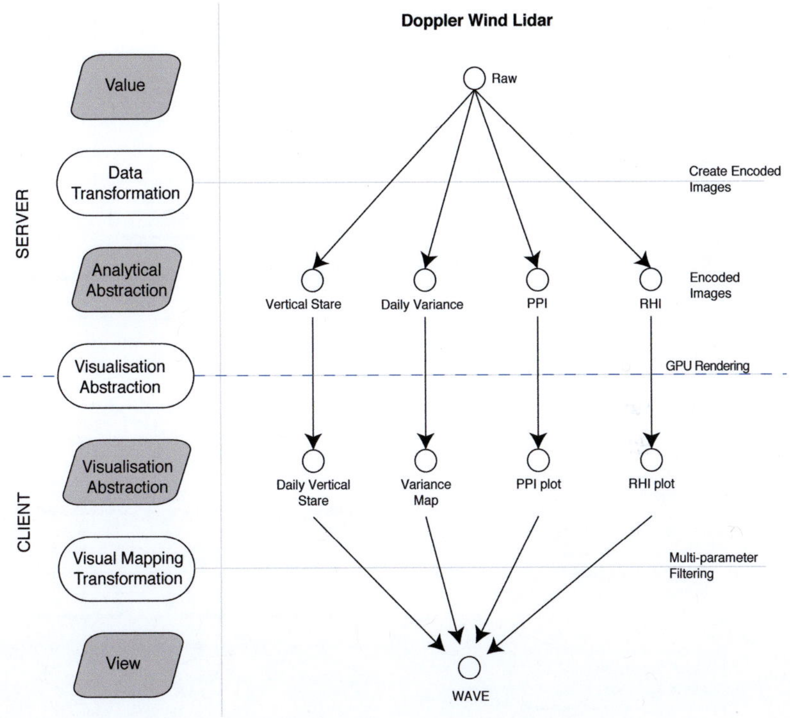

Figure 5.9.: The visual data processing (data state reference model) for the image snapshot, the thumbnail preview, and the 3D visualisation.

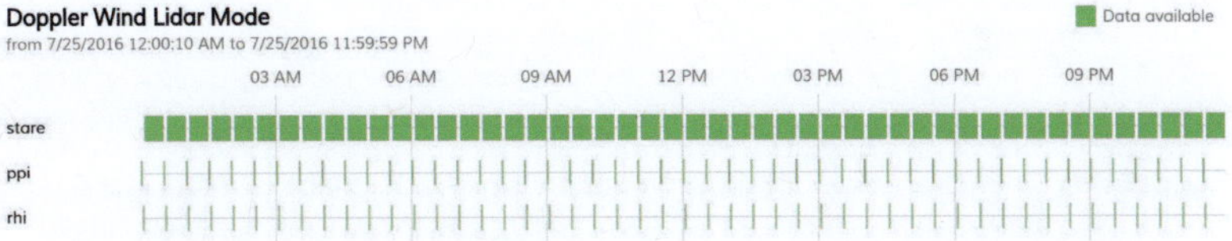

Figure 5.10.: A recursive scanning pattern by the Doppler wind lidar for every 30 minutes for one day (ppi → rhi → stare).

computed cache data (in our case the encoded images) can provide a seamless user experience.

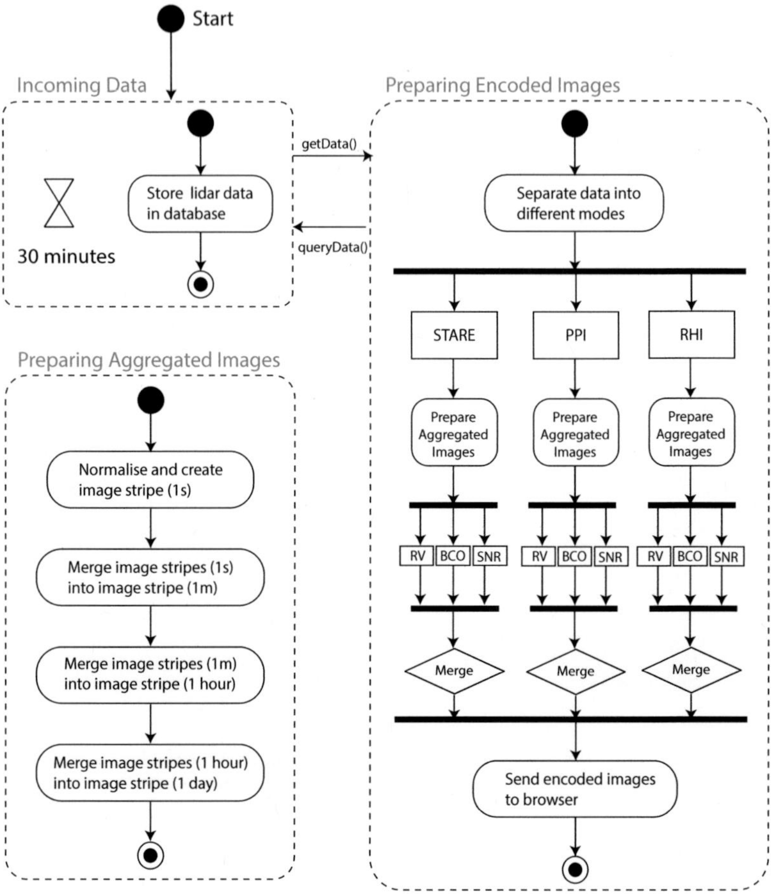

Figure 5.11.: The data preprocessing component which comprises of data classification, data normalisation, data reduction, and data consolidation stages. A_{rad}, A_{bco}, and A_{snr} denote grey images for the wind velocity, the backscattering coefficient, and the signal-noise-ratio attributes, respectively. * I perform data reduction only when the total size of grey images exceeds $1\,\mathrm{MB}$.

Initially, the incoming lidar data are stored in a central database. The data consists of general attributes such as azimuth and elevation angles. However, there is no classification of the scan modes. Hence, I separate the lidar data according to their azimuth and elevation angles into three groups: vertical stare (STARE), PPI, and RHI modes. The sampling time of the incoming data varies based on the measurement requirement. In a situation where there is not much of a change in weather, the sampling time can be set larger to minimise the amount of data being stored; in another situation, the sampling time can be smaller to capture the dynamic variation of weather events. In response, I normalise the time series data using linear interpolation at a regular time interval of one second for later data processing. Even if I interpolate the high-frequency data, the difference is not noticeable due to the limited viewport size.

5.2.2 Data Space

For each group of data, I prepare each aggregated image of the three primary lidar attributes separately: wind radial velocity (RV), backscattering coefficient (BCO), and signal-noise-ratio (SNR). Rather than processing the data of the whole day directly, I perform cascaded operations where I prepare the image stripes of a one-second interval, one-hour interval, and one-day interval. With the one-second interval being assigned to a width of one-pixel, merging the minute image stripes into an hourly image stripe results in a width of 3600 pixels. Here, the hourly image stripe is downscaled by half to accommodate the hourly and daily views. The reason behind downscaling is the limited size of the monitor display where a width of 1800 pixels covers most of the display devices. To generate the daily image stripe, I merge the hourly images and downscale the resulting image stripe to the width of 1800 pixels. For this particular use case, I map the image's x-axis to time (in second) and y-axis to the laser distance of lidar (in metre). The resulting grey image has an image resolution of 1800×1000 pixels, which corresponds to $1800\,\mathrm{s}$ and $10\,000\,\mathrm{m}$, respectively. I select $10\,000\,\mathrm{m}$ to cover the longest possible laser distance for the available lidar scans, in which a pixel height corresponds to $10\,\mathrm{m}$.

To minimise the number of images stored in the GPU texture memory, I merge the primary attributes of lidar into one compact format, in which I refer to the image as an encoded image. From the precomputed aggregated images, I encode the wind velocity attribute onto the red channel, the backscattering coefficient attribute onto the green channel, and the signal-noise-ratio attribute onto the blue channel. Here, I address the restriction presented by the client's GPU requirement regarding the limitation of the texture unit, in which the texture unit defines the number of texture images loadable in the texture memory.

5.2.3 View Space

Apart from the standard lidar displays, I included a variance heat map and 3D PPI scan visualisations to the Visual Display, in which they provide domain experts with an overview [211] and insights [212] of the wind velocity variation of a particular day. The overview aims to show the data structure of the specific day and enables rapid data browsing. The insights, in my use case, are in-depth information of the PPI scan where domain experts can even derive the height information from the 3D PPI visualisation. In this application, I combine the BORA framework (Chapter 4.2.1) and the WAVE framework (Chapter 4.2.3) as the backbone of the system.

Variance Heat Map

To show the wind velocity variance of the day, I use the heat map matrix because it preserves the spatial information of the data attribute concerning time and distance. It allows domain experts to have an instant idea of specific weather events. Figure 5.12 shows the derivation steps of transforming the daily vertical stare profile into a simplified representation.

Within each hourly vertical stare image (Figure 5.12: C), the distance along the lidar's laser consists of smaller segments, known as range gates (depicted along the y-axis). In KITcube, there are 120 range gates, and I summarise

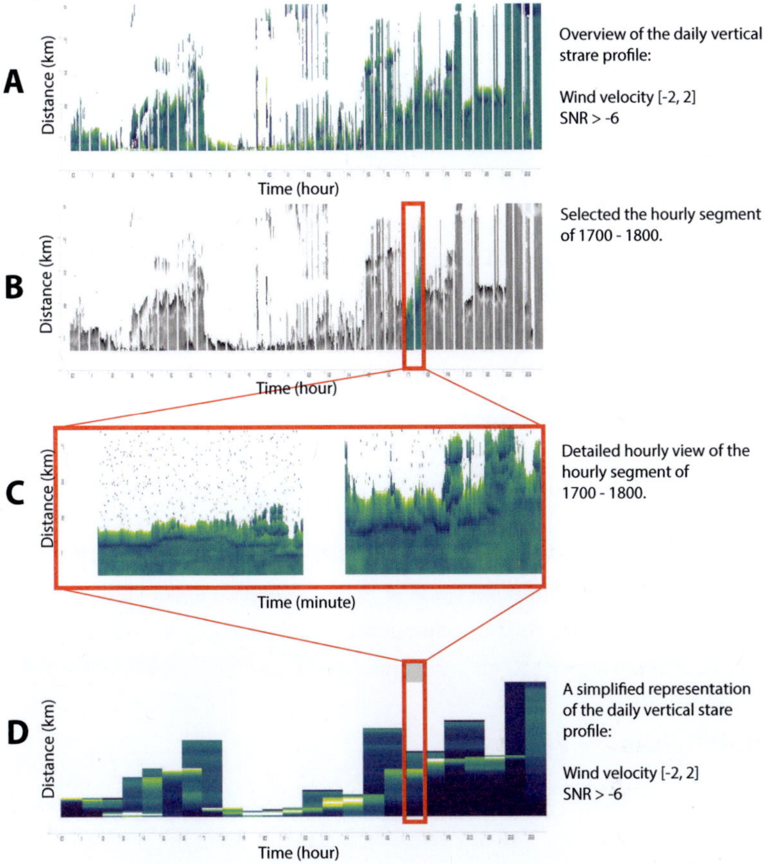

Figure 5.12.: Transformation of a daily vertical stare profile into a simplified representation. (A) shows the original representation of the daily vertical stare profile. (B) highlights the hourly segment (1700-1800). (C) shows the detailed view of the hourly segment. (D) shows the resulting compact representation of the daily vertical stare profile based on the Equation 5.1.

wind velocity attributes along each range gate within an hour's segment as one representative variance according to the Equation 5.1:

$$\sigma^2 = \begin{cases} \frac{\sum_{i=1}^{n}(x_i-\mu)^2}{n}, & \text{if } n > 1800 \\ 0, & \text{otherwise.} \end{cases} \tag{5.1}$$

Across each horizontal range gate segment, I calculate the variance of the wind velocities, but only if there are more than 50 % of the total points present. Altogether for an hourly segment, there are 3600 points along each range gate segment. Half of the total points correspond to 1800 points. In doing so, I suppress the salt-and-pepper noise that might affect the resulting variance. To assign a variance interval, I defined our lower and upper bounds based on the Von Szokefalvi Nagy inequality (lower bound) and the Bhatia-Davis inequality (upper bound) [213]:

$$\frac{(M-m)^2}{2n} \leqslant S^2 \leqslant (M-A)(A-m), \tag{5.2}$$

where S^2 is the variance, M is the maximum value, m is the minimum value, n is the total number of points, and A is the arithmetic mean value. Finally, I colour each unit using the same colour map used throughout our system. Also, I allow domain experts to vary the upper and lower boundaries interactively.

3D PPI Scan

In my visual design, I included a 3D PPI visualisation as an extension to the existing 2D PPI plot. The 3D visualisation offers users the possibility to inspect the PPI scan in a 3D space. Figure 5.13 shows the interactive display that shows the 3D PPI visualisations upon demand. In practice, there are three approaches to visualise a PPI scan in a 3D space: they are point-based rendering, texture wrapping and direct volume rendering.

The point-based rendering method maps the spherical coordinates into the Cartesian system in 3D space. However, data points further from origin have more considerable distance between neighbouring points which results in significant gaps. To mitigate the data sparsity, one could apply an interpolation filter for filling in the empty spaces. In the absence of such a filter, the sparsity

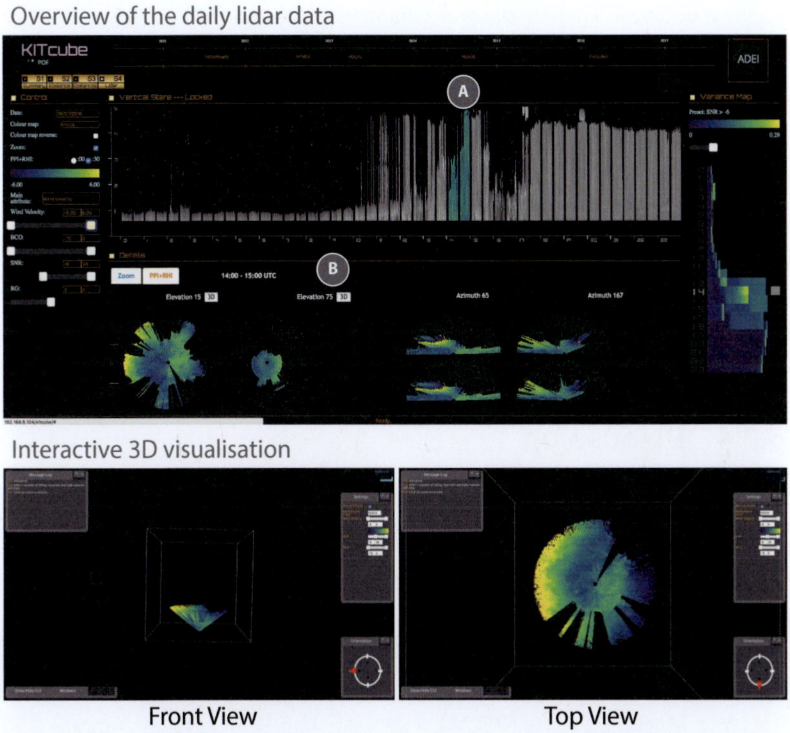

Figure 5.13.: (A) selects an hourly segment. (B) shows the PPI scans of the selected hourly segment. (C) shows the interactive 3D visualisation of the PPI scans. The PPI scan has an elevation angle of $15°$ hence the lower height in the front view and a wide spread in the top view.

of the data set leads to a less appealing visualisation. Although point-based rendering is fast due to its simplicity, filling the data degrades the system's performance [214, 215]. On the other hand, the texture wrapping method wraps the texture image on a 3D geometry. This approach is fast and straightforward given that the final visualisation constitutes a simple geometry. In this regard, a PPI scan can be depicted as a cone geometry. A 2D image is drawn and wrapped on the surface of the cone geometry. However, the 2D image has to be preprocessed. Thus interactive data manipulation is not possible. Instead, the direct volume rendering method [216] is commonly used to display the scientific data set and offers the possibility to perform interactive data rendering. I adopted the direct volume rendering and web-based methods described in Chapter 2.2.2. The direct volume rendering approach enables domain experts to perform data filtering similar to the procedure shown in Figure 5.8.

In the visualisation system, domain experts can select the 3D visualisation by clicking on the 2D PPI scan, where a standalone view appears to allow domain experts to further analyse the behaviour of the particular PPI scan (Figure 5.13).

5.2.4 Discussion

The overall performance of the visualisation system is evaluated based on the responsiveness of the client-side rendering and the latency between server-client interaction. Thus, I performed tests to measure network latency and update rates for various data sizes. To reach this conclusion, I evaluated data reduced by a factor of 5 (7.2 MB), a factor of 10 (3.4 MB), and a factor of 20 (1.3 MB). Using these data sets, I performed a series of multivariate filterings on a MacbookPro (GT750M), a desktop with an integrated graphics card (HD4000), and a high-performance desktop (GTX Titan). I wrote a testbench using Javascript that updates the filtering slider progressively for each attribute and recorded the average update rates. Figure 5.14 (left) shows that update rates are not affected by the data size, but rather by the hardware quality. On the other hand, the data size dictates the performance of the network latency, in which Figure 5.14 (right) shows an improvement in latency the smaller the data size gets. Ideally, setting up the system in a local area network will improve the latency significantly.

The results showed the effectiveness of the system as the update rates are higher than 30 fps [149]. Even the desktop with only an integrated graphics card (HD4000) scored average update rates of 48 fps. Although I reduced the daily vertical stare to fit the viewport, I integrated a variance heatmap

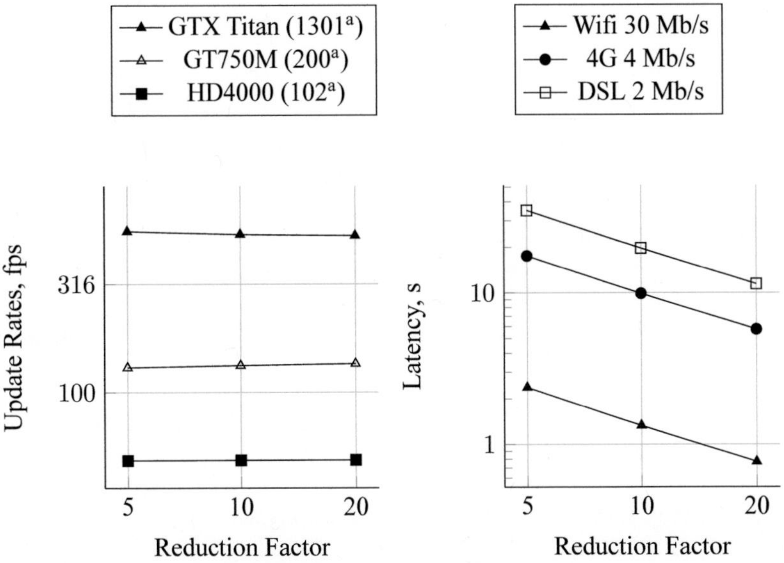

Figure 5.14.: Latency and update rates of reduced data by a factor of 5, 10, and 20 on multiple networks preset and client hardware. [a] refers to frame rates metric of the GPU taken from the WAVE framework (higher the better) [148].

to provide insights into the hourly wind velocity variation. Moreover, the system provides more details with the hourly zoom view (Figure 5.12: C). In Figure 5.15, the domain experts can identify whether there is high wind velocity variation at the lower or upper range gates. Also, one can interpret that a rain event took place between 0800 to 1400 hours based on the missing elements.

The visualisation system was used during the DACCIWA campaign where meteorologists rely on it to explore the acquired data. However, I implemented only the Doppler wind lidar device, and they are other measurement devices such as cloud radar, distrometer, X-band radar, etc. These devices can replicate the design process of Doppler wind lidar. To the best of my knowledge, no visualisation system combines these many devices in a single

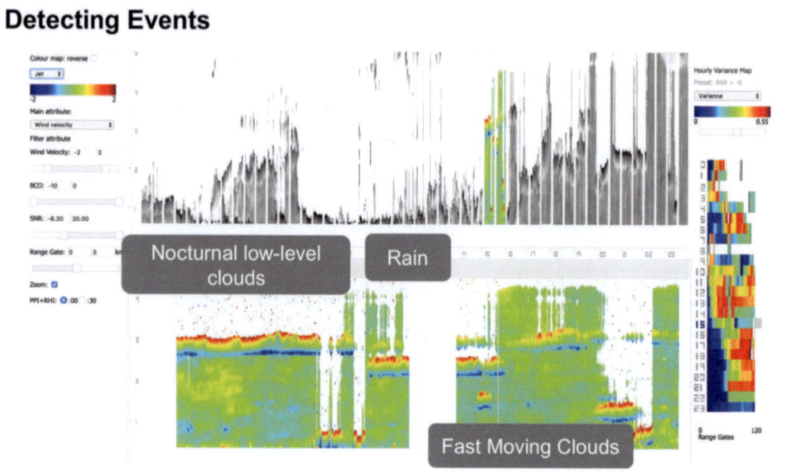

Figure 5.15.: Detecting events from the visualisation system.

platform. The process of implementing visualisation displays for all devices may be cumbersome, but the effort is worthwhile.

5.3 Use Case III: Ultrasound Computer Tomography

One of the most common cancers among women is breast cancer [217]. In the United States, breast cancer continues to rank second after lung cancer [218], and significant efforts have been made to improve early breast cancer detection. Primarily due to the improvement in screening methods and treatments, the mortality from breast cancer has declined steadily since 1995 [219]. A somewhat new and attractive screening method is the ultrasound computer tomography method (USCT) which does not use any ionisation radiation and yet produces high-quality 3D data sets using the 3D synthetic aperture focusing technique [37].

Despite the benefits of the USCT method, most of the research focuses on comparing the screening results to the more familiar mammography screening methods [26, 220]. Although visualisation is a crucial step in diagnosing the data set, less attention is given to improving visualisation techniques which could potentially improve data interpretation. The current state of visualisation tools is still based on analysing a stack of 2D slice images and relies on specific software dependencies, i.e., Matlab MiniViewer [221]. Such an approach requires doctors to mentally imagine the breast anatomy based on a series of 2D images which could lead to mental fatigue.

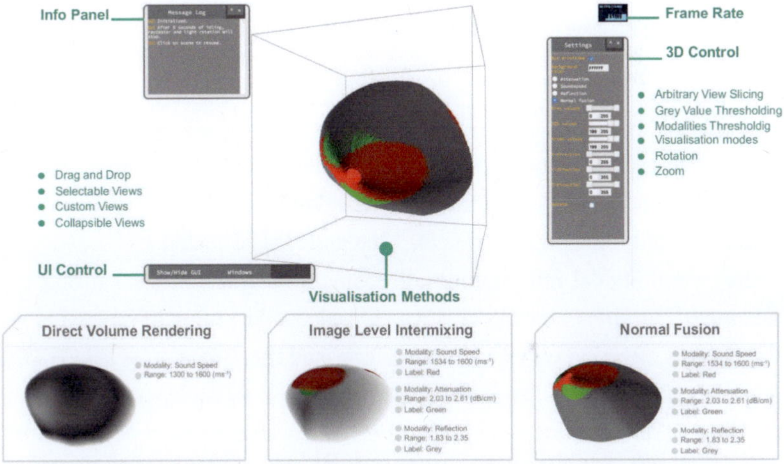

Figure 5.16.: An interactive web-based 3D visualisation tool. The info panel provides information for each action performed by the user. There is also a frame rate panel which shows the performance of the current visualisation. The main panel, 3D control, allows users to set parameters which affect the visualisation directly.

My goal is to merge the multimodality data into a standard web-based 3D visualisation which allows remote and collaborative visualisation. On the one hand, I compromise for lesser quality on client devices with low GPU requirements. In one regard, I adopted the state-of-the-art algorithms in computer

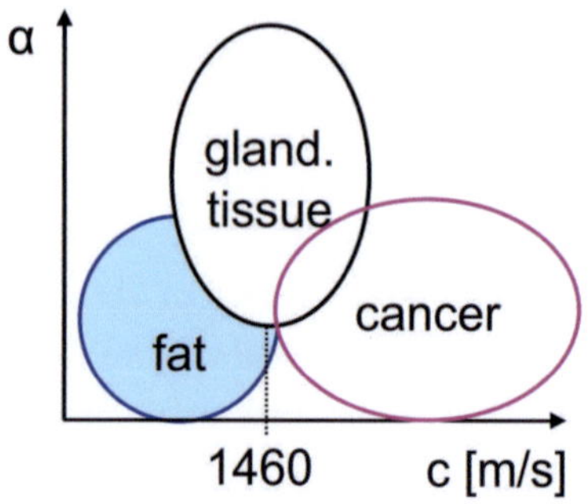

Figure 5.17.: Simplified representation of speed of sound versus attenuation map that classifies fat, glandular and cancer tissue [224]. Reprinted from Gemmeke et al. [225] ©2010 IEEE.

graphics to interactively render the multimodality data using direct volume rendering and surface rendering on client devices with high GPU requirements. To aid the analysis process, I integrated data fusion methods where I merge multimodal information into a single volume. In particular, I use the *normal fusion* approach [222] which projects the region of interest along the *normal* direction on top of the surface, and the *image level intermixing* approach [223] which blends the multimodal information by varying its opacity level. Furthermore, the system allows domain experts to perform arbitrary view slicing, modality grey values thresholding and multiple rendering modes.

The most exciting question, driven by how domain experts view their data, is how we can combine the multimodality data into a single representation, i.e., how can we determine which features are worth showing? Due to the uniqueness of each experiment, there is no general solution to encompass different experiment needs. Therefore, I will use the 3D USCT early breast cancer detection experiment as a use case study. The 3D USCT system provides three imaging modalities: reflection, attenuation, and speed of sound. The goal of the system is to improve diagnostic specificity. Mainly, the standard reflection images are used to inspect the structure. The speed of sound and attenuation images are used to discriminate between cancer and cysts [225]. Greenleaf and Bahn [224] showed that the combination of attenuation and speed of sound allows the discrimination between fat, glandular, and cancer tissue with at least 80 % specificity (Figure 5.17). Similarly, based on 25 patients, Ranger et al. [220] showed that an optimised speed of sound threshold at 1.46 ± 0.1 and 1.52 ± 0.03 km/s best represents the extent of fibroglandular tissue and solid masses. They further characterised the benign from malignant masses by using a threshold of 0.16 ± 0.04 dB/cm of the attenuation threshold.

5.3.1 Design Strategy

Whenever we visualise the multimodal USCT data set, we extract three full range volumes—each volume representing one modality. Despite having 3D models, manually analysing multiple data sets is cumbersome. Instead, I merge the three modalities into a single representation for better data interpretation (data fusion). Mainly, I allow a fusion scheme which determines the projection of each modality, i.e., Ranger's fusion scheme [220]. In this section, I will discuss two data fusion approaches where I utilise both surface and volume rendering techniques interchangeably: the *normal fusion* approach [222] and the *image level intermixing* approach [223] (Figure 5.18). Throughout the data fusion approaches, I label the thresholded region of *sound speed* with an orange colour and *attenuation* with a green colour.

Algorithm 1: The image level intermixing. In the rendering process, I combine the information stored in the slicemap to produce the final image. Mainly, I use the direct volume rendering and extend the classification step where I choose values at each point selectively. The *sound speed* modality is prioritised first, followed by the *attenuation* modality and lastly the *reflection* modality. First, I set the opacity of the background based on the *reflection* modality where the structure of the data can be determined. Then, I consider whether the *sound speed* or the *attenuation* falls within the predefined threshold regions (regions of interest). In a case where any of the two mod-

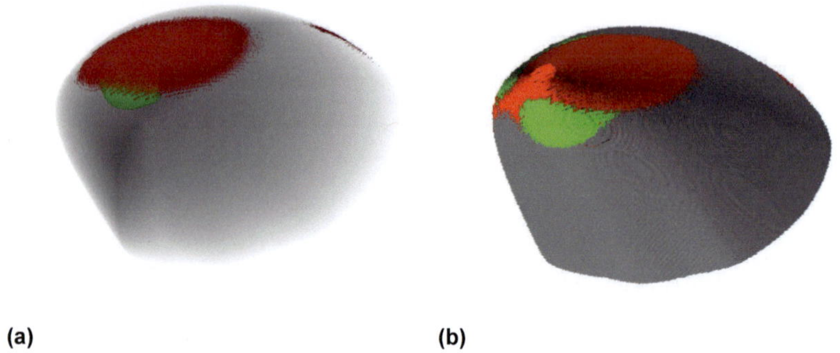

Figure 5.18.: The data fusion approaches: (a) *image level intermixing* and (b) *normal fusion*.

alities are within the region, I set the colour and opacity of the voxel to the corresponding modality opacity and its predefined colour according to the modality priority.

Algorithm 2: The normal fusion approach. The algorithm describes the process of projecting the interior information of the volume onto the surface. Here, I utilise volume rendering to collect information within the volume and surface rendering to produce a realistic image. Similar to the *image level intermixing*, I prioritise the *sound speed* modality over *attenuation* modality, as well as using *reflection* modality to present the structure information. However, if there is an overlapping region, I only show the *sound speed* modality. To produce the final *normal fusion* result, I first cast a ray into the bounding box until there is a hit on the surface of the object. Then, I calculate the normal vector at the intersection point. Rather than continuing in the ray direction, I instead continue to traverse further into the inverted normal direction (secondary ray). Along the secondary ray, I return the orange label if any *sound speed* is detected within the predefined threshold. Otherwise, I return the green label if I find *attenuation* within the predefined threshold with no *sound speed* present. With the colour label ready, I perform the surface rendering using the returned label as the ambient colour.

```
Ray setup (entry position and ray direction);
while ray in volume do
    Interpolate data value at current position;
    if current value (sound speed) within sound speed threshold then
        colour ← orange;
        opacity ← current sound speed opacity;
    else
        if current value (attenuation) within attenuation threshold
          then
            colour ← green;
            opacity ← current attenuation opacity;
        else
            colour ← grey;
            opacity ← current reflection opacity;
        end
    end
    Perform compositing (colour and opacity);
    Propagate position along ray;
end
```

Algorithm 1: Image level intermixing: pseudo code

5.3.2 Data Space

In my use case, I define the speed of sound modality as the primary attribute, followed by the attenuation modality. The reflection modality provides only the geometry information of the data set. Hence I transform the image slices into *slicemap* (Chapter 2.3) which comprises a series of 2D cross-section images stacked in a mosaic gridded format. Figure 5.19 shows a slicemap created from the USCT data set which consists of three modalities: *sound speed*, *attenuation*, and *reflection*. I map each modality into its respective colour channel, where the colour representation of the pixel within the slicemap constitutes a three-tuple $(R, G, B) \in [0, 1]$, where $SoundSpeed \mapsto R$, *attenuation* $\mapsto G$, and *reflection* $\mapsto B$.

```
Ray setup (entry position and ray direction);
Define W as length of the cube;
while ray in volume do
    if intersect then
        calculate normal direction;
        read current position and value;
        output ← grey;
        Secondary ray setup(current position and normal direction);
        while secondary ray less than W/2 do
            if current value within sound speed threshold then
                output ← orange;
                break;
            end
            if current value within attenuation threshold then
                output ← green;
            end
        end
        ambient ← output;
        Perform compositing (ambient + diffuse + specular);
        break;
    else
        propagate position along ray
    end
end
```

Algorithm 2: Normal fusion: pseudo code

To address the diverse client requirements, I introduce the use of multiresolution slicemap—a hierarchy of multiresolution slicemaps differing in image resolution. The main idea is to transfer a suitable size of data that the best performance at the client. We characterise the client by its *texture unit* and *texture size* properties. To deal with the bandwidth limitation, I included the load-on-demand approach where low-resolution data is firstly served followed by a high-resolution data loading in the background [148].

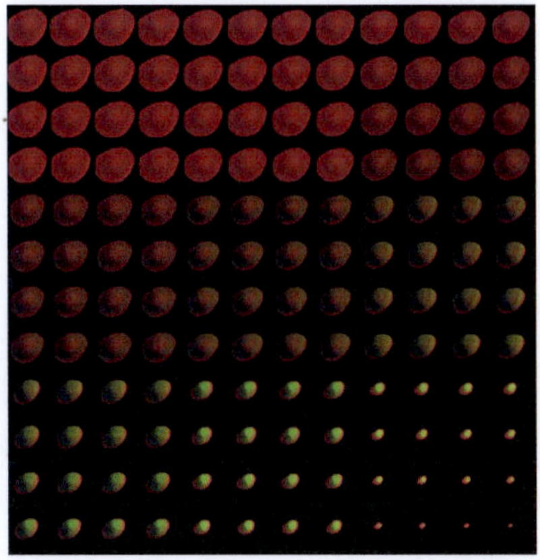

Figure 5.19.: A 12×12 slicemap of a breast data set. A mosaic-format image comprises a stack of 2D slice images. The iteration of the stack images is from left-right and top-bottom. Each slice consists of three modalities—*sound speed*, *attenuation* and *reflection*—that are mapped onto the colour channels respectively ($(R, G, B) \in [0, 1]$, where $SoundSpeed \mapsto R$, *attenuation* $\mapsto G$, and *reflection* $\mapsto B$).

5.3.3 View Space

To address the diverse client requirements, I introduce the use of multiresolution slicemap—a hierarchy of multiresolution slicemaps differing in image resolution. The main idea is to transfer a suitable size of data that the best performance at the client. We characterise the client by its *texture unit* and *texture size* properties. To deal with the bandwidth limitation, I included the load-on-demand approach where low-resolution data is firstly served followed by a high-resolution data loading in the background [148]. The WAVE framework (Chapter 4.2.3) is used for this use case.

5.3.4 Discussion

The basis for all frame rate comparison is the client's local server, which is primarily affected by its available GPU resource. Hence, to measure the efficiency and performance of our tool, I evaluate the mentioned visualisation methods—direct volume rendering (DVR), the *image level intermixing* approach (ILI), the *normal fusion* approach (NF)—on several clients with different GPU resources. The methods are tested on (i) a mobile phone (GPU: Adreno 510), (ii) a standard desktop (GPU: integrated graphics card HD4000), (iii) a laptop (GPU: GT750M), and (iv) a powerful workstation (GPU: Tesla C2). I use the USCT data with a size of $256 \times 256 \times 144$ which is transformed into a single slicemap (Figure 5.19). The three modalities are encoded into the colour channels of the slicemap.

Based on the results shown in Figure 5.20, the direct volume rendering has the best performance due to its simplicity. There is no classification step nor any fusion scheme involved. In the case of the ILI and NF, both fusion methods involve priority-based modality selection to determine the visual output. The ILI is based solely on the volume rendering algorithm and extends the classification step; whereas the NF consists of both volume and surface renderings. Moreover, the NF approach involves a primary ray in the view direction and a secondary ray in the normal direction. In comparison with the ILI approach, the additional secondary ray in the NF approach results in higher traversal steps. However, the performance of the ILI and NF are comparable, which suggests the priority-based selection of the NF serves as an *early secondary ray termination*—the secondary ray terminates upon the detection of *sound speed* modality.

Except for the mobile device, the visualisation methods resulted in an overall frame rate higher than 30 fps which suggest its suitability in clinical or laboratory environments. It is worth noting that the performance shown by the desktop with only an integrated graphics card (integrated GPU HD4000) and no dedicated GPU. Hence, I can conclude that these methods are capable of running on any modern desktop with acceptable performance. On the other hand, the usage of the web-based 3D visualisation in mobile phones in the current state is not feasible. I can optimise the existing algorithm by reducing the sampling step number of the primary ray. Also, I can adopt less resource demanding algorithms such as additive blending. To minimise the processing

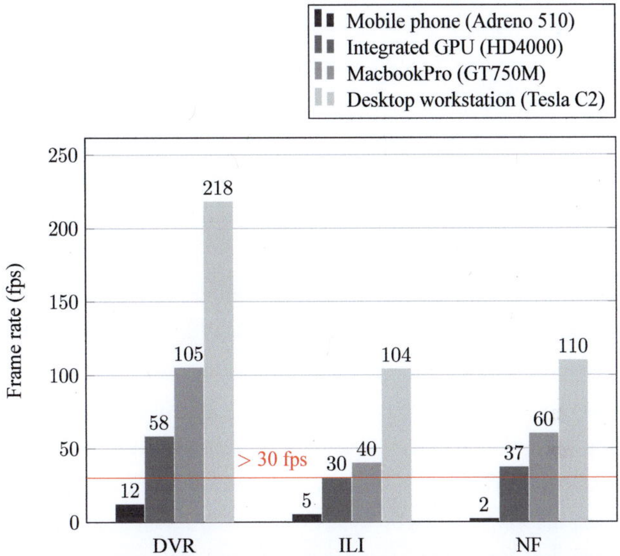

Figure 5.20.: The frame rate of three visualisation methods—the direct volume rendering (DVR), the image level intermixing (ILI) and the normal fusion approach (NF)—tested on the mobile phone, the desktop with integrated GPU, the MacbookPro and the powerful workstation. The higher the frame rate, the better.

load for the client, I can shift the data-intensive operation to the server-side, such as precalculating normal vectors. Also, reducing the data size can improve the client side performance immensely albeit at the cost of the visual quality [148].

The visualisation approaches shown thus far are capable of highlighting a suspicious tumour based on thresholding. However, the projected region on the surface does not show the exact geometry of the tumour size faithfully. The visualisation methods shown might be feasible to serve as an overview, but a visualisation method that depicts the size of the thresholded region can help the diagnosis process immensely.

Future work on our tool encompasses several opportunities. Firstly, given the simple geometry of the USCT data set, fusing the multimodal data is much more interesting. In this section, I have shown a small fraction of the many multimodality visualisations imaginable. For example, we can consider the work by Bramon [226] where he fuses multimodal data using the mutual information approach which requires a probability map of the interested anatomy features. Since the USCT input data are inherently images, I can improve the network latency by introducing compression schemes such as LZO algorithm.

Throughout this section, I assume a simple client-server architecture without a high-performance computer (HPC). With hardware commodity being affordable, it is an exciting prospect to improve the image quality and network latency by deploying an image streaming approach, where the approach shifts computation intensive processes to the server and sends the resulting image to the client. Furthermore, a new trend arises where many applications are emphasising the visual analytic system. It is useful using only multimodality visualisation, but integrating more domain knowledge into the visualisation system can enlighten the doctors or practitioners in their daily work. The WAVE framework proves to be a useful tool and it is possible to extend the visualisation system into a web-based data catalogue.

5.4 Use Case IV: X-ray Computer Tomography

In recent years, X-ray computed tomography (CT) imaging allows biologists to study the internal structure of small animals such as insects and other arthropods [12, 227]. In particular, they can perform high-throughput measurements of 3D and 4D tomographic imaging of dynamic systems and living organisms with submicron spatial and subsecond time resolution [227, 228, 229]. The NOVA [1] project aims to demonstrate, that more efficient use of the facility usage is possible by coordinated research on different organ systems. Since

[1]NOVA stands for Network for Online Visualisation and synergistic Analysis of tomographic data. https://ufo.kit.edu/dis/index.php/project/nova/

different research group specialises in a different biological part of the species, the project encourages collaboration among multiple biological partners.

Using the synchrotron-based X-ray microtomography (SRµCT) imaging technique, the NOVA project [12] serves as an ideal use case where hundreds of small animals are digitised, and their images are turned into Big Data. Each data set size ranges from 2 GB to 15 GB and interactively visualising them is cumbersome. Therefore, the visualisation system suffers from large data latency. Despite the advancement in storage and networking technologies, the bottleneck remains at the network bandwidth—the amount of transferred data exceeds the capacity of the physical network bandwidth [230]. Often, domain experts download the data into an image processing tool like Amira [231], however, the whole process suffers from multiple wait times: wait during network transfer and wait during loading into local machine memory. Moreover, the domain experts have to select optimal parameters to visualise the data efficiently, i.e., the optimal grey value threshold. Figure 5.21 shows the visualisation of five biological specimens which I will use throughout this chapter. Table 5.3 contains the information for each data set . In the figure, the volume renderings are produced by the Amira [231]. The visual outputs consist of a container, the specimen, and a ring artefact. In this section, I will not address the ring artefact because it can be removed by removal algorithms [232, 233, 234]. In the CT application, the noise arises mainly from various sources such as photon detection statistics, detector misalignment, reconstruction algorithms, and so on [235, 236]. Ideally, we would like to produce only the specimen as the final visual output; hence I will address removing the container and the noise in the following sections. Moreover, I apply automatic thresholding to find the optimal threshold value that separates the unwanted details from the specimen.

To improve the efficiency of data and infrastructure usage, we need to establish a clear understanding of the data throughout the tomographic-oriented scientific workflow (Figure 5.22). Hence, the ability to visualise the digitised Big Data during data acquisition is essential. The X-ray tomographic work-

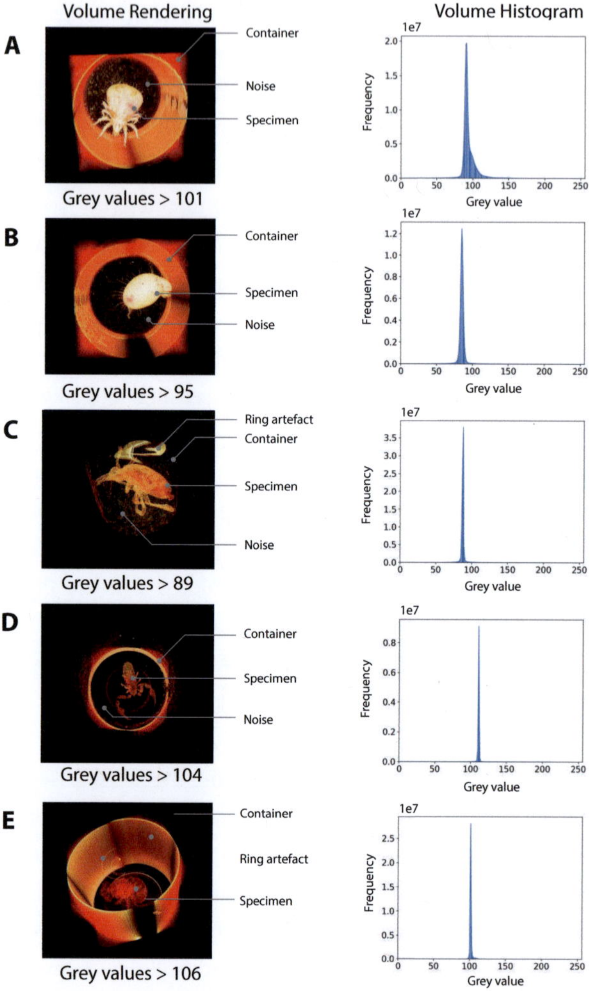

Figure 5.21.: Volume rendering of biological samples with the Amira ® software [231] (left). The labels describe the important features of the data: container, specimen, ring artefact, and noise. The volume histogram is shown at the right to show the frequency distribution of the grey values.

Table 5.3.: The information of data sets used in this chapter.

Label	Type	Description
A	Oribatid mite	*Archegozetes longisetosus* (Aoki, 1965)
B	Box mite	*Euphthiracarus reticulatus* (Berlese, 1913)
C	Gammasid mite	Unidentified species
D	Pseudoscorpion	Unidentified species
E	Tachinid fly	*Gymnosoma nudifrons* (Herting, 1966)

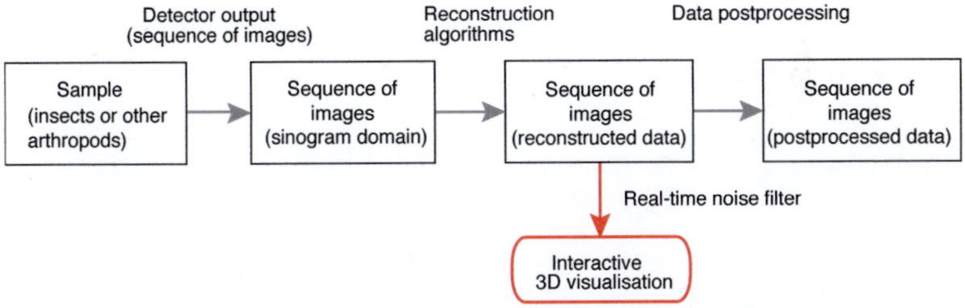

Figure 5.22.: Picture of the image processing pipeline for a tomography-oriented scientific workflow. The red represents the stage, where we enable rapid feedback on data quality visually.

flow starts with the projections of the specimen being recorded continuously by a camera in many angles and thus produces a sequence of images in sinogram domain [237]. The sinograms are then reconstructed into volumetric data for further postprocessing or visualisation. Domain experts act as agents to monitor the correctness of the data visually [238]. If any misconfiguration during the imaging stage occurs, they can remedy the process immediately, improving the utilisation of the infrastructure.

Aside from addressing the large data set size, I also emphasise data availability where the visual information should be available to a wide range of users, each with a different hardware requirement. The hardware requirement refers to the GPU capability where I enable interactive visualisation using parallel computation power. On the one hand, users with lower client requirement would appreciate a recognisable visual preview of the data; on the other hand, users with higher client requirements would expect the best quality of visible contents. In doing so, multiple users can work on the same data set hence encouraging reuse of the experimental data sets. However, loading extensive data to the client would incur long transfer time due to the limited network bandwidth, and rendering large data on the client could be slow due to the limited processing power. Hence, research in Big Data visualisation must address perceptual and interactive scalability [150]. The perceptual scalability refers to how we can achieve the best render quality on arbitrary devices; whereas the interactive scalability refers to smooth data interaction that mainly dictates the data transfer time.

In this section, I discuss methods to provide visual information as part of the digital library framework (Chapter 2.1). Mainly, I focus on delivering best-rendered image quality and provide visual previews to the clients.

5.4.1 Design Strategy

The purpose of integrating visualisation into the digital library (Chapter 2.1) is to provide a better data browsing system that allows domain experts to narrow down and find the relevant data quickly [29]. In the NOVA project, domain experts are interested in *identifying* and *recognising* their scanned sample immediately. Hence, the geometry information is essential during the recognition process. To visualise the data in 3D, we can present the data in meshes or voxels. Meshes represent overall surface details of the data, whereas voxels describe the surface and the inner features as well. However, meshes require prior knowledge to generate the polygon or triangle primitives which are not present during the data exploration process. To allow flexible selection of the region of interest within the data, I opt to use voxel data and provide volume as well as surface renderings (Chapter 2.2.2) in the visualisation system.

For better data transmission, I produce aggregated data which is smaller in size and yet retains the geometry information of the original data. I will study the visual quality of these aggregated data and formulate a strategy to achieve the optimal visual representation of data across diverse client requirements. To design the overall system, I follow the *Visual Information Seeking Mantra* [56] which serves as my initial design guidelines (Chapter 2.1):

Overview first Overview of scanned small animals, e.g., arthropods.

Zoom and filter More information on the selected sample and relate similar scanned samples.

Details-on-demand Allow 3D interactions of the selected sample.

As a result, I devise a visual interaction flow as shown in Figure 5.23. In the Overview First, I provide a list to browse through the scanned specimens by their code names. By selecting any data, domain experts will receive an information page about the selected data (Zoom and Filter). Additionally, there is a thumbnail preview that shows a rotating 3D visualisation. The preview allows domain experts to comprehend the data structure in 3D space. However, the visual presentation has a small viewport, hence can serve only as a quick preview. To inspect the selected data further, the domain expert can launch the Interactive 3D visualisation by clicking on the thumbnail preview, where they can manipulate the grey value threshold, perform arbitrary view slicing, and select different visualisation mode, e.g., surface or volume renderings. To this end, three visual outputs are necessary for this design: image snapshot, thumbnail preview, and interactive 3D visualisation.

To transform the original data into appropriate visual outputs, I map the visual data processing based on the *data state reference model* [64] (Figure 5.24). Also, the model helps in understanding the design space of the scientific domain. In the followings, I will explain the required data processing tasks in the Data Space and the visualisation components in the View Space [2].

[2]The *data state reference model* is discussed in Chapter 3.3.

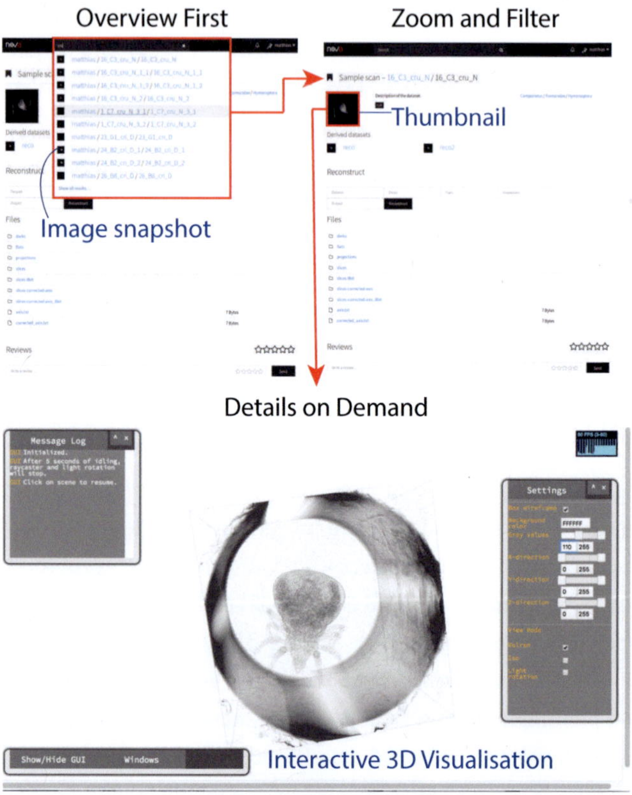

Figure 5.23.: The visual interaction design flow for the NOVA project. The Overview First image shows the browsing list of specimens with code names. The Zoom and Filter image shows the data profile page of the selected code name *16_C3_cru_N*, i.e., an oribatid mite. The Details on Demand image shows the interactive 3D visualisation of the selected specimen. The red arrows show the exploration process of a user, and the blue labels denote the required visual formats for the experiment.

5.4.2 Data Space

Within the Data Space, the Data Transformation describes the data processing pipeline where I remove unwanted details from the data and then provide smal-

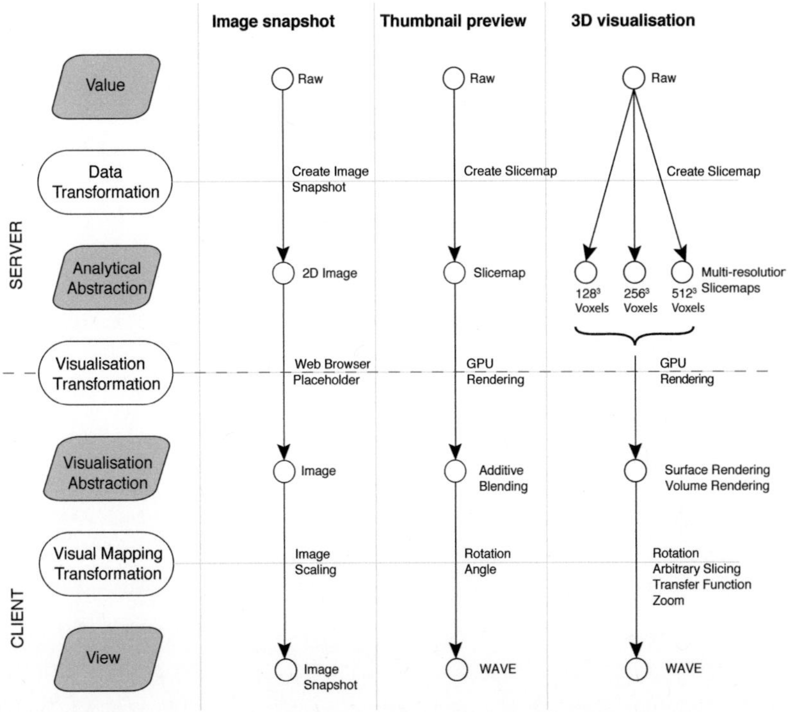

Figure 5.24.: The visual data processing (*data state reference model*) for the image snapshot, the thumbnail preview, and the 3D visualisation. The grey boxes denote the data stages that describe the state of the data; the white, elliptical boxes shows the transformation stage that describes the process of transforming the data from one state to another.

ler aggregated data sets. In this section, I will discuss each processing task and its importance to achieving a useful visualisation output.

I Data Mining

a) Data thresholding

II Data Filtering

a) Container removal

   b) Real time local noise filter

III Data Mapping

   a) Generate slicemap

   b) Generate 3D image

IV Data Reduction

   a) Downscaling

   b) Thumbnail preview

5.4.2.1 Data Mining

Data Thresholding

Initially, the input data set is composed of image stacks where each stack represents a volumetric data set. As the selected use case is dealing with X-ray microtomography images of biological specimens, the data are primarily noisy and low contrasted [239]. Low contrast refers to the narrow region of data in the frequency histogram (Figure 5.21) where there is a limited effective range for thresholding scans. In my application, I visualise the grey values that are greater than the selected threshold. With no prior knowledge of the region of interest, the visualisation system cannot decide on the optimal threshold which ends up showing the full range of grey values. Even if the user sets the threshold manually, essential details could be lost due to the low contrast characteristic. The higher the threshold value is, the more features are removed. In Figure 5.25, the bottom left image shows the visualisation with the threshold value computed by the Otsu-method; the bottom middle image shows the fly data set with well-preserved details. However, the 3D display is surrounded by noise. Even if one performs simple thresholding, the noise might be removed together with data features. For example, setting a threshold value at 109 suppresses the noise but at the expense of eliminating details—the cuticle of the eyes and wings are not visible (Figure 5.25 lower right). If we are visualising 8-bit stack images in the full dynamic range (0 to 255), it results in an opaque volume where each voxel consists of meaningful information, e.g., air or sample container. Hence, a threshold value that separates the scanned sample and its surrounding artefacts are essential.

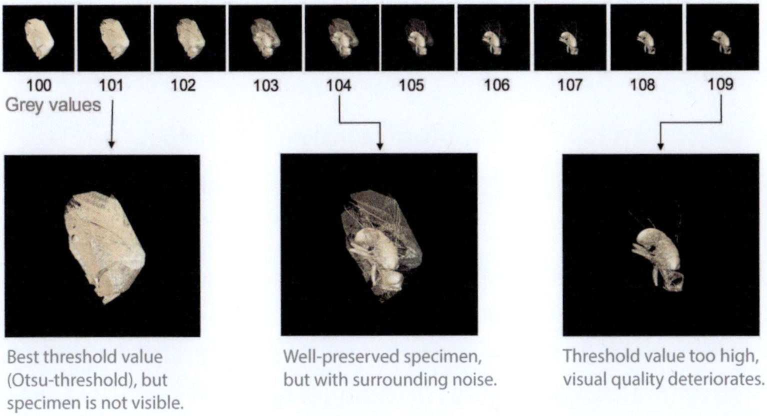

Figure 5.25.: The top images show the final surface 3D visualisation of the tachinid fly *Gymnosoma nudifrons* (Herting, 1966) data set (Table 5.3 E) by varying the lower limit of the threshold.

After applying the data thresholding, visualising the data directly still does not provide a recognisable visual output because of the specimen being occluded by container and noise. The data contain not only the geometry structure of the specimen but also include unwanted details such as sample container or air. Based solely on the distribution of the data histogram, one cannot differentiate between the main features against the irrelevant information—the narrow band of the volume histogram (Figure 5.21). The paradox in removing irrelevant details is that we are eliminating details that we do not have prior knowledge of, which might lead to the removal of essential information. For this reason, I remove the specimen's container during the *Image snapshot* and *Interaction 3D visualisation* visual processes. Then, I enable noise filtering for the *interactive 3D visualisation* visual process during the final View stage. In this section, I describe how I analyse the data to differentiate the data features from the artefact or unwanted details.

To extract the data features, I employ thresholding in which grey values are classified into a bi-tonal data which divides the data distribution into two classes. Particularly, I segment the volumetric data into foreground and background:

$$f(x) = \begin{cases} 0, & \text{if } x \text{ is a foreground voxel} \\ 1, & \text{if } x \text{ is a background voxel} \end{cases} \tag{5.3}$$

The foreground refers to the data distribution on the left side of the threshold; whereas the background relates to the data distribution on the right side of the threshold. Hence, a global threshold, T, is imperative to separate the voxels, x, into their classes. In my application, I show the background and suppress the foreground in the visualisation. To determine the global threshold, I looked into automatic image thresholding methods and extended them to volumetric context—dubbed as *automatic volume thresholding*. The purpose is to subdivide the volume into meaningful non-overlapping regions. In this context, I strive to separate the digitised biological sample from its surroundings, i.e., container. Ideally, we would like to select an optimal threshold based on the distribution of the histogram. Here, I will discuss two approaches and evaluate their validity in my use case: Otsu thresholding [240] and Iterative threshold selection [241].

Otsu thresholding The Otsu thresholding performs a conceptual sweep line to find the optimal threshold, in which a criterion function is used to measure statistical separation between the two classes: foreground and background. The criterion function involves minimising the ratio of the between-classes variance and the total variance, hence:

$$\sigma^2_\omega(T) = \omega_0(T)\sigma^2_0(T) + \omega_1(T)\sigma^2_1(T), \tag{5.4}$$

where ω_0 and ω_1 are the weights which represent the probabilities of the two classes separated by the threshold T. σ_0^2 and σ_1^2 are the variances of the two types. I use the Otsu threshold as the lower limit of the intensity range (Algorithm 3). By starting from the first grey value, $T_{otsu} = 0$, I subdivide the histogram into two regions and select the threshold that maximises the between-class variance (Equation 5.4).

```
T_otsu ← 0, σ_otsu ← 0;
for T_sweep from 0...255 do
    R_a ← histogram[0:T_sweep];
    R_b ← histogram[T_sweep:255];
    W_a ← density(R_a), W_b ← density(R_b);
    U_a ← Mean(R_a), U_b ← Mean(R_b);
    σ ← W_a × W_b × (U_a − U_b)^2 ;          // Between Class Variance
    if σ > σ_otsu then
        σ_otsu ← σ;
        T_otsu ← T_sweep;
    end
end
```

Algorithm 3: Otsu thresholding

Iterative threshold selection The iterative threshold selection (ITS) is akin to greedy algorithms [242] where the algorithm tries to find a global minimum by considering the average of the two clusters: foreground and background. The ITS method comprises five steps, where the second to fourth steps are iterated until a threshold value converges (Algorithm 4). Firstly, the algorithm selects a starting threshold, $T_{it} \in [0, 255]$ (Step 1). Since the histogram distribution concentrates in the middle of the dynamic range, the middle threshold serves as a good starting point. Then, the histogram is divided into two regions, R_1 and R_2, based on the selected threshold T_{it} (Step 2). Thirdly, the mean intensity values, μ_1 and μ_2, are computed for each region respectively (Step 3). In the fourth step, a new threshold is updated based on the average of both mean intensities: $T_{it} = (\mu_1 + \mu_2)/2$ (Step 4). Lastly, Steps

$T_{it} \leftarrow T_{start}$;
$r \leftarrow T_{start}$; // T_{it} converges if $r = 0$
while $r \neq 0$ **do**
  $R_a \leftarrow$ histogram[0:T_{it}];
  $R_b \leftarrow$ histogram[T_{it}:255];
  $\mu_1 \leftarrow$ MeanIntensity(R_a);
  $\mu_2 \leftarrow$ MeanIntensity(R_b);
  $T_{tmp} \leftarrow (\mu_1 + \mu_2)/2$;
  $r \leftarrow |r - T_{tmp}|$;
  $T_{it} \leftarrow T_{tmp}$;
end

Algorithm 4: Iterative threshold selection (ITS)

2—4 are repeated until the mean values μ_1 and μ_2 do not change in successive iterations (Step 5).

Evaluation and Discussion The main difference between the two approaches lies in the number of iterations. In the case of Otsu thresholding, the algorithm always performs a full scan across the dynamic range, i.e., a range from 0 to 255 for an 8-bit data, whereas the ITS method terminates upon finding the global minimum where the number of iterations is often much smaller. I compare the two thresholding approaches using the data sets described in Table 5.3 and their visual results are shown in Figure 5.26. For the first three data sets, the Otsu and ITS methods are providing the same threshold values, thus highlights the shape of the samples. However, the last two data sets cannot extract the biological specimens, where they failed to find the optimum value due to narrow histogram distribution. Since Otsu and ITS methods rely on discrete increments of threshold values, a small shift in the narrow dynamic range results in a considerable change to the variance spreads (Otsu) or the mean intensities (ITS).

To evaluate the performance of each method, I take the average of 10 computation times on the MacbookPro with a 64 bit Quad-Core Intel(R) Core i7 CPU at 2.60 GHz and 16 GB of DDR3 memory. Figure 5.27 shows the av-

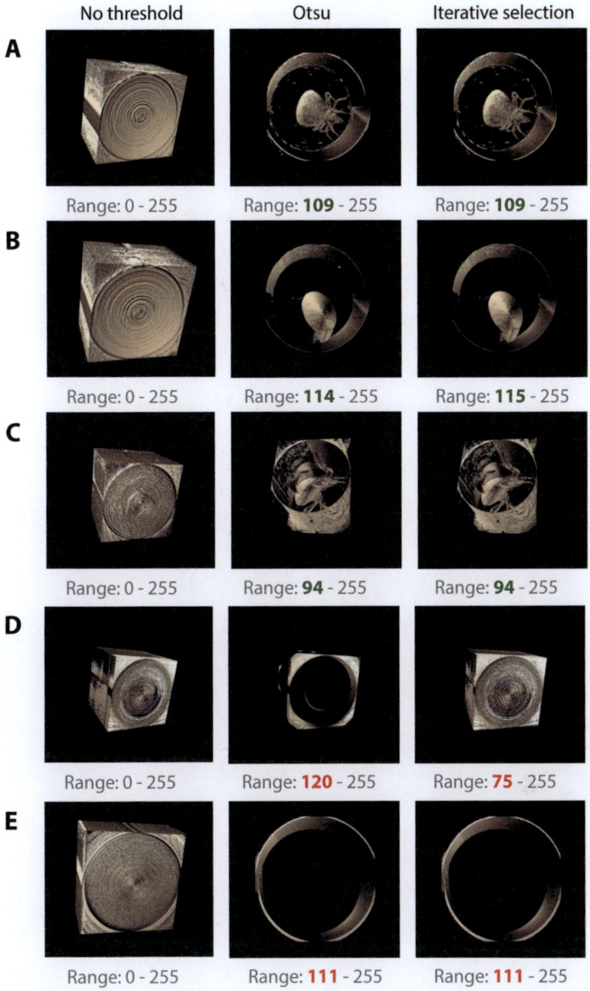

Figure 5.26.: The visual results of data sets when applying threshold values calculated by the Otsu and iterative threshold selection (ITS) methods. The red colour shows the values that are under- or over-thresholded. The green colour shows the optimal threshold for each particular data set.

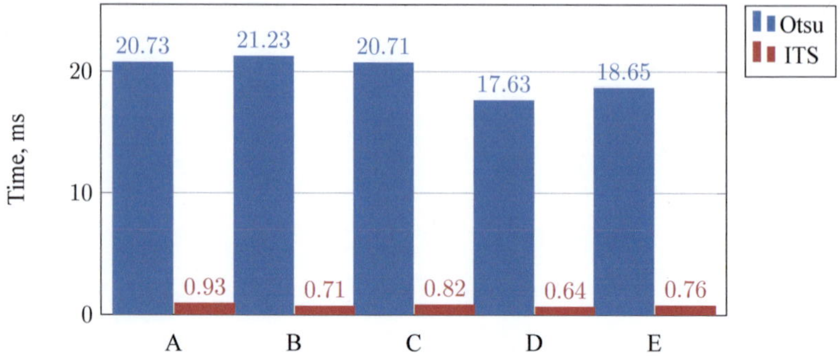

Figure 5.27.: The performances of the Otsu and the iterative threshold selection methods on a series of data sets described in Table 5.3.

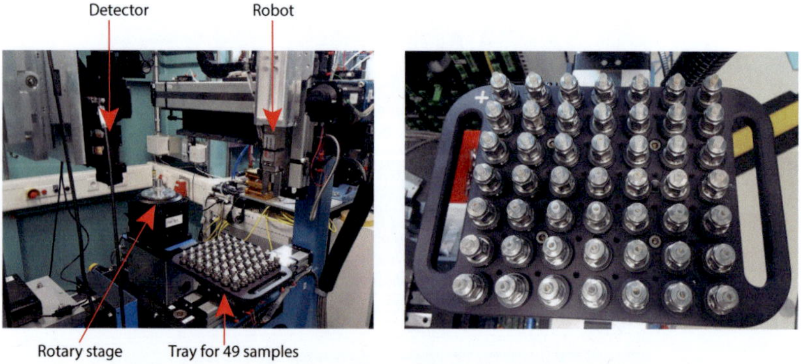

Figure 5.28.: The experiment setup of the KIT Imaging Cluster [22] that is equipped with a fully automated data acquisition system (left). The biological samples are placed within the 3D printed containers (right) and each container is placed on top of the rotary stage for scanning. Photographs by Thomas van de Kamp.

erage computation time for each of the data set. The Otsu threshold has a much higher computation time due to the complete sweep of the image's dynamic range. The ITS method depended solely on the iteration convergence and based on these data sets, and the threshold converges after approximately ten iterations where the ITS method performs 20 times faster than the Otsu method.

Insofar, the visual results included the sample container where the container contributed to the overall volume histogram, thus affected the global histogram analysis. Interestingly, for the Pseudoscorpion and the tachinid fly *Gymnosoma nudifrons* (Herting, 1966) data sets (Table 5.3: D and E), the Otsu method extracted the sample container from their background. Hence, removing the sample container before the thresholding scan can result in a better and faithful histogram analysis. Fortunately, the sample container is a cylinder shape, and I will discuss the container removal approach in the next section.

5.4.2.2 Data Filtering

Specifically for the NOVA experiment, the data sets come with a sample container and process noise. In this section, I will discuss the container removal approach and the real-time local noise filter that help to improve the data recognition.

Container Removal

During the data acquisition stage, the biological samples are placed inside 3D printed containers (Figure 5.28). Then, the samples are placed on top of the rotary stage using the robot's assistance. Hence, the geometry of the container is scanned as part of the acquired data. A viable approach is to define the geometry of the sample container and remove it from the data. Although the sample container has a simple cylindrical geometry, the primary challenge lies in finding the exact position and radius of the geometry. In response, I use the Hough Circle Transform [243] to identify a circle from the top slice image. Since the samples sit at the bottom of the container, I assume that the above images describe the geometry information.

Figure 5.29 shows the detected circle from the top slice image. In particular, the Hough Circle Transform detects multiple rings which represent the sample

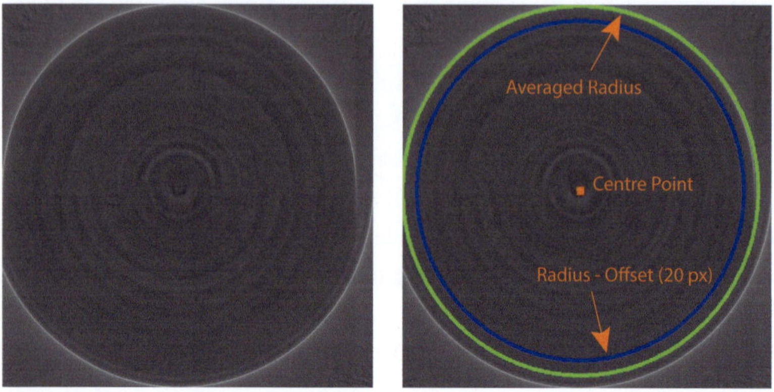

Figure 5.29.: The left image shows the top slice image and the right image highlights the averaged radius (computed from the detected radii), the offset radius, and the centre point. The blue radius is the output circular geometry.

container wall, and I average the identified centre points and radii. I also account for the thickness of the container wall by reducing the radius further by 20 pixels. I then crop the outer part of the circle geometry from the image and repeat for the whole volume. Figure 5.30 shows the visual results on the data sets after cropping. The previous Pseudoscorpion and the tachinid fly *Gymnosoma nudifrons* (Herting, 1966) data sets (Table 5.3: D and E) are showing the shape of the samples which proves the importance of removing the sample container. However, the ITS method for the Pseudoscorpion data set (Table 5.3: D) still fails. By excluding the sample container details from the histogram, Otsu and ITS methods performed better and can extract the shape of samples. However, the ITS method still fails on the Pseudoscorpion data set (Table 5.3: D) while the Otsu method is robust even when dealing with narrow histogram distribution. Given the current dynamic range of the data (8-bit image), the Otsu thresholding method is more reliable, hence a better thresholding method to be applied throughout all data sets. If we have data sets with higher dynamic range, the ITS method might be a better option.

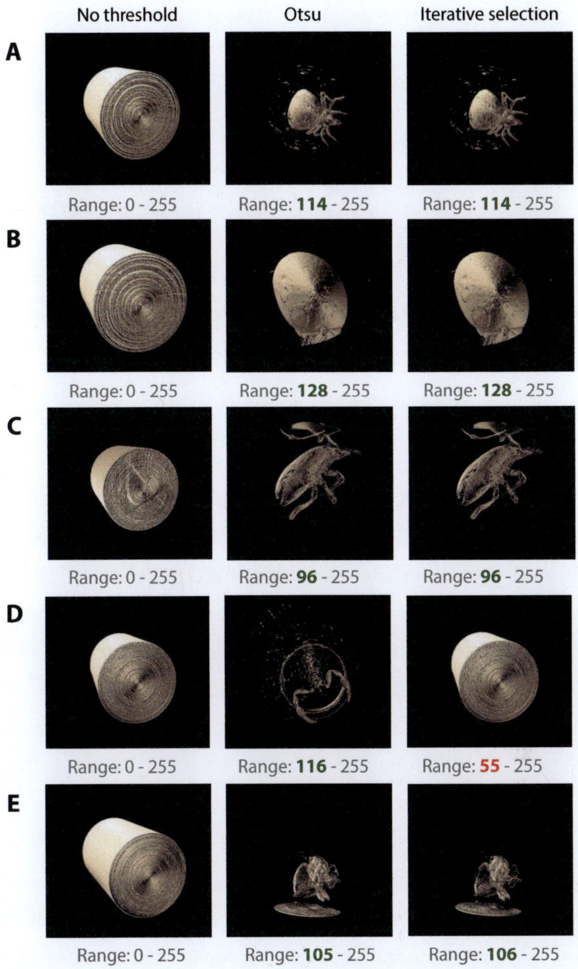

Figure 5.30.: The visual results of cropped data sets when applying threshold values calculated by the Otsu and iterative threshold selection (ITS) methods. The red colour shows the values that are under- or over-thresholded. The green colour shows the optimal threshold for each particular data set.

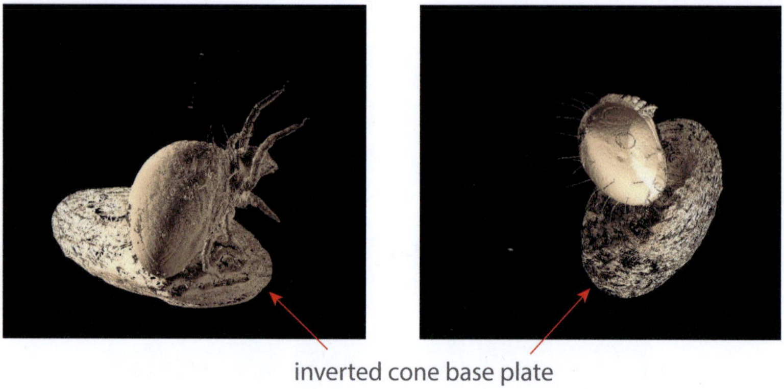

Figure 5.31.: Archie and pseudoskorpion with an inverted cone base geometry.

To this end, I can extract the shape of the samples using Otsu thresholding. The acquired threshold value allows users to have a fast preview without any manual intervention. The method proposed is optimal for 8-bit data sets. Some improvement prospects are worth discussing, for example, despite the container removal method which bases the shape registration on cylindrical geometry, the 3D printed containers have an inverted cone base plate that helps the samples to position themselves within the sample container (Figure 5.31). The cropping of the data sets which is based solely on the cylindrical geometry cannot detect nor remove the base plate. If we can eliminate the base plate, the overall thresholding scan will improve. Moreover, we need a broader dynamic range for better analysis, i.e., tone mapping [244, 245]. By using 16-bits or 32-bits cross-sectional data sets (higher dynamic range), we can stretch the region of interest wider. Also, in the presence of a broad dynamic range of the data, the ITS method will be an attractive option where it performs much faster than the Otsu thresholding.

Real-time Noise Filtering

Removing noise in CT data for an interactive 3D visualisation is vital to improving the quality of the final display. It is essential for the surface rendering mode within the interactive 3D visualisation process. However, noise is inevitable in data produced by CT. Hence, the visualisation of the original CT data with the inherited noise obscures the user from identifying the structures and features contained in the data. Even when the user filters the information manually (data thresholding), essential details could be lost due to the broad spectral range of the CT noise, overlapping with the signal frequencies, which are of interest.

I aim to provide a fast preview of the original CT data in real-time where the noisy data must be concocted within the millisecond range. I consider some form of spatially variant filtering of CT volume based upon the differences between the frequency characteristics of the noise and the signal. There are two primary approaches for spatial filtering of CT noise. In the first approach, the projection data is processed (before the reconstruction step) [246, 247]; in the second approach, the reconstructed data is processed (after the reconstruction step) [248, 249]. I chose the latter approach to have a general solution, which is independent of the diverse requirements of CT scanners [250].

Most studies of spatial filtering are performed offline with two-dimensional CT images. Since the CT volume is a stack of 2D cross-sectional images [251], 2D filters are commonly applied to remove the CT noise. I study these filters and extend them in a 3D context. Throughout the discussion of related works, I will henceforth use the term point rather than voxel. Low-pass filtering is the most common filter that replaces each point with the average values of the defined kernel size [252, 253]. Low-pass filtering removes the high frequencies from the volume data which reduces the noise and improves the detectability of the data structure. However, the filter reduces the intrinsic resolution of the data, i.e., smoothes edges and decreases the visibility of small structures. Since the low-pass filter is non-deterministic, an increasing kernel size will lead to the unintended removal of data. Okada [254] presented an approach based on the assumption that significant differences between neighbouring voxels are unlikely to be noise. Okada's approach smoothes only the adjacent voxels with a grey value difference below the predefined threshold. Lee et al. [255] presented the sigma filter which assumes a Gaussian distribution of CT noise. They showed the effectiveness of the sigma filter in preserving subtle details and line features as long as the intensity difference between them and their background is lesser than the two-sigma intensity range. In other words, the sigma filter only considers grey values that fall within the 2-sigma intensity range. Similarly, McDonnell [256] presented an extended box-filtering approach that defines the intensity region empirically. Apart from spatial filtering, I also consider an entropy-based approach which calculates the information entropy of a given kernel [257, 258, 259]. I use the Shannon-Wiener entropy criterion [175] to characterise the noise distribution within the kernel. However, the influence of random effects can adversely affect the accuracy of entropy calculation [260]. To provide the final 3D surface rendering, I adopted the GPU direct volume rendering approach [181] by terminating the ray casting iteration at the surface intersection point. Since the CT data are voxel data, I compute the normal vector using the 3D Sobel operator and apply illumination models on the surface points, i.e., the Phong illumination model (refer to Chapter 2.2.2).

Method In my approach, I perform spatial filtering in real-time that suppresses the noise at the first surface intersection point within the volume rendering framework. Hence, I consider spatial voxels in the 3D space. Throughout this section, I will refer to my approach as the optimised filter.

Most filters discussed earlier are applied to 2D cross-sectional images of volumetric data and remove noise permanently. Instead, I emphasise in suppressing the noise for fast preview and let users decide upon the noise filter usage. The flexibility to choose noise filter usage is essential, especially when users are interested in performing analysis of the data which might require analysis of the noise distribution. Hence, a primary goal is to provide users with optimal visual quality without any manual intervention. Firstly, I determine the optimal threshold by using the Otsu thresholding method [240]. Based on the thresholded data, I detect a wide array of surface intersection points. Each intersection surface point serves as the central voxel where we determine whether the corresponding voxel is noise. Hence, I compute the average value based on the central voxel together with its adjacent neighbouring voxels within the kernel size, M:

$$S_0 = \frac{1}{3 \cdot M} \left(\sum_{i=0}^{M-1} P(s_x + \Delta i, s_y, s_z) + \sum_{i=0}^{M-1} P(s_x, s_y + \Delta i, s_z) + \sum_{i=0}^{M-1} P(s_x, s_y, s_z + \Delta i) \right), \tag{5.5}$$

with

$$\Delta i = i - \frac{M-1}{2}. \tag{5.6}$$

The grey value of the central voxel with a spatial coordinate of (s_x, s_y, s_z) is assigned P_0; Δi represents the offset value from the central voxel. Let S_0 be the *average cluster* at the central voxel (Figure 5.32 left). I then take eight additional *average clusters* ($S_1 ... S_8$) that are spread diagonally around the central voxel with a distance of $\sqrt{3}$ units (Figure 5.32 right). I replace the corresponding voxel value with the resulting average value from the nine clusters.

3D Spatial Noise Filters For completeness, I extend other 2D spatial noise filters discussed earlier in a 3D context. In particular, I consider the low-pass filtering (mean filter), Okada filter, Sigma filter and the entropy filter. Similar to my method, the filters start at the surface intersection point.

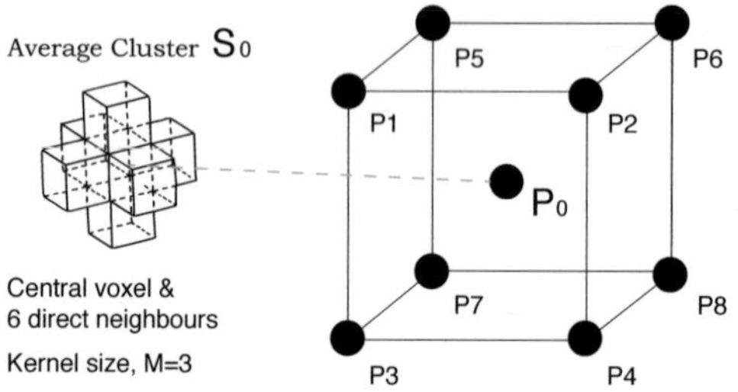

Figure 5.32.: Illustration of the *average cluster* which takes the average of central voxels and their adjacent neighbours. The average of nine *average clusters* ($P_0 ... P_8$) is used to represent the surface intersection point.

Mean Filter I calculate the average of voxel values that lie within the kernel size, M:

$$S = \frac{1}{M^3} \left(\sum_{i=0}^{M-1} \sum_{j=0}^{M-1} \sum_{k=0}^{M-1} P(s_x + \Delta i, s_y + \Delta j, s_z + \Delta k) \right), \tag{5.7}$$

where P is the grey value of the voxel with the spatial coordinate of (s_x, s_y, s_z). The Δi represents the offset value from the central voxel which is defined as $(i * 1 - 1)$.

Sigma Filter Within the predefined kernel size M, the sigma filter only considers n voxel values that fall within the intensity range specified by the global standard deviation. Specifically, the intensity range must be within the 2σ region:

$$S = \frac{1}{n} \sum_{i=0}^{n-1} P_i, \quad \forall P_i \in [-2\sigma, 2\sigma]. \tag{5.8}$$

Okada Filter The Okada filter studies the difference between the central voxel value, P_0, with its neighbouring voxel values, P_i. I consider only the neighbouring voxels when the difference value is lower than the predefined threshold T_d:

$$S = \begin{cases} \frac{1}{n}\sum_{i=0}^{n-1} P_i, & \text{if } |P_0 - P_i| < T_d \\ 0, & \text{otherwise,} \end{cases} \tag{5.9}$$

where n is the total number of voxels that satisfies the condition $|P_0 - P_i| < T_d$.

Entropy Filter I calculate the first order entropy H from m voxels within the kernel size M. Then, I set an entropy threshold of T_e to determine the noise range. Before filtering, I precompute the normalised frequency distribution of the data to assign a probability of p_i to each grey level. If the entropy criterion [259] exceeds my predefined threshold, then I choose instead to display the central voxel value, P_0.

$$S = \begin{cases} P_0, & \text{if } -\sum_{i=0}^{m-1} p_i \log_2(p_i) > T_e \\ 0, & \text{otherwise.} \end{cases} \tag{5.10}$$

Evaluation To evaluate the quality of the filters, I compare the visual results and frame rates of the filters presented earlier. In the previous section (Section 5.4.2.2), we see how artefacts such as the sample container can affect the thresholding result. Hence, I will evaluate the filters with a container free data set that is prepared by using Amira ® 5.6.0. I use the tachinid fly *Gymnosoma nudifrons* (Herting, 1996) data set (Table 5.3: E), where the outer container and base plate are manually removed. The Otsu-threshold for the data is 101, and I will apply this threshold setting across the filters. Figure 5.33 shows the visual quality of the tachinid fly filtered by numerous filters. The entropy filter has the worst quality because the noise and the useful data regions are overlapping. On the other hand, the mean filter, the sigma filter and the Okada filter can suppress the noise considerably well and outline the details of the

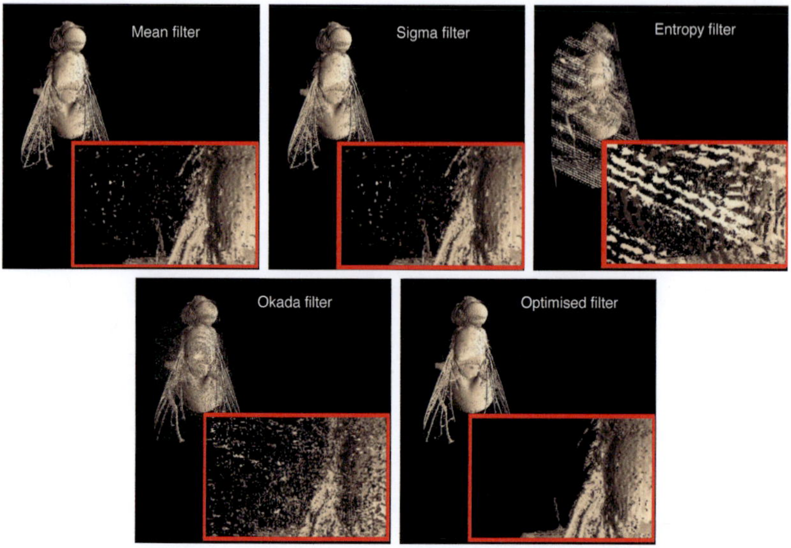

Figure 5.33.: A visual comparison of the tachinid fly *Gymnosoma nudifrons* (Herting, 1966) data set between the reference surface mesh model (top left), the mean filter (top middle), the sigma filter (top right), the entropy filter (bottom left), the Okada filter (bottom middle) and the optimised filter (bottom right). The entropy filter fails to suppress the noise completely. Also, there is still spot noise in the mean, sigma and Okada filters which my approach (the optimised filter) is able to suppress.

tachinid fly. However, stubborn spot noise persists around the subject. In my approach, I included not only the average value at the central voxel but also eight uniformly spread *average clusters* for better noise-to-information analysis. As a result, the optimised filter suppresses most of the noise including spot noise. I further evaluate the final visual quality by calculating the entropy value on the resulting 3D images (Figure 5.34). The lower the entropy value, the better the visual quality. The optimised filter has the lowest entropy value which indicates the effectiveness of the tuned filter in suppressing even spot noise.

The performance of the filters (Figure 5.35) are measured using an Intel ® Core ™ i5-4670 CPU (4 x 3.40GHz) with a NVIDIA Tesla C2070. The mean

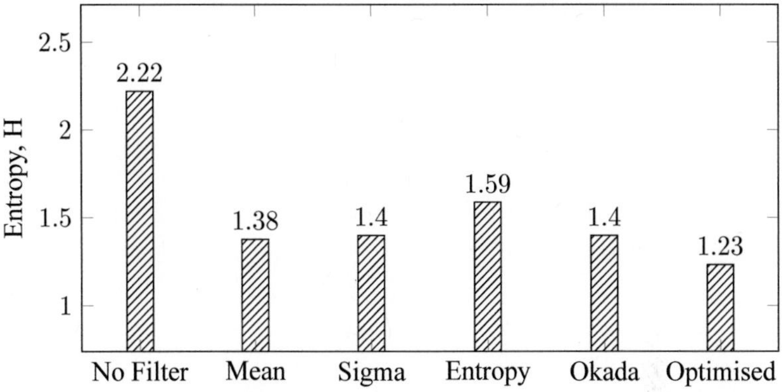

Figure 5.34.: Visual comparison: Entropy value of the final 3D images produced without any filter, with the mean filter, the sigma filter, the entropy filter, the Okada filter and my approach. The lower the entropy value the better.

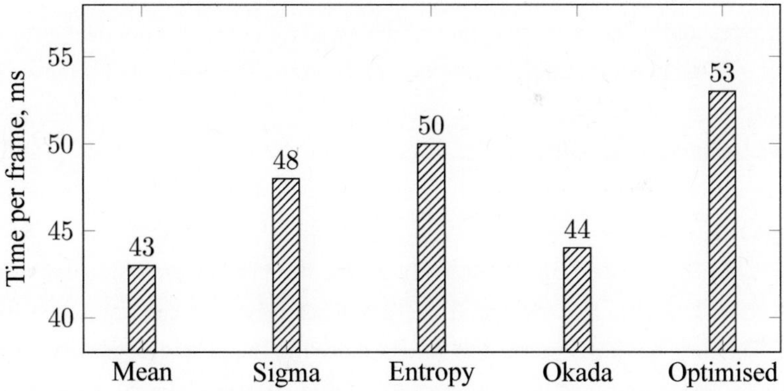

Figure 5.35.: Performance: Time measurement per frame of the mean filter, the sigma filter, the entropy filter, the Okada filter and the optimised filter. Less time indicates a better performance.

filter is the fastest due to its simplicity in taking all voxel values within the kernel and performing straight averaging. The Okada filter involves constant checking of the difference value between the neighbouring voxel and the central voxel which leads to a slower time. Also, the Okada filter only takes the six direct adjacent voxels into consideration. On the other hand, the sigma filter considers all the voxels within the defined kernel size, in which its grey values fall within the 2σ range. The entropy filter performs an entropy computation (Equation 5.10) that increases the overall complexity and hence the time needed for computation. The time per frame for my approach is the highest among the filters because of the additional *average cluster* fetching around the central voxel. The idea is to cover a broader spatial region to identify the characteristic of the current central voxel accurately. Although my approach takes longer in comparison to the other spatial filters, the visual quality is greatly improved while taking only 10 ms longer (mean filter).

Since the data have a narrow histogram distribution, the intensity range within the 2σ region covers most of the grey values, and the result is similar to the mean filter. Also, the Okada filter requires strenuous effort to find the best threshold of T_d for each data set. Hence, I will consider only the entropy filter, the mean filter and the optimised filter on the five data sets (Table 5.3).

Comparison with other data sets I compare the discussed filters with other different data sets from the experiment (Table 5.3). The specimen container is removed by the container removal approach described in Section 5.4.2.2. Figure 5.36 respectively shows the visual outputs of the data sets after applying the entropy filter, the mean filter and the optimised filter. The thresholding approaches demonstrated in the previous section (Section 5.4.2.1) result in an optimal threshold value. However, the filters require more details to analyse. Thus I reduce the optimal threshold (Otsu threshold) by an offset to allow more grey values to be included in the filtering process. The new threshold T is defined as:

$$T = T_{otsu} - \text{Offset}, \tag{5.11}$$

where

$$\text{Offset} = \left\lceil \frac{\mu}{\sigma} * k \right\rceil. \tag{5.12}$$

The μ and σ are the maximum likelihood estimates of the volume histogram. The k parameter is a control parameter and is set at 41.22 based on the five data sets. Also, the resulting offset is rounded by the nearest integer function. In the visual output, the entropy filter preserves fine details such as hairs but at the expense of having more noise in the background. The Pseudoscorpion data set (Table 5.3 D) have so much noise in the background that the noise completely covers the sample. The mean filter reduces the noise slightly and the delicate features as well. The optimised filter is an extension of the mean filter, where the filter can suppress the stubborn surrounding noise. When applying the entropy filter on data set A and B, one can see the hairs on the legs and body of the small animals. To this end, there is no one-size-fits-all filter presented. If users are interested in fine details, they can use the entropy filter; and if users are interested in a noise-free visualisation, they can use the optimised filter.

Discussion Based on the evaluation, the optimised filter serves as an extension to the arsenal of filters within the visualisation system, where users can choose the appropriate filter interactively. Since the optimised filter combines the concepts from the Okada and the mean filters, it is therefore slightly different than a plain mean filter. The filters presented are based on one pass, whereas the mean filter usually involves multiple passes to smooth or remove the noise. Often, the question is how many passes are necessary to achieve the desired output. Different data sets with different histogram distribution will require a different number of passes. The optimised filter fits the one pass requirement and produces the effect similar to multiple passes of the mean filter.

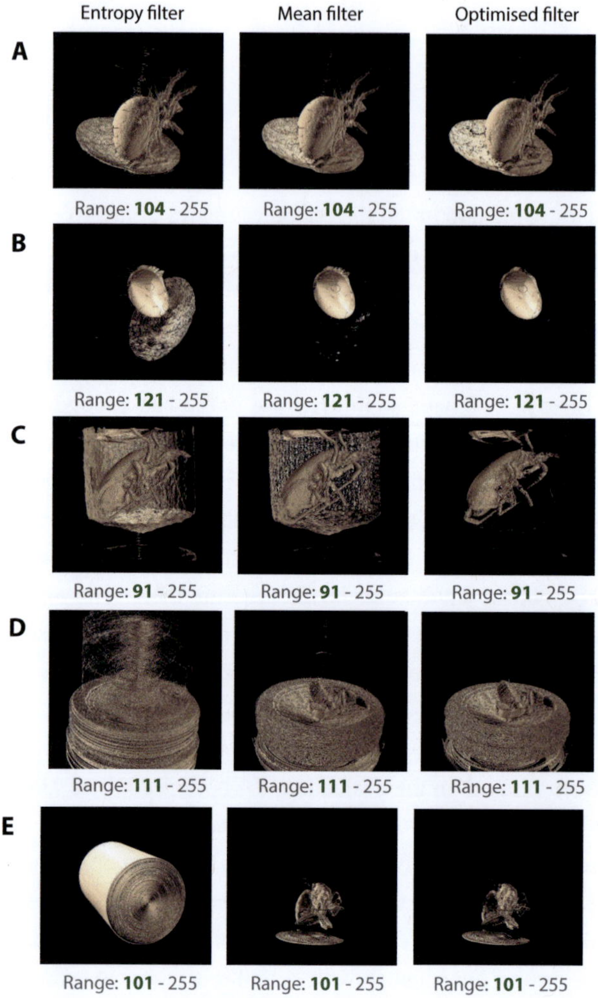

Figure 5.36.: The visual results of data sets when applying the entropy filter, the mean filter and the optimised filter on the data sets. A container removal algorithm is applied to the data sets prior to filtering. The green colour shows the optimal threshold for each particular data set.

Although the optimised filter is useful for the data sets from the NOVA experiment, the layout used in determining the average neighbourhood clusters can vary on different scanners with different noise characteristics.

5.4.2.3 Data Mapping

At the server-side, the raw data have to undergo a series of processing tasks and lastly will be transformed into a visual data object. The visual data object is the required format to render the final visualisation at the client-side. In this thesis, I propose to use a 2D image and slicemap [3] formats as discussed in Chapter 4.1. The 2D image will be placed directly onto the web browser (Chapter 4.1.1); whereas the slicemap is loaded into the texture memory of the GPU for interactive visualisation (Chapter 4.1.2).

5.4.2.4 Data Reduction

Downscaling

Due to the large data size, I downscale the raw data before transforming it into a slicemap. I use the Lanczos filter from ImageMagick to perform the downscaling operation. After downscaling the raw data, I transform them into a PNG-format slicemap. For example, a raw data set of a carpenter ant [261] with $2016 \times 2016 \times 2016$ voxels (7.7 GB) can be downscaled and transformed into a low-resolution slicemap with $256 \times 256 \times 256$ voxels (2 MB). To prepare the multi-resolution hierarchy of cache data, I prepare the slicemaps in three level-of-details: $128 \times 128 \times 128$ voxels (LOD 0), $256 \times 256 \times 256$ voxels (LOD 1), and $512 \times 512 \times 512$ voxels (LOD 2).

Thumbnail Preview

To provide a minimalistic view of the scanned sample, I present a method to generate an aggregated data set (thumbnail preview) that is much smaller

[3] Slicemap is the input 3D data required for the client-side rendering. Refer to Chapter 2.3: Web-based Visualisation.

in size and yet able to represent the structure of the sample adequately. It is worth noting that the format of the aggregated data is a slicemap (3D input data) which allows an interactive 3D visualisation, i.e., continuously rotating. The idea is based on the assumption that the sample consists of unique grey values. It is derived from my observation where I extract the features by using the thresholding approaches (Section 5.4.2.1).

The data obtained from the X-ray tomography yields a 3D structure with each voxel representing a scalar value ranging from 0 to 255 (8-bit image resolution). The Thumbnail Preview assumes that the top 3 slices of the volume describe the non-sample grey values (surrounding artefacts), which can be air or the sample container. The assumption is valid since the specimen does not fill up the whole space within the container and sits at the bottom of the sample container. Ideally, the unwanted data (namely, artefacts) have to be discarded and have unique grey values. Henceforth, I will describe the grey values of the top 3 slices as *noise signature* (Figure 5.37: middle), which I will remove from the original data.

In this approach, the *noise signature* consists of grey value components that will be removed from the original data, resulting in reduced data. As a result, only the sample features remained but at the cost of fine details. The result showed a rough surface where fine details were missing. I chose to render the reduced data using the additive blending approach which outlines the structure of the specimen. Moreover, the thumbnail preview has a small viewport where fine details are not noticeable by users. Also, extensive user interactions on the data sets are not required because I only provide the necessary 3D controls to the preview, i.e., rotation.

To this end, I perform the Thumbnail Preview approach to the five data sets (Table 5.3), and the visual results are shown in Figure 5.38. The figures on the left row show the surface rendering of the container-removed data sets. The middle and right rows show the surface rendering and additive blending modes of reduced data sets where the Thumbnail Preview approach is applied. For a quick preview, the reduced data resembles the original data, but with coarser

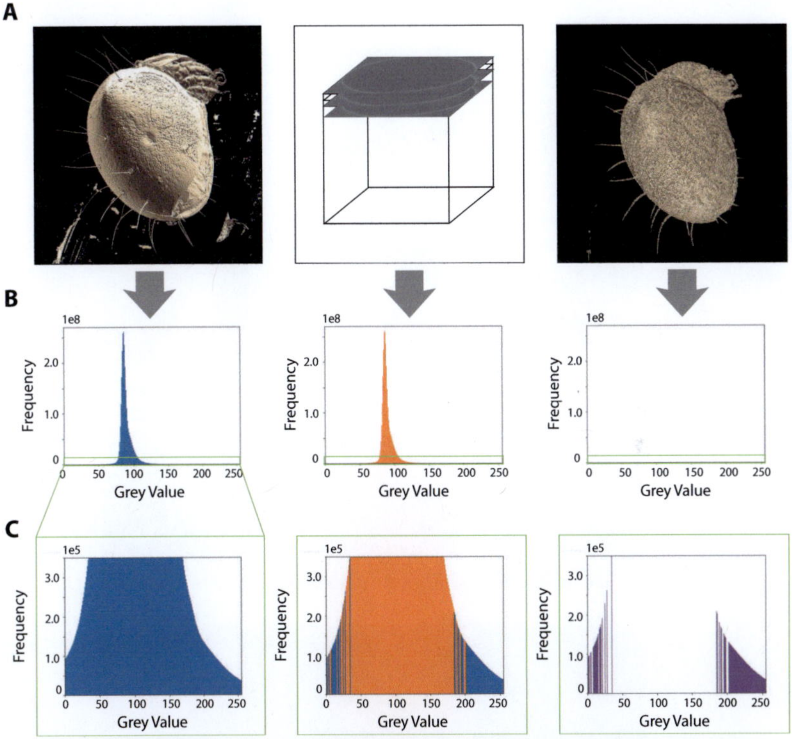

Figure 5.37.: The left column shows the original data (histogram distribution shown in blue colour) where row A displays the surface rendering of the oribatid mite data set, row B shows the histogram of the volumetric data set, and row C shows the zoom region of the respective histogram distribution. The middle column shows the histogram distribution of the first three cross-section images (orange colour)—known as the *noise signature*. The right column shows the resulting surface rendering of the filtered data (histogram distribution is shown in purple colour), where the noise signature is extracted from the original data.

details, which is a collateral data that highlights the subtle features more vibrantly (caricature approach), i.e., the hair in the samples are enlarged. The additive blending mode is optimal because the visual results emphasise the structure of the data and at the same time reduces the visibility of surround-

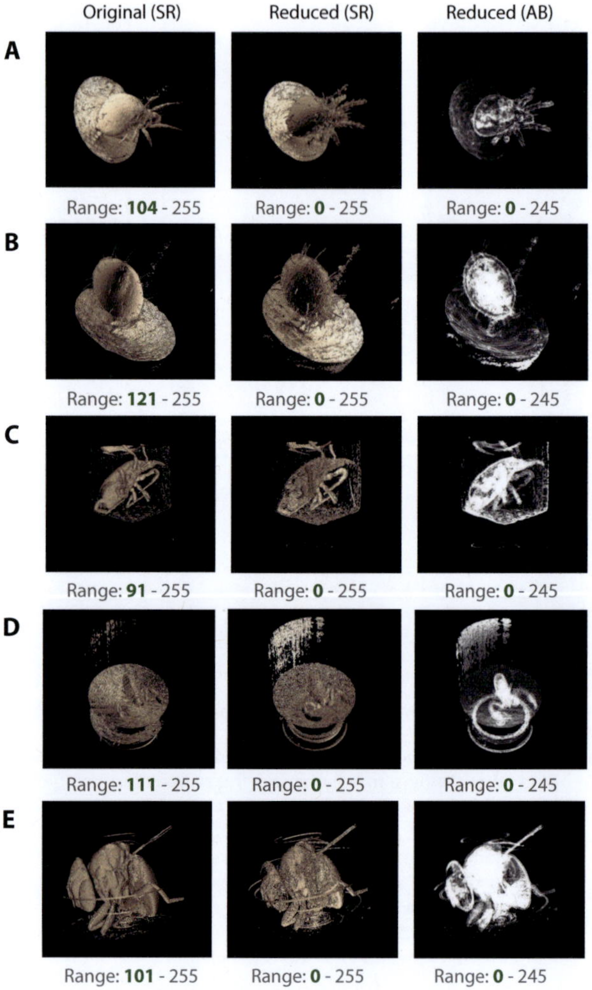

Figure 5.38.: A visual comparison between the original data sets and the downscaled thumbnail previews. SR stands for surface rendering and AB stands for additive blending mode. The green colour shows the optimal threshold for each particular data set.

ing artefacts. It is worth noting that the Thumbnail Preview approach does not require any thresholding and the data is shown in its full dynamic range. For now, my method can extract the essential features from the data, and in conjunction, opens up numerous research directions, i.e., classification of the data.

5.4.3 View Space

5.4.3.1 Visualisation Abstraction Operator

I present the data using the 3D projection method, the additive blending method, the volume rendering method, and the surface rendering method. The 3D projection produces a 2D image based on the viewing position and angle towards the 3D structure (Chapter 4.1.1). The additive blending is used as a complementary visualisation method to compensate for the information loss of a reduced data set (Section 5.4.2.4). The surface and volume renderings are used to visualise the details of the 3D structure where users can interact with the data in real-time (Chapter 2.2.2).

5.4.3.2 View Operator

To address the latency and resource issues of designing a Big Data system (Chapter 3.3.3), I combine the WAVE framework and the image snapshot system to offer a flexible setup. Notably, the WAVE framework addresses the offline mode where users can query the Big Data in a resource constraint environment, Base on the client requirements; WAVE will serve the slicemap with the appropriate size to ensure an interactive system. The client requirements refer to the network condition and the hardware capability of the client. The NOVA project has dedicated visualisation server which allows online Big Data streaming. Here, the raw data (3D) is projected onto a 3D image which is later served to the client (Chapter 4.2.2). Rather than serving the projected images continuously, I allow high-quality images to be streamed only on-demand.

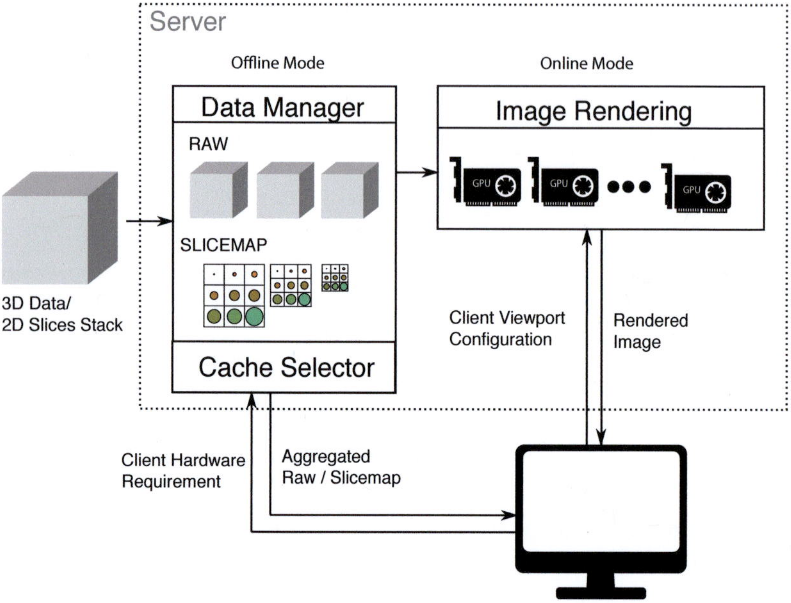

Figure 5.39.: The architecture of the system with online and offline rendering components for visualising large 3D data.

Since the WAVE server serves cache slicemaps, the quality of the final visualisation suffers in exchange for a better system response time. Hence, in my setup, users can query for the projected 3D image from the server to improve the visual quality of the final visualisation. Figure 5.39 shows the architecture of the setup, where offline mode refers to the WAVE framework, and the online mode refers to the image snapshot system.

Visualising Segmented Data Within the tomographic-oriented scientific workflow, the acquired raw data will be further processed into multiple modalities where each modal represents a feature of the specimen. In this section, I discuss the postprocessing stage where the 3D volumetric data is segmented into various parts to describe the original specimen. Particularly, Lösel and Heuveline [262] described a parameter-free semi-automated

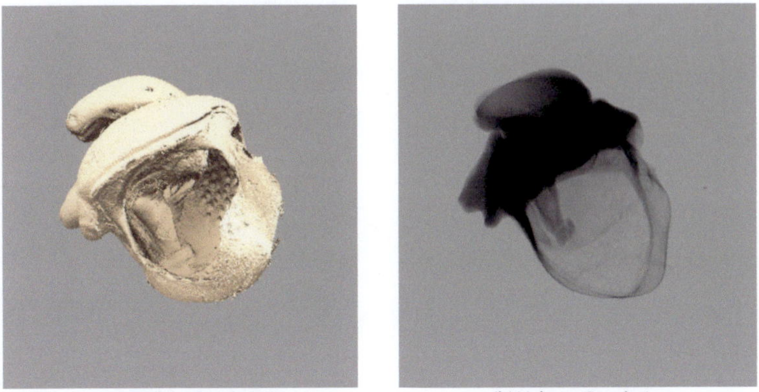

Figure 5.40.: Visualisation of the biological screw in the beetle's leg using the surface and volume renderings.

segmentation approach based on the random walk algorithm. They provided a web-based segmentation service that allows domain experts to generate multiple segmented data conveniently. Each segmented data is assigned a unique grey value and putting numerous segmented data together gives a discrete histogram distribution. I describe the visualisation of the segmented data using the transfer function. A transfer function (TF) maps the scalar values of a volumetric data to optical properties, and it is part of the surface and volume renderings [263]. Within the visualisation pipeline, the TF defines the colour and opacity to be assigned for a particular grey value. Thus, the TF is used to highlight essential regions of volumetric data.

To visualise a biological specimen with its various segmented data, I take the data that shows the biological screw in a beetle's leg [264] as an example. The Figure 5.40 shows the surface and volume renderings of the volumetric data set. The biological screw data set consists of two segments: the screw and the joint. In the segmented data sets, each data attribute is assigned a unique grey value. In this case, the screw is assigned the value of one, and the joint is assigned a value of two. By applying a one-dimensional TF [263], the

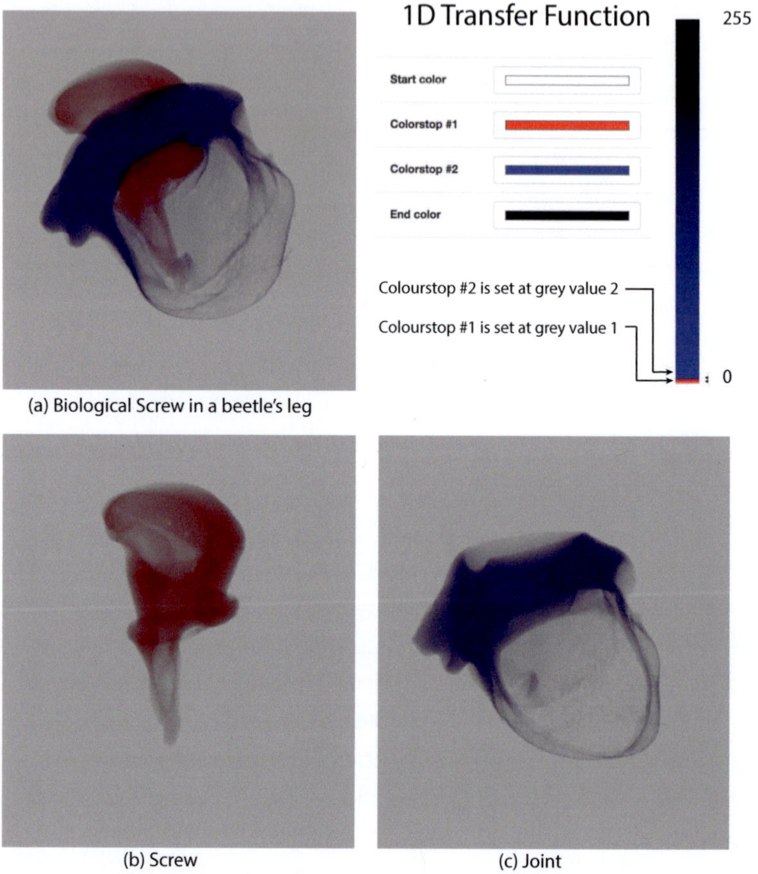

Figure 5.41.: Visualisation of the biological screw in the beetle's leg using the surface and volume renderings.

scalar values are assigned its appropriate colour depending on the TF definition. Figure 5.41 shows the volume rendering of the biological screw data set with its defined 1D TF. A red label is set at grey value one to highlight the screw feature; whereas a blue label is set at grey value two onwards to show the joint of the data set.

Rather than merging the multimodal data into one representation, the TF allows domain experts to select the segmented data interactively. This approach is useful to verify the correctness of the segmentation process. In this thesis, the segmented data are prepared as slicemaps, and the segmentation labels are treated as the new grey values.

5.4.4 Discussion

In this use case study, I addressed the Big Data challenge within the digital library framework where the large size of the data impedes the performance of the system. This section shed light on how one strives to visualise the Big Data and how one design a framework. I introduce a general workflow that fits into most situations, namely the workflow of the knowledge discovery process [139]. I then propose a guideline on how one can design the flow of data processing and visualisation methods that fit into the general workflow. Mainly, I emphasise the *Visual Information Seeking Mantra* [56] that guides the user to design a user-specific workflow, in which the user defines a series of primary visual data processing steps. I further organise the methods and actions using the *data state reference model* [64] that serves as a clear operational map to manage the processes efficiently.

The WAVE framework is used within the Biomedisa online segmentation service as a visualisation tool [262], and within the NOVA project as the data catalogue preview. Since the WAVE framework supports multiple client hardware, characterising the client requirements is not trivial because the client hardware advances continuously. To date, the WAVE framework can deliver the best visual quality according to the client hardware requirements.

6
Conclusions

In this dissertation, I introduce the challenges faced by research institutions where significant amounts of data are stored in the data repositories. In turn, we are facing a Big Data phenomena where the data is large (more than gigabytes) and disperse (multifaceted) that impedes the reuse of the stored information. Mainly, there is no guarantee that we can extract information from the provided digital library—a user interface gateway between users and data sets. In this chapter, I scrutinise the issues raised and considerations demonstrated from the earlier chapters. First, I discuss Big Data experiments where I show the necessary methods to provide an interactive visualisation system that highlights the main features of the data. Then, I describe the design considerations of developing a data sharing software and a web-based visualisation library, both of which extract and share the data information to a mass audience, independent of the users' geographic location.

6.1 Research Objectives

My work focusses on effectively visualising the prominent features of the Big Data and the subsequent steps to manage them. Inevitably, I can only show a portion of the Big Data due to the massive data size and the number of dispersing items. My propositions allow domain experts to grasp the gist of the data through my designed visualisation tools without the need to explore the data further. Comprehensive visualisation is an important step to explore a large data repository. Although Big Data refers to the four domains (Volume, Variety, Velocity, Value), I focus on two essential areas where we either deal with data that is too large in size (i.e., gigabytes or petabytes) or with too many small data sets (i.e., 100 parameters per second).

My goal is helping domain experts dealing with large amounts of data by means of data management and visualisation procedures. Hence, the central question is:

How can visualisation help in searching and understanding Big Data during data acquisition?

Visualisation in this thesis refers to the user interface provided in the digital library framework. A visualisation that helps domain experts in *searching* and *understanding* their data. In the next section, I discuss the progress towards each specific research question which as a whole answer the central question.

6.2 Progress on Thesis Contributions

The primary objective of this thesis is to provide a solution to Big Data challenges and to demonstrate how visualisation can help improve the data exploration of a digital library. The challenges are diverse and generalising these different requirements into a generic design is a daunting task. I meet this challenge by addressing three research questions, to which I provide summaries below.

6.2.1 Big Data: Volume

Question 1: How can we visualise Big Data without downloading the whole original copy itself?

I use the NOVA experiment [12] as a case study of the Big Data dilemma where the size of data is causing additional system latencies. Particularly, I helped domain experts in designing a workflow to visualise their large data set. Although I am not dealing with data in the range of petabytes, the size of each NOVA data set lies within the range of gigabytes. Preparing and visualising these data sets cause high system latency. Despite the system and network latencies, I aim to visualise the data set in less than 1 s. The workflow is based on the *Visual Information Seeking Mantra* [56] and the *data state reference model* [64]. I proposed methods to download visual data of appropriate size according to its final visualisation platform. I also presented methods to improve the clarity of visualisation by removing artefacts and noise.

The dissertation contributes to providing a richer understanding of the methods and considerations in dealing with Big Data (Volume) experiments. Chapter 5.4 showed the diversity in addressing the large data size from managing the input data in the database up to visualisation the data on the screen. Also, I developed the WAVE framework (Chapter 4.2.3) and the optimal 3D viewpoint system (Chapter 4.2.2) that help in the architecture design. However, the overall system is based on the selected processing methods and may not be sufficient in a different Big Data application. Hence, more processing methods can be added to improve the usefulness of the current system. Also, the system is not coupled with other data acquisition systems. Building an interface between the current visualisation system with other common data acquisition framework such as TANGO [265] will be beneficial for the scientific community.

The workflow proves to be a reliable guideline to design a new visualisation system. There are multiple data stages in the workflow, and each data stage can be studied separately. Hence, researchers can focus on a specific task rather than overwhelmed by different tasks. The proposed workflow is a generic solution for many experiments, but the processing tasks within the data stages are customised. Still, designing a new system is cumbersome regardless of the nature of the experiment. Moreover, a sound knowledge of the research domain is necessary throughout the process. The developed software frameworks can help enlighten the design process, but domain experts should be involved to incorporate domain-specific knowledge. An interface that allows transferring the domain-specific knowledge into the frameworks is not addressed in this thesis. The approaches discussed in this thesis are successful, and I practised the guideline and implemented the frameworks in other experiments such as the Biomedisa online segmentation tool [262].

6.2.2 Big Data: Variety

> *Question 2:* How can we represent and extract scientific insights from heterogeneous data?

> *Question 3:* How can we merge multimodal and multivariate data into one visual representation?

I addressed the two questions using the KITcube experiment [25] and the 3D USCT project [37]. On the one hand, the KITcube experiment [25] (climate research) aims to resolve all relevant atmospheric processes and allows detailed process studies and to form a better knowledge for model-based predictions. On the other hand, the 3D ultrasound computed tomography (USCT) project (medical diagnosis) aims to provide for early breast cancer diagnosis [26]. In both use cases, rather than analysing many different parameters, I aim to help domain experts to study their heterogeneous using visualisation techniques, e.g., combining multiple parameters in a single display.

Mainly in the KITcube experiment, I visualised the Doppler wind lidar data across multiple measurement campaigns (Chapter 5.2). To provide an interactive visualisation and data monitoring system, I demonstrated various tasks of data management according to the proposed design guideline. For this particular use case, domain experts are keen on having conventional plots. Thus, I chose conventional plots and a 3D volume rendering as the outputs of the visualisation system. The conventional plots are essential as these are the plots that domain experts have been relying on for most of their research career. Hence, designing a visualisation system cannot neglect the familiarity of domain experts on the conventional plots. Due to the limited display size, it is not possible to show all available data attributes. Instead, I selected prominent parameters that give a comprehensive overview of the data. The parameters are chosen based on continuous discussions with domain experts, and this step is essential to narrow down the parameters. The visualisation system is effective and conveys a summary of the daily overview. Here, I used the WAVE and BORA frameworks as the building blocks of the visualisation system. The BORA framework is used to monitor the status of measurement devices during active campaigns, and the WAVE framework (2D and 3D displays) is used to visualise the wind variation based on the Doppler wind lidar. Visualisation for climate research has a broad spectrum of applications where each measurement device can be treated as a single application. The proposed guideline serves as a good starting point, and the use case study of Doppler wind lidar serves as an example for other devices. My main contribution is by dealing with disperse data and summarising multiple parameters into a compact visualisation.

In KITcube, Doppler wind lidar is one of the many measurement devices. Hence, it is desirable to include the data of all devices into a single platform. The amount of effort to add one measurement device is high because I not only have to design the visualisation system, but I also need to parse the different data formats. Often, the data format of each device is unique. To create a visualisation system for a device, the final picture of the visualisation is not clear since meteorologists want to view all the data. Thus, selecting a few prominent parameters for the Overview is difficult. The methods shown in this thesis serve as a good starting point, and other measurement devices can learn from the Doppler wind lidar use case.

To merge multimodal data, I discussed the 3D USCT project using the breast tumour multimodal data (Chapter 5.3) and a use case of multi-spectral imagery (Chapter 5.1). In contrast to the climate study, we are facing data with multimodality. In the use case study with multi-spectral imaging, I designed an interactive visualisation where users can choose up to three bands of information to be visualised simultaneously. In the 3D USCT project, I discussed two algorithms that merge the multimodal data into a single representation. To this end, I demonstrated methods of combining multimodality data into a single representation, either by using an interactive approach or by merge algorithms. Given the variety of combining multimodality data, this dissertation contributes to understanding the complexity of Big Data challenges regarding Variety. Notably, use cases that fall under the same category require different approaches to achieve the domain experts' desired result. For the KITcube experiment, the 3D USCT project, and the multi-spectral imagery use cases, I use the WAVE framework to provide 2D and 3D displays.

The fusion methods discussed do not represent the actual size of a tumour, but rather an oversized region that is projected onto the surface. The visualisation from these methods is suitable as a visual preview of data catalogues, where the oversized region can attract attention from doctors. Then, doctors can retrieve the details of that particular data set for further diagnosis. For future work, visualisation of a breast tumour that represents the actual size has to be implemented. The WAVE framework provides an excellent platform to improve the visualisation technique where visualisation experts can focus on developing visual outputs. In comparison to other standard visualisation tools such as Amira or DICOM, the WAVE framework is easy to use because it built as a web-based platform.

6.2.3 Data Availability

Question 4: How can we exchange data among international research communities?

I address the data availability by choosing a web browser as the client platform. Web browsers are available on the most major client system, and users can access the data independently to their geographical location—limited only by network bandwidth. Hence, reducing the size of raw data can ensure responsive data latency. Providing data of smaller size also means that only a limited number of features are preserved. I emphasise providing data with different level-of-detail that differ in data resolution. The idea is to preserve the structure of the data that makes it still identifiable. Also, I propose to use progressive loading to improve the responsiveness of the system. Despite the web-based approach being a convenient platform, the dissertation mentions the downsides that have to be addressed. Mainly, data transfer suffers from limited network bandwidth. Despite the technology advancement regarding network infrastructures, the amounts of data transferred through the network far exceed the network bandwidth, in which this mismatch remains as the bottleneck for the web-based system.

The BORA framework is developed to encourage collaboration among researchers by ensuring high data availability. Particularly, BORA allows multiple research groups to share their data monitoring displays. Given the uniqueness of each experiment, any attempt to generalise the diverse requirements seems impossible. Using BORA, I successfully generalise the different experiment requirements by identifying commonalities among them. Mainly, regardless of any experiment, the data is inherently stored in a central data repository, and I choose to display the data displays on the standard web browser. BORA was initially developed to solve the massive server queries, but later gained popularity and it is implemented in 13 experiment groups, i.e., ten subgroups from the KATRIN experiment [164] and three sub-groups from the KIT 1 MW photovoltaics facility [28]. The reason lies in the simplicity of the BORA framework that allows domain experts to create any custom data display without in-depth knowledge of web technologies; therefore it enables domain experts to concentrate on their research endeavours.

6.2.4 Non-textual Metadata

> *Question 5:* How can we search for non-textual content such as 3D images?

Often, Big Data is not present in a textual format. Traditionally, domain experts have to include textual descriptions that accompany their data sets [39, 51, 57, 58, 59, 60, 61]. Thus, this scenario places the responsibility onto the shoulders of domain experts to maintain a well-described repository. There are ongoing researches that address exploring non-textual data content such as videos or images [266, 267, 268] that can enrich the search capabilities in a digital library. I discuss the non-textual metadata by proposing the selection of 3D data set that provides the most information. I describe this approach as part of the view operator (Chapter 4.2.2). Each view operator has a predefined data processing workflow. The view operator can be a standalone system or combined with other view operators.

In this dissertation, I demonstrated one of the many possible non-textual content search approaches where I searched for the best view angle of the 3D data. The selected rendered image contains most information that enables domain experts to identify their data sets. Also, the key to defining new search criteria is having a fluent and interactive visualisation of multidimensional data sets. Thus, the WAVE framework is an ideal platform to attach advance algorithms, and can be extended to apply deep learning of specific characteristics.

6.3 Thesis Contributions

Throughout this thesis, I provide a richer understanding of the Big Data dilemma faced by the research institutions. Below, I list my contributions that help support my research topic, *Big Data Management and Visualisation.*

1. **Design considerations for experiment-driven visualisation systems as part of the digital library framework.** Given the diverse scientific experiments, the proposed design considerations help domain experts design a visualisation system that best interprets their data. Mainly, I demonstrated with four different use cases that employ a similar strategy to provide the final visualisation within a digital library framework.

2. **Data management for a web-based system.** Despite the high data availability through the web browser, the limited network bandwidth introduces an overarching challenge to load large data sets—larger data size renders a better visual quality. Hence, I discussed the significance of progressive loading to improve the system response. Also, I showed throughout the different use cases how I prepare the visual input data that can be downscaled for better data transmission.

3. **Real-time noise filtering method.** An important feature in visualising data is to minimise noise. I introduced a local-noise filter that can suppress the noise in real-time. The filter is an extension of the mean filter that achieves effects similar to multi-pass mean filtering.

4. **Interactive image-based visual analytic system.** In this dissertation, I process primary experiment data into image-based data, where images are loaded into the GPU of the client system. Hence, users can update content interactively. The image-based data discussed in this work are slicemaps and encoded images.

5. **Personalised collaborative data display.** I identified the common problem in most research institutions that domain experts rely heavily

on computer engineers to build multiple data monitoring displays. The confluence between different domain expertise is cumbersome. Instead, I developed a generic personalised data display that allows domain experts to build their displays independently.

6. **A web-based Big Data visualisation library.** I developed three view operators that adapt converting multi-dimensional data into 1D, 2D, and 3D displays. The operators allow domain experts from different research area to contribute and visualise their data.

6.4 Future Research

This dissertation encompasses a small fraction of the possible topic within the scope of Big Data visualisation. In particular, I addressed only two subsets of the Big Data features: Volume and Variety. There are many open research directions as below:

6.4.1 The third Big Data feature: Velocity

Laney [9] described the three Big Data features, which are Volume, Variety, and Velocity. Since then, the "three Vs" have been treated as the common framework to describe Big Data [269], and later "four Vs" with an additional feature called Veracity [10]. The Velocity has been the main feature of Big Data, and it is common in a research institution. KAPTURE [270], which is a high-speed detector used in X-ray synchrotron radiation facility, serves as an ideal use case that introduces the Big Data challenge regarding Velocity. The detector allows domain experts to scan machine parameters and gain insights into the behaviour at different threshold settings and the change of spectrograms [271].

The system emphasises continuous sampling of very short pulses generated by terahertz (THz) detectors and produces a high data rate of 6.5 GB/s. The sampled data are stored and later analysed by domain experts. However, domain experts cannot interpret nor analyse the fast incoming data in real-time. Offline data analysis takes a long time to produce any viable results. Ideally, we would like to detect the features immediately during real-time data acquisition. In this context, the WAVE library can be used in this application where the difference lies only at the data model, where the feature detection algorithm has to be implemented at the data acquisition hardware. It is thus attractive to study how WAVE can be applied to a project that faces the challenge of the high data rate. Mainly, the data model consists of algorithms that have to be implemented in a hardware language, i.e., Verilog or VHDL for FPGA platforms.

6.4.2 Virtual Reality

This dissertation emphasises displaying data on mobile phones or computer desktops, in which they are displayed on a 2D screen. An exciting research direction is to study the impact of Big Data in different viewing dimension. Mainly, how can we visualise Big Data directly within a 3D environment such as virtual reality? I co-developed two virtual reality prototypes, i.e., the NOVA [12] and the 3D USCT [37] projects, that represent the actual experimental setup in a virtual 3D environment. The prototypes are presented at conferences and university events to introduce each experiment to the mass audience. The data presented is large in size which leads to a huge upload time (approximately 30 minutes for one data set of 200 MB). Once the data set is uploaded, users will not suffer from high data latency since the data set resides in the client memory. However, the client memory is limited, and it is not possible to fit large data sets. Hence, it is interesting to study how we handle large data sets in a virtual reality environment. Also, it is worth investigating the acceptance of users on methods such as progressive loading. In the context of WAVE, the execution model and modules require virtual reality implementation. The extension complies with the interaction model for beyond-desktop visualisations proposed by Jansen and Dragicevic [272]. To accommodate the virtual 3D environment, the WAVE architecture might need to be adjusted accordingly and extended to other settings such as augmented reality or large displays.

6.5 Conclusion

In this dissertation, I have shown the diversity of each Big Data challenge that each use case uses different preprocessing and visualisation methods to achieve its desired visualisation outputs. Over the course of this dissertation, I have observed increasing interest in web-based Big Data visualisation from the reoccurring conferences and workshops such as Big Data Visual and Immersive Analytics (BDVA), IEEE Big Data, International Joint Conference on Computer Vision, Imaging and Computer Graphics Theory and Applications (IVAPP), World Wide Web Conference (WWW), EuroVis and IEEE Visualization (VIS). Over recent years, Big Data has become a common challenge faced by many different research domains, where managing the vast and complex data becomes the prior requirement before any further research direction can take place. Hence, I propose supporting data exploration by using visualisation techniques. To this end, my position in tackling the topic is to enable visualisation of various Big Data applications by using the proposed workflow and frameworks. Also, I promote the availability of data by providing the final visualisation on a web browser.

References

[1] R. Agarwal and V. Dhar, "Big data, data science, and analytics: The opportunity and challenge for is research," 2014.

[2] C. Dobre and F. Xhafa, "Intelligent services for big data science," *Future Generation Computer Systems*, vol. 37, pp. 267–281, 2014.

[3] G. Brumfiel, "High-energy physics: Down the petabyte highway," *Nature News*, vol. 469, no. 7330, pp. 282–283, 2011.

[4] C. P. Chen and C.-Y. Zhang, "Data-intensive applications, challenges, techniques and technologies: A survey on big data," *Information Sciences*, vol. 275, pp. 314–347, 2014.

[5] M. Hilbert and P. López, "The world's technological capacity to store, communicate, and compute information," *science*, vol. 332, no. 6025, pp. 60–65, 2011.

[6] T. Hey, S. Tansley, and K. Tolle, "Jim gray on escience: A transformed scientific method," *Fourth Paradigm*, pp. xvii–xxxi, 2009.

[7] W. G. Wesley, "The accuracy of tycho brahe's instruments," *Journal for the History of Astronomy*, vol. 9, no. 1, pp. 42–53, 1978.

[8] V. Kantere, "A holistic framework for big scientific data management," in *IEEE International Congress on Big Data*, pp. 220–226, June 2014.

[9] D. Laney, "3d data management: Controlling data volume, velocity and variety," *META Group Research Note*, vol. 6, p. 70, 2001.

[10] M. Schroeck, R. Shockley, J. Smart, D. Romero-Morales, and P. Tufano, "Analytics: The real-world use of big data," *IBM Global Business Services*, pp. 1–20, 2012.

[11] G. Bell, T. Hey, and A. Szalay, "Beyond the data deluge," *Science*, vol. 323, no. 5919, pp. 1297–1298, 2009.

[12] S. Schmelzle, M. Heethoff, V. Heuveline, P. Lösel, J. Becker, F. Beckmann, F. Schluenzen, J. U. Hammel, A. Kopmann, W. Mexner, M. Vogelgesang, N. Tan Jerome, O. Betz, R. Beutel, B. Wipfler, A. Blanke, S. Harzsch, M. Hörnig, T. Baumbach, and T. van de Kamp, "The NOVA project: maximizing beam time efficiency through synergistic analyses of SRμCT data," in *Developments in X-Ray Tomography XI*, vol. 10391, pp. 10391 – 10391 – 17, International Society for Optics and Photonics, 2017.

[13] D. M. South, I. D. S. Group, *et al.*, "Data preservation in high energy physics," in *Journal of Physics: Conference Series*, vol. 331, p. 012005, IOP Publishing, 2011.

[14] S. Gražulis, D. Chateigner, R. T. Downs, A. F. T. Yokochi, M. Quirós, L. Lutterotti, E. Manakova, J. Butkus, P. Moeck, and A. Le Bail, "Crystallography Open Database – an open-access collection of crystal structures," *Journal of Applied Crystallography*, vol. 42, pp. 726–729, Aug 2009.

[15] R. Akeson, X. Chen, D. Ciardi, M. Crane, J. Good, M. Harbut, E. Jackson, S. Kane, A. Laity, S. Leifer, *et al.*, "The NASA exoplanet archive: data and tools for exoplanet research," *Publications of the Astronomical Society of the Pacific*, vol. 125, no. 930, p. 989, 2013.

[16] D. J. Eisenstein, D. H. Weinberg, E. Agol, H. Aihara, C. A. Prieto, S. F. Anderson, J. A. Arns, É. Aubourg, S. Bailey, E. Balbinot, *et al.*, "Sdss-iii: Massive spectroscopic surveys of the distant universe, the milky

way, and extra-solar planetary systems," *The Astronomical Journal*, vol. 142, no. 3, p. 72, 2011.

[17] C. Tominski, *Event based visualization for user centered visual analysis.* PhD thesis, University of Rostock, 2006.

[18] D. Thompson, J. A. Levine, J. C. Bennett, P.-T. Bremer, A. Gyulassy, V. Pascucci, and P. P. Pébay, "Analysis of large-scale scalar data using hixels," in *Large Data Analysis and Visualization (LDAV), 2011 IEEE Symposium on*, pp. 23–30, IEEE, 2011.

[19] N. Tan Jerome, S. Chilingaryan, A. Shkarin, A. Kopmann, M. Zapf, A. Lizin, and T. Bergmann, "WAVE: A 3d online previewing framework for big data archives," in *Proceedings of the 12th International Joint Conference on Computer Vision, Imaging and Computer Graphics Theory and Applications - Volume 3: IVAPP, (VISIGRAPP 2017)*, pp. 152–163, INSTICC, ScitePress, 2017.

[20] E. W. Bethel, M. Greenwald, K. K. van Dam, M. Parashar, S. M. Wild, and H. S. Wiley, "Management, analysis, and visualization of experimental and observational data—the convergence of data and computing," in *e-Science (e-Science), 2016 IEEE 12th International Conference on*, pp. 213–222, IEEE, 2016.

[21] S. John Walker, "Big data: A revolution that will transform how we live, work, and think," 2014.

[22] R. Simon, G. Buth, and M. Hagelstein, "The X-ray-fluorescence facility at ANKA, Karlsruhe: minimum detection limits and micro probe capabilities," *Nuclear Instruments and Methods in Physics Research Section B: Beam Interactions with Materials and Atoms*, vol. 199, pp. 554–558, 2003.

[23] M. Q. Wang Baldonado, A. Woodruff, and A. Kuchinsky, "Guidelines for using multiple views in information visualization," in *Proceedings*

of the Working Conference on Advanced Visual Interfaces, AVI '00, (New York, NY, USA), pp. 110–119, ACM, 2000.

[24] R. Bonney, C. B. Cooper, J. Dickinson, S. Kelling, T. Phillips, K. V. Rosenberg, and J. Shirk, "Citizen science: a developing tool for expanding science knowledge and scientific literacy," *BioScience*, vol. 59, no. 11, pp. 977–984, 2009.

[25] N. Kalthoff, B. Adler, A. Wieser, M. Kohler, K. Träumner, J. Handwerker, U. Corsmeier, S. Khodayar, D. Lambert, A. Kopmann, N. Kunka, G. Dick, M. Ramatschi, J. Wickert, and C. Kottmeier, "KITcube–a mobile observation platform for convection studies deployed during HyMeX," *Meteorologische Zeitschrift*, vol. 22, no. 6, pp. 633–647, 2013.

[26] N. Ruiter, M. Zapf, R. Dapp, T. Hopp, W. Kaiser, and H. Gemmeke, "First results of a clinical study with 3d ultrasound computer tomography," in *Ultrasonics Symposium (IUS), 2013 IEEE International*, pp. 651–654, IEEE, 2013.

[27] L. Bornschein, KATRIN-Collaboration, *et al.*, "The KATRIN experiment-a direct measurement of the electron antineutrino mass in the sub-eV region," *Nuclear Physics A*, vol. 752, pp. 14–23, 2005.

[28] J. Barry, N. Munzke, and J. Thomas, "Power fluctuations in solar-storage clusters: spatial correlation and battery response times," *Energy Procedia*, vol. 135, pp. 379–390, 2017.

[29] M. Tory and T. Moller, "Human factors in visualization research," *IEEE transactions on visualization and computer graphics*, vol. 10, no. 1, pp. 72–84, 2004.

[30] R. E. Kahn and V. G. Cerf, *An open architecture for a digital library system and a plan for its development.* Corporation for National Research Initiatives, 1988.

[31] H. Kaur, "Role of Digital Libraries in the Present Era: Challenges and Issues," in *Handbook of Research on Inventive Digital Tools for Collection Management and Development in Modern Libraries* (S. Thanuskodi, ed.), pp. 86–102, Hershey, PA, USA: IGI Global, 2015.

[32] P. Lyman, "What is a digital library? technology, intellectual property, and the public interest," in *Books, Bricks and Bytes*, pp. 1–34, Routledge, 2017.

[33] M. Seadle and E. Greifeneder, "Defining a digital library," *Library Hi Tech*, vol. 25, no. 2, pp. 169–173, 2007.

[34] M. Trivedi, "Digital libraries: functionality, usability, and accessibility," *Library Philosophy and Practice (e-journal)*, p. 381, 2010.

[35] C. Lynch and H. Garcia-Molina, "Interoperability, scaling, and the digital libraries research agenda.," *Microcomputers for Information Management*, vol. 13, no. 2, pp. 85–132, 1996.

[36] G. Cleveland, *Digital libraries: definitions, issues and challenges*. IFLA, Universal dataflow and telecommunications core programme, 1998.

[37] H. Gemmeke, T. Hopp, M. Zapf, C. Kaiser, and N. V. Ruiter, "3D ultrasound computer tomography: Hardware setup, reconstruction methods and first clinical results," *Nuclear Instruments and Methods in Physics Research Section A: Accelerators, Spectrometers, Detectors and Associated Equipment*, 2017.

[38] J. Bernard, *Exploratory search in time-oriented primary data*. PhD thesis, Technische Universität, 2015.

[39] L. E. Good, A. C. Popat, W. C. Janssen, and E. A. Bier, "A fluid interface for personal digital libraries," in *International Conference on Theory and Practice of Digital Libraries*, pp. 162–173, Springer, 2005.

[40] A. Veerasamy and R. Heikes, "Effectiveness of a graphical display of retrieval results," in *ACM SIGIR Forum*, vol. 31, pp. 236–245, ACM, 1997.

[41] N. Dushay, "Visualizing metadata: A virtual book spine viewer," *D-Lib Magazine*, vol. 10, no. 10, 2004.

[42] G. Mathew, A. Agarwal, and T. Menzies, "Trends in topics at SE conferences (1993-2013)," *CoRR*, vol. abs/1608.08100, 2016.

[43] K. Shubankar, A. Singh, and V. Pudi, "A frequent keyword-set based algorithm for topic modeling and clustering of research papers," in *Data Mining and Optimization (DMO), 2011 3rd Conference on*, pp. 96–102, IEEE, 2011.

[44] P. Isenberg, T. Isenberg, M. Sedlmair, J. Chen, and T. Möller, "Visualization as seen through its research paper keywords," *IEEE transactions on visualization and computer graphics*, vol. 23, no. 1, pp. 771–780, 2017.

[45] T. L. Griffiths and M. Steyvers, "Finding scientific topics," *Proceedings of the National academy of Sciences*, vol. 101, no. suppl 1, pp. 5228–5235, 2004.

[46] S. Mesbah, K. Fragkeskos, C. Lofi, A. Bozzon, and G.-J. Houben, "Facet embeddings for explorative analytics in digital libraries," in *International Conference on Theory and Practice of Digital Libraries*, pp. 86–99, Springer, 2017.

[47] C. Ahlberg and B. Shneiderman, "Visual information seeking using the FilmFinder," in *Conference Companion on Human Factors in Computing Systems*, CHI '94, (New York, NY, USA), pp. 433–434, ACM, 1994.

[48] C. Williamson and B. Shneiderman, "The dynamic HomeFinder: Evaluating dynamic queries in a real-estate information exploration system," in *Proceedings of the 15th annual international ACM SIGIR conference on Research and development in information retrieval*, pp. 338–346, ACM, 1992.

[49] B. Kim, J. Scott, and S. Kim, "Exploring digital libraries through visual interfaces," in *Digital Libraries-Methods and Applications*, InTech, 2011.

[50] N. Tan Jerome and A. Kopmann, "Digital visual exploration library," in *Proceedings of the 13th International Joint Conference on Computer Vision, Imaging and Computer Graphics Theory and Applications - Volume 4: IVAPP, (VISIGRAPP 2018)*, INSTICC, ScitePress, 2018.

[51] E. Clarkson, K. Desai, and J. Foley, "Resultmaps: Visualization for search interfaces," *IEEE Transactions on Visualization and Computer Graphics*, vol. 15, no. 6, 2009.

[52] M. F. De Oliveira and H. Levkowitz, "From visual data exploration to visual data mining: a survey," *IEEE Transactions on Visualization and Computer Graphics*, vol. 9, no. 3, pp. 378–394, 2003.

[53] M. A. Hearst, "Tilebars: visualization of term distribution information in full text information access," in *Proceedings of the SIGCHI conference on Human factors in computing systems*, pp. 59–66, ACM Press/Addison-Wesley Publishing Co., 1995.

[54] S. K. Card, J. D. Mackinlay, and B. Shneiderman, *Readings in information visualization: using vision to think*. Morgan Kaufmann, 1999.

[55] K. Börner and C. Chen, "Visual interfaces to digital libraries: Motivation, utilization, and socio-technical challenges," *Visual interfaces to digital libraries*, pp. 1–9, 2002.

[56] B. Shneiderman, "The eyes have it: A task by data type taxonomy for information visualizations," in *Visual Languages, 1996. Proceedings., IEEE Symposium on*, pp. 336–343, IEEE, 1996.

[57] L. T. Nowell and D. Hix, "Visualizing search results: user interface development for the Project Envision database of computer science literature," *Advances in Human Factors Ergonomics*, vol. 19, p. 56, 1993.

[58] K. Borner, A. Dillon, and M. Dolinsky, "LVis—digital library visualizer," in *Information Visualization, 2000. Proceedings. IEEE International Conference on*, pp. 77–81, IEEE, 2000.

[59] H.-y. Shiaw, R. J. Jacob, and G. R. Crane, "The 3D vase museum: a new approach to context in a digital library," in *Proceedings of the 4th ACM/IEEE-CS joint conference on Digital libraries*, pp. 125–134, ACM, 2004.

[60] L. Marks, J. A. Hussell, T. M. McMahon, and R. E. Luce, "ActiveGraph: A digital library visualization tool," *International Journal on Digital Libraries*, vol. 5, no. 1, pp. 57–69, 2005.

[61] S. Chandna, F. Rindone, C. Dachsbacher, and R. Stotzka, "Quantitative exploration of large medieval manuscripts data for the codicological research," in *Large Data Analysis and Visualization (LDAV), 2016 IEEE 6th Symposium on*, pp. 20–28, IEEE, 2016.

[62] S. Few, "The surest path to visual discovery," 2006.

[63] D. A. Keim, "Information visualization and visual data mining," *IEEE transactions on Visualization and Computer Graphics*, vol. 8, no. 1, pp. 1–8, 2002.

[64] E. H.-h. Chi, "A taxonomy of visualization techniques using the data state reference model," in *Information Visualization, 2000. InfoVis 2000. IEEE Symposium on*, pp. 69–75, IEEE, 2000.

[65] N. Tan Jerome, S. Chilingaryan, A. Kopmann, and A. Wieser, "An interactive web-based doppler wind lidar visualisation system," in *Workshop on Visualisation in Environmental Sciences (EnvirVis)* (K. Rink, A. Middel, D. Zeckzer, and R. Bujack, eds.), The Eurographics Association, 2017.

[66] M. Tobiasz, P. Isenberg, and S. Carpendale, "Lark: Coordinating co-located collaboration with information visualization," *IEEE transactions on visualization and computer graphics*, vol. 15, no. 6, pp. 1065–1072, 2009.

[67] J. M. Brunetti, S. Auer, R. García, J. Klímek, and M. Nečaskỳ, "Formal linked data visualization model," in *Proceedings of International Conference on Information Integration and Web-based Applications & Services*, p. 309, ACM, 2013.

[68] J. A. Cottam, A. Lumsdaine, and C. Weaver, "Watch this: A taxonomy for dynamic data visualization," in *Visual Analytics Science and Technology (VAST), 2012 IEEE Conference on*, pp. 193–202, IEEE, 2012.

[69] L. Treinish, "A function-based data model for visualization," in *Proceedings of the IEEE Visualization 1999 Conference Late Breaking Hot Topics*, pp. 73–76, 1999.

[70] N. Elmqvist and J.-D. Fekete, "Hierarchical aggregation for information visualization: Overview, techniques, and design guidelines," *IEEE Transactions on Visualization and Computer Graphics*, vol. 16, no. 3, pp. 439–454, 2010.

[71] G. Aad, E. Abat, J. Abdallah, A. Abdelalim, A. Abdesselam, O. Abdinov, B. Abi, M. Abolins, H. Abramowicz, E. Acerbi, *et al.*, "The ATLAS experiment at the CERN large hadron collider," *Journal of Instrumentation*, vol. 3, no. S08003, 2008.

[72] A. Ailamaki, V. Kantere, and D. Dash, "Managing scientific data," *Communications of the ACM*, vol. 53, no. 6, pp. 68–78, 2010.

[73] N. Kurachi, *The Magic of Computer Graphics*. Natick, MA, USA: A. K. Peters, Ltd., 1st ed., 2011.

[74] W. E. L. Grimson, G. J. Ettinger, S. J. White, T. Lozano-Perez, W. Wells, and R. Kikinis, "An automatic registration method for frameless stereotaxy, image guided surgery, and enhanced reality visualization," *IEEE Transactions on medical imaging*, vol. 15, no. 2, pp. 129–140, 1996.

[75] M. S. Falk, *Visualization and mesoscopic simulation in systems biology*. PhD thesis, Visualisierungsinstitut der Universität Stuttgart, 4 2013.

[76] A. Kaufman and K. Mueller, "Overview of volume rendering," *The visualization handbook*, vol. 7, pp. 127–174, 2005.

[77] M. Jonsson, "Volume rendering," Master's thesis, Umeå University, 2005.

[78] N. Max, "Optical models for direct volume rendering," *IEEE Transactions on Visualization and Computer Graphics*, vol. 1, no. 2, pp. 99–108, 1995.

[79] J. F. Blinn, "Light reflection functions for simulation of clouds and dusty surfaces," *Acm Siggraph Computer Graphics*, vol. 16, no. 3, pp. 21–29, 1982.

[80] P. Lacroute and M. Levoy, "Fast volume rendering using a shear-warp factorization of the viewing transformation," in *Proceedings of the 21st Annual Conference on Computer Graphics and Interactive Techniques*, SIGGRAPH '94, (New York, NY, USA), pp. 451–458, ACM, 1994.

[81] W. E. Lorensen and H. E. Cline, "Marching cubes: A high resolution 3d surface construction algorithm," in *Proceedings of the 14th Annual*

Conference on Computer Graphics and Interactive Techniques, SIGGRAPH '87, (New York, NY, USA), pp. 163–169, ACM, 1987.

[82] S. D. Roth, "Ray casting for modeling solids," *Computer graphics and image processing*, vol. 18, no. 2, pp. 109–144, 1982.

[83] R. A. Drebin, L. Carpenter, and P. Hanrahan, "Volume rendering," in *Proceedings of the 15th Annual Conference on Computer Graphics and Interactive Techniques*, SIGGRAPH '88, (New York, NY, USA), pp. 65–74, ACM, 1988.

[84] P. Sabella, "A rendering algorithm for visualizing 3d scalar fields," *SIGGRAPH Comput. Graph.*, vol. 22, pp. 51–58, June 1988.

[85] M. Levoy, "Display of surfaces from volume data," *IEEE Comput. Graph. Appl.*, vol. 8, pp. 29–37, May 1988.

[86] B. T. Phong, "Illumination for computer generated pictures," *Communications of the ACM*, vol. 18, no. 6, pp. 311–317, 1975.

[87] J. F. Blinn and M. E. Newell, "Texture and reflection in computer generated images," *Commun. ACM*, vol. 19, pp. 542–547, Oct. 1976.

[88] A. Nischwitz, M. Fischer, P. Haberäcker, and G. Socher, *Computergrafik und Bildverarbeitung*. Springer, 2007.

[89] R. L. Cook and K. E. Torrance, "A reflectance model for computer graphics," *ACM Transactions on Graphics (TOG)*, vol. 1, no. 1, pp. 7–24, 1982.

[90] C. Schlick, "An inexpensive brdf model for physically-based rendering," *Computer graphics forum*, vol. 13, no. 3, pp. 233–246, 1994.

[91] R. Mullick, R. N. Bryan, and J. Butman, "Confocal volume rendering: Fast segmentation-free visualization of internal structures," in *Proceedings of SPIE*, pp. 144–154, 2000.

[92] I. Sobel and G. Feldman, “A 3x3 isotropic gradient operator for image processing,” *a talk at the Stanford Artificial Project in*, pp. 271–272, 1968.

[93] M. J. Bentum, B. B. A. Lichtenbelt, and T. Malzbender, “Frequency analysis of gradient estimators in volume rendering,” *IEEE Transactions on Visualization and Computer Graphics*, vol. 2, no. 3, pp. 242–254, 1996.

[94] H. Childs, B. Geveci, W. Schroeder, J. Meredith, K. Moreland, C. Sewell, T. Kuhlen, and E. W. Bethel, “Research challenges for visualization software,” *Computer*, vol. 46, no. 5, pp. 34–42, 2013.

[95] F. Mwalongo, M. Krone, G. Reina, and T. Ertl, “State-of-the-art report in web-based visualization,” *Computer Graphics Forum*, vol. 35, no. 3, pp. 553–575, 2016.

[96] F. Mwalongo, M. Krone, G. Reina, and T. Ertl, “State-of-the-art report in web-based visualization,” *Computer Graphics Forum*, vol. 35, no. 3, pp. 553–575, 2016.

[97] Khronos, “WebGL - OpenGL ES 2.0 for the Web, https://www.khronos.org/webgl/,” 2011.

[98] J. Congote, A. Segura, L. Kabongo, A. Moreno, J. Posada, and O. Ruiz, “Interactive visualization of volumetric data with webgl in real-time,” in *Proceedings of the 16th International Conference on 3D Web Technology*, Web3D ’11, (New York, NY, USA), pp. 137–146, ACM, 2011.

[99] J. M. Noguera and J.-R. Jiménez, *Visualization of very large 3D volumes on mobile devices and WebGL*. Václav Skala-UNION Agency, 2012.

[100] C. P. Chen and C.-Y. Zhang, “Data-intensive applications, challenges, techniques and technologies: A survey on Big Data,” *Information Sciences*, vol. 275, pp. 314–347, 2014.

[101] L. Williams, "Pyramidal parametrics," in *ACM Siggraph Computer Graphics*, vol. 17, pp. 1–11, ACM, 1983.

[102] R. Kitchin, "Big data, new epistemologies and paradigm shifts," *Big Data & Society*, vol. 1, no. 1, p. 2053951714528481, 2014.

[103] M. Rivi, L. Calori, G. Muscianisi, and V. Slavnic, "In-situ visualization: State-of-the-art and some use cases," *PRACE White Paper*, pp. 1–18, 2012.

[104] S. G. Parker and C. R. Johnson, "SCIRun: a scientific programming environment for computational steering," in *Proceedings of the 1995 ACM/IEEE conference on Supercomputing*, p. 52, ACM, 1995.

[105] T. Tu, H. Yu, L. Ramirez-Guzman, J. Bielak, O. Ghattas, K.-L. Ma, and D. R. O'hallaron, "From mesh generation to scientific visualization: An end-to-end approach to parallel supercomputing," in *Proceedings of the 2006 ACM/IEEE conference on Supercomputing*, p. 91, ACM, 2006.

[106] M. J. Turk, B. D. Smith, J. S. Oishi, S. Skory, S. W. Skillman, T. Abel, and M. L. Norman, "yt: A multi-code analysis toolkit for astrophysical simulation data," *The Astrophysical Journal Supplement Series*, vol. 192, no. 1, p. 9, 2011.

[107] F. Zhang, C. Docan, M. Parashar, S. Klasky, N. Podhorszki, and H. Abbasi, "Enabling in-situ execution of coupled scientific workflow on multi-core platform," in *Parallel & Distributed Processing Symposium (IPDPS), 2012 IEEE 26th International*, pp. 1352–1363, IEEE, 2012.

[108] M. Dorier, R. Sisneros, T. Peterka, G. Antoniu, and D. Semeraro, "Damaris/viz: A nonintrusive, adaptable and user-friendly in situ visualization framework," in *Large-Scale Data Analysis and Visualization (LDAV), 2013 IEEE Symposium on*, pp. 67–75, IEEE, 2013.

[109] A. Esnard, N. Richart, and O. Coulaud, "A steering environment for online parallel visualization of legacy parallel simulations," in *Distributed Simulation and Real-Time Applications, 2006. DS-RT'06. Tenth IEEE International Symposium on*, pp. 7–14, IEEE, 2006.

[110] F. Zheng, H. Abbasi, C. Docan, J. Lofstead, Q. Liu, S. Klasky, M. Parashar, N. Podhorszki, K. Schwan, and M. Wolf, "Predata–preparatory data analytics on peta-scale machines," in *Parallel & Distributed Processing (IPDPS), 2010 IEEE International Symposium on*, pp. 1–12, IEEE, 2010.

[111] J. F. Lofstead, S. Klasky, K. Schwan, N. Podhorszki, and C. Jin, "Flexible io and integration for scientific codes through the adaptable io system (adios)," in *Proceedings of the 6th international workshop on Challenges of large applications in distributed environments*, pp. 15–24, ACM, 2008.

[112] P. Malakar, V. Natarajan, and S. S. Vadhiyar, "An adaptive framework for simulation and online remote visualization of critical climate applications in resource-constrained environments," in *Proceedings of the 2010 ACM/IEEE International Conference for High Performance Computing, Networking, Storage and Analysis*, pp. 1–11, IEEE Computer Society, 2010.

[113] B. Lorendeau, Y. Fournier, and A. Ribes, "In-situ visualization in fluid mechanics using catalyst: A case study for code saturne," in *Large-Scale Data Analysis and Visualization (LDAV), 2013 IEEE Symposium on*, pp. 53–57, IEEE, 2013.

[114] M. Larsen, E. Brugger, H. Childs, J. Eliot, K. Griffin, and C. Harrison, "Strawman: A batch in situ visualization and analysis infrastructure for multi-physics simulation codes," in *Proceedings of the First Workshop on In Situ Infrastructures for Enabling Extreme-Scale Analysis and Visualization*, pp. 30–35, ACM, 2015.

[115] S. Jourdain, U. Ayachit, and B. Geveci, "Paraviewweb, a web framework for 3d visualization and data processing," *IJCISIM*, vol. 3, pp. 870–7, 2011.

[116] J. Ahrens, S. Jourdain, P. O'Leary, J. Patchett, D. H. Rogers, and M. Petersen, "An image-based approach to extreme scale in situ visualization and analysis," in *Proceedings of the International Conference for High Performance Computing, Networking, Storage and Analysis*, pp. 424–434, IEEE Press, 2014.

[117] S. Burigat and L. Chittaro, "On the effectiveness of Overview+Detail visualization on mobile devices," *Personal and ubiquitous computing*, vol. 17, no. 2, pp. 371–385, 2013.

[118] A. Cockburn, A. Karlson, and B. B. Bederson, "A review of overview+ detail, zooming, and focus+ context interfaces," *ACM Computing Surveys (CSUR)*, vol. 41, no. 1, p. 2, 2009.

[119] D. Lu, D. Zhu, Z. Wang, and J. Gao, "Efficient level of detail for texture-based flow visualization," *Computer Animation and Virtual Worlds*, 2015.

[120] J. Kimball, M. Duchaineau, and F. Kuester, "Interactive visualization of large scale atomistic and cosmological particle simulations," in *Aerospace Conference, 2013 IEEE*, pp. 1–9, IEEE, 2013.

[121] M. Zinsmaier, U. Brandes, O. Deussen, and H. Strobelt, "Interactive level-of-detail rendering of large graphs," *IEEE Transactions on Visualization and Computer Graphics*, vol. 18, no. 12, pp. 2486–2495, 2012.

[122] W. J. Schroeder, B. Lorensen, and K. Martin, *The visualization toolkit: an object-oriented approach to 3D graphics*. Kitware, 2004.

[123] W. J. Schroeder, K. M. Martin, and W. E. Lorensen, "The design and implementation of an object-oriented toolkit for 3d graphics and visu-

alization," in *Proceedings of the 7th conference on Visualization'96*, pp. 93–ff, IEEE Computer Society Press, 1996.

[124] A. Vitali, D. Regazzoni, C. Rizzi, and G. Colombo, "Extending vtk library to dynamically modify polygonal meshes in medical applications," *Computer-Aided Design and Applications*, vol. 15, no. 2, pp. 203–210, 2018.

[125] A. M. Noecker, K. S. Choi, P. Riva-Posse, R. E. Gross, H. S. Mayberg, and C. C. McIntyre, "Stimvision software: examples and applications in subcallosal cingulate deep brain stimulation for depression," *Neuromodulation: Technology at the Neural Interface*, vol. 21, no. 2, pp. 191–196, 2018.

[126] J. Cercos-Pita, I. Cal, D. Duque, and G. S. de Moreta, "Nasal-geom, a free upper respiratory tract 3d model reconstruction software," *Computer Physics Communications*, vol. 223, pp. 55–68, 2018.

[127] H. Childs, E. Brugger, B. Whitlock, J. Meredith, S. Ahern, D. Pugmire, K. Biagas, M. Miller, G. H. Weber, H. Krishnan, *et al.*, "Visit: An end-user tool for visualizing and analyzing very large data," tech. rep., Ernest Orlando Lawrence Berkeley National Laboratory, Berkeley, CA (US), 2012.

[128] M. Dreher and T. Peterka, "Decaf: Decoupled dataflows for in situ high-performance workflows," tech. rep., Argonne National Lab.(ANL), Argonne, IL (United States), 2017.

[129] M. Larsen, J. Ahrens, U. Ayachit, E. Brugger, H. Childs, B. Geveci, and C. Harrison, "The alpine in situ infrastructure: Ascending from the ashes of strawman," in *Proceedings of the In Situ Infrastructures on Enabling Extreme-Scale Analysis and Visualization*, pp. 42–46, ACM, 2017.

[130] X. Zhu, A. Zelmer, and S. Wellmann, “Visualization of protein-protein interaction in nuclear and cytoplasmic fractions by co-immunoprecipitation and in situ proximity ligation assay.,” *Journal of visualized experiments: JoVE*, no. 119, 2017.

[131] D. Rantzau, U. Lang, R. Lang, H. Nebel, A. Wierse, and R. Ruehle, “Collaborative and interactive visualization in a distributed high performance software environment,” in *High Performance Computing for Computer Graphics and Visualisation*, pp. 207–216, Springer, 1996.

[132] M. Miller, C. D. Hansen, and C. R. Johnson, “The scirun problem solving environment: Implementation within a distributed environment.,” in *PPSC*, 1999.

[133] J. Woodring, J. P. Ahrens, J. Patchett, C. Tauxe, and D. H. Rogers, “High-dimensional scientific data exploration via cinema,” in *Data Systems for Interactive Analysis (DSIA), 2017 IEEE Workshop on*, pp. 1–5, IEEE, 2017.

[134] J. M. Patchett, B. Nouanesengsy, G. Gisler, J. Ahrens, and H. Hagen, “In situ and post processing workflows for asteroid ablation studies,” in *Eurographics Conference on Visualization (EuroVis)*, 2017.

[135] J. R. Wendelberger, D. Banesh, L. J. Wendelberger, and J. P. Ahrens, “Detecting changes in simulations,” tech. rep., Los Alamos National Lab.(LANL), Los Alamos, NM (United States), 2017.

[136] J. Behr, P. Eschler, Y. Jung, and M. Zöllner, “X3dom: a dom-based html5/x3d integration model,” in *Proceedings of the 14th international conference on 3D web technology*, pp. 127–135, ACM, 2009.

[137] J. Behr, C. Mouton, S. Parfouru, J. Champeau, C. Jeulin, M. Thöner, C. Stein, M. Schmitt, M. Limper, M. de Sousa, *et al.*, “webvis/instant3dhub: visual computing as a service infrastructure to deliver adaptive, secure and scalable user centric data visualisation,” in

Proceedings of the 20th International Conference on 3D Web Technology, pp. 39–47, ACM, 2015.

[138] A. Arbelaiz, A. Moreno, L. Kabongo, and A. García-Alonso, "Volume visualization tools for medical applications in ubiquitous platforms," in *eHealth 360°*, pp. 443–450, Springer, 2017.

[139] J. Han, J. Pei, and M. Kamber, *Data mining: concepts and techniques*. Elsevier, 2011.

[140] D. Agrawal, P. Bernstein, E. Bertino, S. Davidson, U. Dayal, M. Franklin, J. Gehrke, L. Haas, A. Halevy, J. Han, *et al.*, "Challenges and opportunities with big data 2011-1," 2011.

[141] R. T. Kouzes, G. A. Anderson, S. T. Elbert, I. Gorton, and D. K. Gracio, "The changing paradigm of data-intensive computing," *Computer*, vol. 42, no. 1, pp. 26–34, 2009.

[142] D. A. Keim, "Visual exploration of large data sets," *Communications of the ACM*, vol. 44, no. 8, pp. 38–44, 2001.

[143] M. O. Ward, "A taxonomy of glyph placement strategies for multidimensional data visualization," *Information Visualization*, vol. 1, no. 3-4, pp. 194–210, 2002.

[144] T. Nocke, S. Schlechtweg, and H. Schumann, "Icon-based visualization using mosaic metaphors," in *Information Visualisation, 2005. Proceedings. Ninth International Conference on*, pp. 103–109, IEEE, 2005.

[145] E. R. Tufte, N. H. Goeler, and R. Benson, *Envisioning information*, vol. 126. Graphics press Cheshire, CT, 1990.

[146] S. van den Elzen and J. J. van Wijk, "Small multiples, large singles: A new approach for visual data exploration," *Computer Graphics Forum*, vol. 32, no. 3pt2, pp. 191–200, 2013.

[147] S. Chilingaryan, A. Beglarian, A. Kopmann, and S. Vöcking, "Advanced data extraction infrastructure: Web based system for management of time series data," *Journal of Physics: Conference Series*, vol. 219, no. 4, p. 042034, 2010.

[148] N. Tan Jerome, S. Chilingaryan, A. Shkarin, A. Kopmann, M. Zapf, A. Lizin, and T. Bergmann, "WAVE: A 3D online previewing framework for big data archives," in *VISIGRAPP*, 2017.

[149] M. Claypool and K. Claypool, "Latency and player actions in online games," *Communications of the ACM*, vol. 49, no. 11, pp. 40–45, 2006.

[150] Z. Liu, B. Jiang, and J. Heer, "imMens: Real-time Visual Querying of Big Data," *Computer Graphics Forum*, vol. 32, no. 3pt4, pp. 421–430, 2013.

[151] S. Agarwal, B. Mozafari, A. Panda, H. Milner, S. Madden, and I. Stoica, "BlinkDB: queries with bounded errors and bounded response times on very large data," in *Proceedings of the 8th ACM European Conference on Computer Systems*, pp. 29–42, ACM, 2013.

[152] J. M. Hellerstein, P. J. Haas, and H. J. Wang, "Online aggregation," *Acm Sigmod Record*, vol. 26, no. 2, pp. 171–182, 1997.

[153] D. Fisher, "Hotmap: Looking at geographic attention," *IEEE Transactions on Visualization & Computer Graphics*, no. 6, pp. 1184–1191, 2007.

[154] C. Barnes, M. Best, B. Bornhold, S. Juniper, B. Pirenne, and P. Phibbs, "The NEPTUNE Project-a cabled ocean observatory in the NE Pacific: Overview, challenges and scientific objectives for the installation and operation of stage i in canadian waters," in *Underwater Technology and Workshop on Scientific Use of Submarine Cables and Related Technologies, 2007. Symposium on*, pp. 308–313, IEEE, 2007.

[155] P. Isenberg, N. Elmqvist, J. Scholtz, D. Cernea, K.-L. Ma, and H. Hagen, "Collaborative visualization: definition, challenges, and research agenda," *Information Visualization*, vol. 10, no. 4, pp. 310–326, 2011.

[156] N. Panagiotou, N. Zygouras, I. Katakis, D. Gunopulos, N. Zacheilas, I. Boutsis, V. Kalogeraki, S. Lynch, and B. O'Brien, "Intelligent urban data monitoring for smart cities," in *Joint European Conference on Machine Learning and Knowledge Discovery in Databases*, pp. 177–192, Springer, 2016.

[157] V. Kantere, "A holistic framework for big scientific data management," in *Big Data (BigData Congress), 2014 IEEE International Congress on*, pp. 220–226, IEEE, 2014.

[158] M. Bostock, V. Ogievetsky, and J. Heer, "D^3 data-driven documents," *IEEE transactions on visualization and computer graphics*, vol. 17, no. 12, pp. 2301–2309, 2011.

[159] Nicolas Garcia Belmonte, "JavaScript InfoVis Toolkit," 2013.

[160] R. Barga, J. Jackson, N. Araujo, D. Guo, N. Gautam, and Y. Simmhan, "The trident scientific workflow workbench," in *eScience, 2008. eScience'08. IEEE Fourth International Conference on*, pp. 317–318, IEEE, 2008.

[161] B. Beran, C. van Ingen, and D. R. Fatland, "Sciscope: a participatory geoscientific web application," *Concurrency and Computation: Practice and Experience*, vol. 22, no. 17, pp. 2300–2312, 2010.

[162] A. Beglarian, H. Gemmeke, C. Lefhalm, S. Wuestling, and T. Schonitz, "3D temperature monitoring for ultra-high vacuum spectrometers in KATRIN experiment," in *Real Time Conference, 2005. 14th IEEE-NPSS*, pp. 2–pp, IEEE, 2005.

[163] G. W. Johnson, *LabVIEW Graphical Programming: Practical Applications in Instrumentation and Control. Hauptbd.* McGraw-Hill, 1994.

[164] J. Amsbaugh, J. Barrett, A. Beglarian, T. Bergmann, H. Bichsel, L. Bodine, J. Bonn, N. Boyd, T. Burritt, Z. Chaoui, *et al.*, "Focal-plane detector system for the KATRIN experiment," *Nuclear Instruments and Methods in Physics Research Section A: Accelerators, Spectrometers, Detectors and Associated Equipment*, vol. 778, pp. 40–60, 2015.

[165] UC Berkeley Visualization Lab, "Flare." http://flare.prefuse.org/, 2008.

[166] C. Reas and B. Fry, *Processing: a programming handbook for visual designers and artists*. Mit Press, 2007.

[167] K. Cook, G. Grinstein, and M. Whiting, "The VAST Challenge: history, scope, and outcomes: An introduction to the special issue," 2014.

[168] J. Dirksen, *Three. js essentials*. Packt Publishing Ltd, 2014.

[169] D. D. Chamberlin, "Document convergence in an interactive formatting system," *IBM journal of research and development*, vol. 31, no. 1, pp. 58–72, 1987.

[170] K. A. Hinum, *Gravi++: an interactive information visualization for high dimensional, temporal data*. na, 2006.

[171] P. M. Martin-Sanchez, C. Gebhardt, J. Toepel, J. Barry, N. Munzke, J. Günster, and A. A. Gorbushina, "Monitoring microbial soiling in photovoltaic systems: A qpcr-based approach," *International Biodeterioration & Biodegradation*, 2018.

[172] S. Pousty and K. Miller, *Getting Started with OpenShift: A Guide for Impatient Beginners*. " O'Reilly Media, Inc.", 2014.

[173] B. Vasilescu, Y. Yu, H. Wang, P. Devanbu, and V. Filkov, "Quality and productivity outcomes relating to continuous integration in github," in *Proceedings of the 2015 10th Joint Meeting on Foundations of Software Engineering*, pp. 805–816, ACM, 2015.

[174] E. T. Barr, C. Bird, P. C. Rigby, A. Hindle, D. M. German, and P. Devanbu, "Cohesive and isolated development with branches," in *International Conference on Fundamental Approaches to Software Engineering*, pp. 316–331, Springer, 2012.

[175] D. Applebaum, *Probability and information: An integrated approach.* Cambridge University Press, 1996.

[176] A. Lizin, "Lightweight framework for 3D web visualization," Master's thesis, Tomsk Polytechnic University, Russia, 2016.

[177] F. Schultze, "Scalable visualization of large tomographic 3D volumes on the web," Master's thesis, Karlsruhe Institute of Technology, Germany, 2015.

[178] A. Tukalo, "Generic interactive user interface for medical data using multimodality slicemaps," tech. rep., Savonia University of applied sciences, Finnland, 2015.

[179] N. P. Rougier, "Antialiased 2D grid, marker, and arrow shaders," *Journal of Computer Graphics Techniques*, vol. 3, no. 4, p. 52, 2013.

[180] J. Jomier, S. Jourdain, U. Ayachit, and C. Marion, "Remote visualization of large datasets with midas and paraviewweb," in *Proceedings of the 16th International Conference on 3D Web Technology*, pp. 147–150, ACM, 2011.

[181] J. Kruger and R. Westermann, "Acceleration techniques for GPU-based volume rendering," in *Proceedings of the 14th IEEE Visualization 2003 (VIS'03)*, p. 38, IEEE Computer Society, 2003.

[182] M. Claypool, K. Claypool, and F. Damaa, "The effects of frame rate and resolution on users playing first person shooter games," in *Electronic Imaging 2006*, pp. 607101–607101, International Society for Optics and Photonics, 2006.

[183] Kishonti, "Gfxbench 4.0." https://gfxbench.com/, 2011.

[184] J. Díaz-García, P. Brunet, I. Navazo, and P.-P. Vázquez, "Progressive ray casting for volumetric models on mobile devices," *Computers & Graphics*, 2018.

[185] A. Arbelaiz, A. Moreno, L. Kabongo, and A. García-Alonso, "X3dom volume rendering component for web content developers," *Multimedia Tools and Applications*, vol. 76, no. 11, pp. 13425–13454, 2017.

[186] X. Zou, G. Zhao, J. Li, Y. Yang, and Y. Fang, "3d land cover classification based on multispectral lidar point clouds," *The International Archives of Photogrammetry, Remote Sensing and Spatial Information Sciences*, vol. 41, p. 741, 2016.

[187] C. Ünsalan and K. L. Boyer, "A system to detect houses and residential street networks in multispectral satellite images," *Computer Vision and Image Understanding*, vol. 98, no. 3, pp. 423–461, 2005.

[188] S. Bouraoui and A. Deruyver, "A system to detect residential area in multispectral satellite images," in *Image and Vision Computing New Zealand (IVCNZ), 2010 25th International Conference of*, pp. 1–5, IEEE, 2010.

[189] E. Tarantino, "Land cover classification of quickbird multispectral data with an object-oriented approach," *WIT Transactions on Information and Communication Technologies*, vol. 32, 2004.

[190] F. Yao, C. Wang, D. Dong, J. Luo, Z. Shen, and K. Yang, "High-resolution mapping of urban surface water using zy-3 multi-spectral imagery," *Remote Sensing*, vol. 7, no. 9, pp. 12336–12355, 2015.

[191] B. Adler, N. Kalthoff, and L. Gantner, "Nocturnal low-level clouds over southern west africa analysed using high-resolution simulations," *Atmospheric Chemistry and Physics*, vol. 17, no. 2, pp. 899–910, 2017.

[192] A. Fink, R. Schuster, P. Knippertz, and R. van der Linden, "Climatology and dynamics of nocturnal low-level stratus over the southern west african monsoon region," in *AGU Fall Meeting Abstracts*, 2013.

[193] B. Schneider and T. Nocke, *Image politics of climate change: visualizations, imaginations, documentations*, vol. 55. transcript Verlag, 2014.

[194] T. Nocke, T. Sterzel, M. Böttinger, and M. Wrobel, "Visualization of climate and climate change data: An overview," *Digital earth summit on geoinformatics*, pp. 226–232, 2008.

[195] C. Tominski, J. F. Donges, and T. Nocke, "Information visualization in climate research," in *Information Visualisation (IV), 2011 15th International Conference on*, pp. 298–305, IEEE, 2011.

[196] S. Madden, "From databases to big data," *IEEE Internet Computing*, vol. 16, no. 3, pp. 4–6, 2012.

[197] J. Cohen, B. Dolan, M. Dunlap, J. M. Hellerstein, and C. Welton, "MAD skills: new analysis practices for big data," *Proceedings of the VLDB Endowment*, vol. 2, no. 2, pp. 1481–1492, 2009.

[198] P. Fox and J. A. Hendler, "Semantic escience: encoding meaning in next-generation digitally enhanced science.," *The Fourth Paradigm*, vol. 2, 2009.

[199] S. W. Henderson and S. M. Hannon, "Advanced coherent lidar system for wind measurements," in *Optics & Photonics 2005*, pp. 58870I–58870I, International Society for Optics and Photonics, 2005.

[200] P. G. Hofmeister, C. Bollig, S. Fayed, M. Kunze, and R. Reuter, "A compact doppler wind lidar for controlling the operation of wind turbines," *EARSeL eProceedings*, vol. 14, no. 1, p. 1, 2015.

[201] N. S. Prasad, R. Sibell, S. Vetorino, R. Higgins, and A. Tracy, "An all-fiber, modular, compact wind lidar for wind sensing and wake vortex

applications," in *SPIE Defense+ Security*, pp. 94650C–94650C, International Society for Optics and Photonics, 2015.

[202] MATLAB, *version 7.10.0 (R2010a)*. Natick, Massachusetts: The MathWorks Inc., 2010.

[203] S. Hankin, D. Harrison, J. Osborne, J. Davidson, and K. Obrien, "A strategy and a tool, ferret, for closely integrated visualization and analysis," *Journal of Visualization and Computer Animation*, vol. 7, no. 3, pp. 149–157, 1996.

[204] Y. Wang, G. Huynh, and C. Williamson, "Integration of google maps/earth with microscale meteorology models and data visualization," *Computers & Geosciences*, vol. 61, pp. 23–31, 2013.

[205] N. W. Cherukuru and R. Calhoun, "Augmented reality based doppler lidar data visualization: Promises and challenges," in *EPJ Web of Conferences*, vol. 119, p. 14006, EDP Sciences, 2016.

[206] T. Bergmann, M. Balzer, T. Hopp, T. van de Kamp, A. Kopmann, N. Tan Jerome, and M. Zapf, "Inspiration from VR gaming technology: Deep immersion and realistic interaction for scientific visualization," in *VISIGRAPP*, 2017.

[207] P. Knippertz, H. Coe, J. C. Chiu, M. J. Evans, A. H. Fink, N. Kalthoff, C. Liousse, C. Mari, R. P. Allan, B. Brooks, *et al.*, "The dacciwa project: Dynamics–aerosol–chemistry–cloud interactions in west africa," *Bulletin of the American Meteorological Society*, vol. 96, no. 9, pp. 1451–1460, 2015.

[208] N. Elmqvist, N. Henry, Y. Riche, and J.-D. Fekete, "Melange: space folding for multi-focus interaction," in *Proceedings of the SIGCHI Conference on Human Factors in Computing Systems*, pp. 1333–1342, ACM, 2008.

[209] J. Zhao, F. Chevalier, E. Pietriga, and R. Balakrishnan, "Exploratory analysis of time-series with chronolenses," *IEEE Transactions on Visualization and Computer Graphics*, vol. 17, no. 12, pp. 2422–2431, 2011.

[210] R. Roberts, C. Tong, R. Laramee, G. A. Smith, P. Brookes, and T. D'Cruze, "Interactive analytical treemaps for visualisation of call centre data," in *Proceedings of the Conference on Smart Tools and Applications in Computer Graphics*, pp. 109–117, Eurographics Association, 2016.

[211] B. Craft and P. Cairns, "Beyond guidelines: what can we learn from the visual information seeking mantra?," in *Information Visualisation, 2005. Proceedings. Ninth International Conference on*, pp. 110–118, IEEE, 2005.

[212] Y. Song, J. Ye, N. Svakhine, S. Lasher-Trapp, M. Baldwin, and D. Ebert, "An atmospheric visual analysis and exploration system," *IEEE Transactions on Visualization and Computer Graphics*, vol. 12, no. 5, pp. 1157–1164, 2006.

[213] R. Sharma, M. Gupta, and G. Kapoor, "Some better bounds on the variance with applications," *J. Math. Inequal*, vol. 4, no. 3, pp. 355–363, 2010.

[214] M. Stamminger and G. Drettakis, "Interactive sampling and rendering for complex and procedural geometry," in *Rendering Techniques 2001*, pp. 151–162, Springer, 2001.

[215] R. L. Cook, L. Carpenter, and E. Catmull, "The Reyes image rendering architecture," *ACM SIGGRAPH Computer Graphics*, vol. 21, no. 4, pp. 95–102, 1987.

[216] M. Levoy, "Display of surfaces from volume data," *IEEE Computer graphics and Applications*, vol. 8, no. 3, pp. 29–37, 1988.

[217] L. A. Torre, F. Bray, R. L. Siegel, J. Ferlay, J. Lortet-Tieulent, and A. Jemal, "Global cancer statistics, 2012," *CA: a cancer journal for clinicians*, vol. 65, no. 2, pp. 87–108, 2015.

[218] K. C. Oeffinger, E. T. Fontham, R. Etzioni, A. Herzig, J. S. Michaelson, Y.-C. T. Shih, L. C. Walter, T. R. Church, C. R. Flowers, S. J. LaMonte, *et al.*, "Breast cancer screening for women at average risk: 2015 guideline update from the american cancer society," *Jama*, vol. 314, no. 15, pp. 1599–1614, 2015.

[219] R. L. Siegel, K. D. Miller, and A. Jemal, "Cancer statistics, 2016," *CA: a cancer journal for clinicians*, vol. 66, no. 1, pp. 7–30, 2016.

[220] B. Ranger, P. J. Littrup, N. Duric, P. Chandiwala-Mody, C. Li, S. Schmidt, and J. Lupinacci, "Breast ultrasound tomography versus mri for clinical display of anatomy and tumor rendering: preliminary results," *American Journal of Roentgenology*, vol. 198, no. 1, pp. 233–239, 2012.

[221] T. Hopp, G. Schwarzenberg, M. Zapf, and N. V. Ruiter, "A matlab gui for the analysis and exploration of signal and image data of an ultrasound computer tomograph," in *Advances in Computer-Human Interaction, 2008 First International Conference on*, pp. 53–58, IEEE, 2008.

[222] R. Stokking, K. J. Zuiderveld, and M. A. Viergever, "Integrated volume visualization of functional image data and anatomical surfaces using normal fusion," *Human Brain Mapping*, vol. 12, no. 4, pp. 203–218, 2001.

[223] W. Cai and G. Sakas, "Data intermixing and multi-volume rendering," *Computer Graphics Forum*, vol. 18, no. 3, pp. 359–368, 1999.

[224] J. F. Greenleaf and R. C. Bahn, "Clinical imaging with transmissive ultrasonic computerized tomography," *IEEE Transactions on Biomedical Engineering*, no. 2, pp. 177–185, 1981.

[225] H. Gemmeke, L. Berger, M. Birk, G. Goebel, A. Menshikov, D. Tcherniakhovski, M. Zapf, and N. Ruiter, "Hardware setup for the next generation of 3d ultrasound computer tomography," in *Nuclear Science Symposium Conference Record (NSS/MIC), 2010 IEEE*, pp. 2449–2454, IEEE, 2010.

[226] R. Bramon, I. Boada, A. Bardera, J. Rodriguez, M. Feixas, J. Puig, and M. Sbert, "Multimodal data fusion based on mutual information," *IEEE Transactions on Visualization and Computer Graphics*, vol. 18, no. 9, pp. 1574–1587, 2012.

[227] O. Betz, U. Wegst, D. Weide, M. Heethoff, L. Helfen, W.-K. Lee, and P. Cloetens, "Imaging applications of synchrotron X-ray phase-contrast microtomography in biological morphology and biomaterials science. I. General aspects of the technique and its advantages in the analysis of millimetre-sized arthropod structure," *Journal of Microscopy*, vol. 227, no. 1, pp. 51–71, 2007.

[228] S. Schmelzle, R. A. Norton, and M. Heethoff, "Mechanics of the ptychoid defense mechanism in Ptyctima (Acari, Oribatida): One problem, two solutions," *Zoologischer Anzeiger-A Journal of Comparative Zoology*, vol. 254, pp. 27–40, 2015.

[229] T. Van de Kamp, A. Ershov, T. dos Santos Rolo, A. Riedel, and T. Baumbach, "Insect imaging at the ANKA synchrotron radiation facility," *Entomologie heute*, vol. 25, pp. 147–160, 2013.

[230] J. Ahrens, B. Hendrickson, G. Long, S. Miller, R. Ross, and D. Williams, "Data-intensive science in the us doe: case studies and future challenges," *Computing in Science & Engineering*, vol. 13, no. 6, pp. 14–24, 2011.

[231] D. Stalling, M. Westerhoff, H.-C. Hege, *et al.*, "Amira: A highly interactive system for visual data analysis," *The visualization handbook*, vol. 38, pp. 749–67, 2005.

[232] P. Thalmann, C. Bikis, G. Schulz, P. Paleo, A. Mirone, A. Rack, S. Siegrist, E. Cörek, J. Huwyler, and B. Müller, "Removing ring artefacts from synchrotron radiation-based hard x-ray tomography data," in *Developments in X-Ray Tomography XI*, vol. 10391, p. 1039114, International Society for Optics and Photonics, 2017.

[233] S. Bruns, S. L. S. Stipp, and H. O. Sørensen, "Looking for the signal: A guide to iterative noise and artefact removal in x-ray tomographic reconstructions of porous geomaterials," *Advances in water resources*, vol. 105, pp. 96–107, 2017.

[234] X. Liang, Z. Zhang, T. Niu, S. Yu, S. Wu, Z. Li, H. Zhang, and Y. Xie, "Iterative image-domain ring artifact removal in cone-beam ct," *Physics in Medicine & Biology*, vol. 62, no. 13, p. 5276, 2017.

[235] F. E. Boas and D. Fleischmann, "CT artifacts: causes and reduction techniques," *Imaging Med*, vol. 4, no. 2, pp. 229–240, 2012.

[236] A. Borsdorf, *Adaptive filtering for noise reduction in X-ray computed tomography*. Logos, 2009.

[237] A. Rack, T. Weitkamp, S. B. Trabelsi, P. Modregger, A. Cecilia, T. dos Santos Rolo, T. Rack, D. Haas, R. Simon, R. Heldele, *et al.*, "The micro-imaging station of the TopoTomo beamline at the ANKA synchrotron light source," *Nuclear Instruments and Methods in Physics Research Section B: Beam Interactions with Materials and Atoms*, vol. 267, no. 11, pp. 1978–1988, 2009.

[238] A. Endert, M. S. Hossain, N. Ramakrishnan, C. North, P. Fiaux, and C. Andrews, "The human is the loop: new directions for visual analytics," *Journal of Intelligent Information Systems*, vol. 43, pp. 411–435, Dec 2014.

[239] N. Coudray, J.-L. Buessler, and J.-P. Urban, "Robust threshold estimation for images with unimodal histograms," *Pattern Recognition Letters*, vol. 31, no. 9, pp. 1010–1019, 2010.

[240] N. Otsu, "A threshold selection method from gray-level histograms," *IEEE transactions on systems, man, and cybernetics*, vol. 9, no. 1, pp. 62–66, 1979.

[241] J. Kittler, J. Illingworth, and J. Föglein, "Threshold selection based on a simple image statistic," *Computer vision, graphics, and image processing*, vol. 30, no. 2, pp. 125–147, 1985.

[242] J. Edmonds, "Matroids and the greedy algorithm," *Mathematical programming*, vol. 1, no. 1, pp. 127–136, 1971.

[243] D. Ioannou, W. Huda, and A. F. Laine, "Circle recognition through a 2d hough transform and radius histogramming," *Image and vision computing*, vol. 17, no. 1, pp. 15–26, 1999.

[244] P. Debevec and S. Gibson, "A tone mapping algorithm for high contrast images," in *13th Eurographics Workshop on Rendering: Pisa, Italy*, Citeseer, 2002.

[245] P. Ledda, A. Chalmers, T. Troscianko, and H. Seetzen, "Evaluation of tone mapping operators using a high dynamic range display," *ACM Transactions on Graphics (TOG)*, vol. 24, no. 3, pp. 640–648, 2005.

[246] S.-c. Huang, M. E. Phelps, E. J. Hoffman, and D. E. Kuhl, "Cubic splines for filter design in computed tomography," *IEEE Transactions on Nuclear Science*, vol. 27, no. 5, pp. 1368–1374, 1980.

[247] P. King, K. Hubner, W. Gibbs, and E. Holloway, "Noise identification and removal in positron imaging systems," *IEEE Transactions on Nuclear Science*, vol. 28, no. 1, pp. 148–151, 1981.

[248] S. J. Riederer, N. J. Pelc, and D. A. Chesler, "The noise power spectrum in computed X-ray tomography," *Physics in medicine and biology*, vol. 23, no. 3, p. 446, 1978.

[249] G. Henrich, "A simple computational method for reducing streak artifacts in CT images," *Computerized tomography*, vol. 4, no. 1, pp. 67–71, 1980.

[250] M. Schaap, A. M. Schilham, K. J. Zuiderveld, M. Prokop, E.-J. Vonken, and W. J. Niessen, "Fast noise reduction in computed tomography for improved 3-D visualization," *IEEE transactions on medical imaging*, vol. 27, no. 8, pp. 1120–1129, 2008.

[251] S. Hu, E. A. Hoffman, and J. M. Reinhardt, "Automatic lung segmentation for accurate quantitation of volumetric X-ray CT images," *IEEE transactions on medical imaging*, vol. 20, no. 6, pp. 490–498, 2001.

[252] E. Chew, G. Weiss, R. Brooks, and G. Di Chiro, "Effect of CT noise on detectability of test objects," *American Journal of Roentgenology*, vol. 131, no. 4, pp. 681–685, 1978.

[253] R. Rutherford, B. Pullan, and I. Isherwood, "Measurement of effective atomic number and electron density using an EMI scanner," *Neuroradiology*, vol. 11, no. 1, pp. 15–21, 1976.

[254] M. Okada, "Noise evaluation and filter design in CT images," *IEEE transactions on biomedical engineering*, no. 9, pp. 713–719, 1985.

[255] J.-S. Lee, "Digital image smoothing and the sigma filter," *Computer vision, graphics, and image processing*, vol. 24, no. 2, pp. 255–269, 1983.

[256] M. McDonnell, "Box-filtering techniques," *Computer Graphics and Image Processing*, vol. 17, no. 1, pp. 65–70, 1981.

[257] A. S. Abutaleb, "Automatic thresholding of gray-level pictures using two-dimensional entropy," *Computer vision, graphics, and image processing*, vol. 47, no. 1, pp. 22–32, 1989.

[258] M. Borda, *Fundamentals in information theory and coding*. Springer Science & Business Media, 2011.

[259] C. Thum, "Measurement of the entropy of an image with application to image focusing," *Journal of Modern Optics*, vol. 31, no. 2, pp. 203–211, 1984.

[260] B. Likar, J. A. Maintz, M. A. Viergever, F. Pernus, *et al.*, "Retrospective shading correction based on entropy minimization," *Journal of Microscopy*, vol. 197, no. 3, pp. 285–295, 2000.

[261] F. H. Garcia, E. Wiesel, and G. Fischer, "The ants of kenya (hymenoptera: Formicidae)-faunal overview, first species checklist, bibliography, accounts for all genera, and discussion on taxonomy and zoogeography," *Journal of East African Natural History*, vol. 101, no. 2, pp. 127–222, 2013.

[262] P. Lösel and V. Heuveline, "Enhancing a diffusion algorithm for 4d image segmentation using local information," in *Medical Imaging: Image Processing*, p. 97842L, 2016.

[263] P. Ljung, J. Krüger, E. Groller, M. Hadwiger, C. D. Hansen, and A. Ynnerman, "State of the art in transfer functions for direct volume rendering," *Computer Graphics Forum*, vol. 35, no. 3, pp. 669–691, 2016.

[264] T. van de Kamp, P. Vagovič, T. Baumbach, and A. Riedel, "A biological screw in a beetle's leg," *Science*, vol. 333, no. 6038, pp. 52–52, 2011.

[265] A. Götz, E. Taurel, J. Pons, P. Verdier, J. Chaize, J. Meyer, F. Poncet, G. Heunen, E. Götz, A. Buteau, *et al.*, "Tango a corba based control system," *ICALEPCS2003, Gyeongju, October*, 2003.

[266] P. Abend, T. Thielmann, R. Ewerth, D. Seiler, M. Mühling, J. Döring, M. Grauer, and B. Freisleben, "Geobrowsing behaviour in google earth-a semantic video content analysis of on-screen navigation," *GI_Forum*, pp. 2–13, 2012.

[267] M. Mühling, R. Ewerth, J. Zhou, and B. Freisleben, "Multimodal video concept detection via bag of auditory words and multiple kernel learning," in *International Conference on Multimedia Modeling*, pp. 40–50, Springer, 2012.

[268] C. Henning and R. Ewerth, "Estimating the information gap between textual and visual representations," *International Journal of Multimedia Information Retrieval*, vol. 7, no. 1, pp. 43–56, 2018.

[269] H. Chen, R. H. Chiang, and V. C. Storey, "Business intelligence and analytics: from big data to big impact," *MIS quarterly*, pp. 1165–1188, 2012.

[270] M. Caselle, L. A. Perez, M. Balzer, A. Kopmann, L. Rota, M. Weber, M. Brosi, J. Steinmann, E. Bründermann, and A.-S. Müller, "Kapture-2. a picosecond sampling system for individual thz pulses with high repetition rate," *Journal of Instrumentation*, vol. 12, no. 01, p. C01040, 2017.

[271] M. Brosi, M. Schuh, E. Blomley, J. Steinmann, P. Schönfeldt, M. Schedler, N. Hiller, B. Kehrer, A.-S. Müller, and E. Bründermann, "Systematic studies of short bunch-length bursting at ANKA," 2016.

[272] Y. Jansen and P. Dragicevic, "An interaction model for visualizations beyond the desktop," *IEEE Transactions on Visualization and Computer Graphics*, vol. 19, no. 12, pp. 2396–2405, 2013.

A

Datasets

Multispectral Satellite Images

- Owner: Visual Analytics Benchmark Repository
- Experiment/Project: VAST Challenge 2018
- Methods: Satellite Imaging
- Resolution: 651 × 651 px (per image)
- Challenge: Multimodal (6 Modalities)

Wind Velocity

- Owner: Andreas Wieser
- Experiment/Project: KITcube
- Methods: Doppler wind lidar
- Challenge: Multivariate (102 parameters per second)
- Total: 4 billion datasets per campaign (duration of 2 months)
- Types: Vertical stare, Plan Position Indicator (PPI), and Range Height Indicator (RHI)

Breast Cancer Tumour

- Owner: Nicole Ruiter, Michael Zapf, and Torsten Hopp
- Experiment/Project: 3D Ultrasound Computer Tomography (USCT)
- Methods: Ultrasound Computer Tomography
- Resolution: 256 × 256 × 128 voxels
- Challenge: Multimodal (3 Modalities: sound of speed, attenuation, and reflection signals)

Oribatid mite *Archegozetes longisetosus*

- Owner: Sebastian Schmelzle
- Experiment/Project: Network for Online Visualisation and synergistic Analysis of tomographic data (NOVA)
- Methods: X-ray Synchrotron Tomography
- Resolution: 1536 × 1536 × 1152 voxels
- Challenge: Web-based visualisation with data latency lesser than 1 s (bottleneck at the limited network bandwidth)

Box mite *Euphthiracarus reticulatus*

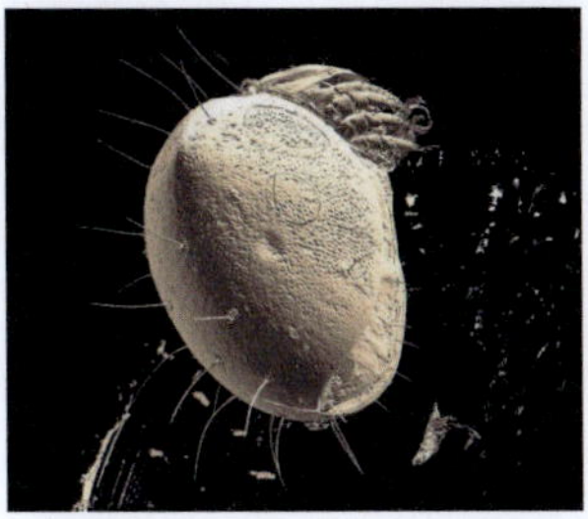

- Owner: Sebastian Schmelzle
- Experiment/Project: Network for Online Visualisation and synergistic Analysis of tomographic data (NOVA)
- Methods: X-ray Synchrotron Tomography
- Resolution: 1536 × 1536 × 1152 voxels
- Challenge: Web-based visualisation with data latency lesser than 1 s (bottleneck at the limited network bandwidth)

Gammasid mite

- Owner: Sebastian Schmelzle
- Experiment/Project: Network for Online Visualisation and synergistic Analysis of tomographic data (NOVA)
- Methods: X-ray Synchrotron Tomography
- Resolution: 2016 × 2016 × 2016 voxels
- Challenge: Web-based visualisation with data latency lesser than 1 s (bottleneck at the limited network bandwidth)

Pseudoscorpion

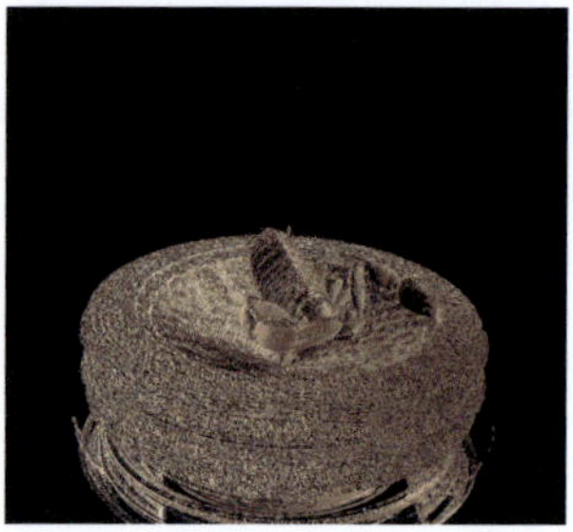

- Owner: Sebastian Schmelzle
- Experiment/Project: Network for Online Visualisation and synergistic Analysis of tomographic data (NOVA)
- Methods: X-ray Synchrotron Tomography
- Resolution: 2016 × 2016 × 1692 voxels
- Challenge: Web-based visualisation with data latency lesser than 1 s (bottleneck at the limited network bandwidth)

Tachinid fly *Gymnosoma nudifrons*

- Owner: Sebastian Schmelzle
- Experiment/Project: Network for Online Visualisation and synergistic Analysis of tomographic data (NOVA)
- Methods: X-ray Synchrotron Tomography
- Resolution: 1968 × 1968 × 1456 voxels
- Challenge: Web-based visualisation with data latency lesser than 1 s (bottleneck at the limited network bandwidth)

Biological Screw in a Weevil's Leg

- Owner: Thomas van de Kamp
- Experiment/Project: Network for Online Visualisation and synergistic Analysis of tomographic data (NOVA)
- Methods: X-ray Synchrotron Tomography
- Resolution: 512 × 512 × 486 voxels
- Challenge: Web-based visualisation with data latency lesser than 1 s (bottleneck at the limited network bandwidth)